THE LIFE AND TIMES
OF SUKARNO

THE LIFE AND TIMES OF SUKARNO

C. L. M. PENDERS, M.A., Ph.D.

Department of History,
University of Queensland

Fairleigh Dickinson

Rutherford · Madison · Teaneck
Fairleigh Dickinson University Press

Library of Congress Catalogue Card Number: 74-369
ISBN 0-8386-1546-5

Printed in Great Britain

To
THERESA

Preface

THIS book is intended primarily to provide the general reader as well as the student embarking on a study of modern South-East Asia with background information and insights into the life and times of the late President Sukarno of Indonesia—the *enfant terrible* of the newly emerging nations of Asia.

Sukarno died in 1970 and this study so close to the events can only be tentative in many of its conclusions, in particular those dealing with the later years of his life.

Most of the background information has been drawn from printed sources; but much of the data and many of the views about Sukarno himself have emerged from hundreds of interviews which I was able to conduct with a politically and ideologically representative cross-section of Indonesians during 1963, 1967, and 1970. The majority of those interviewed were prepared to give information on the basis of personal trust and requested that their names should not be published. I wish to thank these people here for the kindness, helpfulness and the great hospitality extended to me during my Indonesian tours. In addition I am greatly indebted for the helpful suggestions and information given by: Dr Ali Sastroamidjojo, Dr Abu Hanifah, Prof. Achmad Subardjo, Pak Said, Anwar Tjokroaminoto, Rusni, Prof. G. Reesink, I Gusti Bagus Oka, Dr Soebardi, Achdiat K. Mihardja, and the late Dr Soetjipto Wirjosuparto. It should be stressed, however, that all evaluations and judgements are my own.

I am also thankful to my colleagues Prof. D. P. Singhal, Prof. Gordon Greenwood, and Dr Glen Barclay for their help and encouragement. I also wish to record my gratefulness to Mrs Kooyman and Mrs Craig for dealing so cheerfully with my idiosyncrasies and with a manuscript which was positively chaotic.

C. Penders
March 1972

Contents

Illustrations

Photographs are by courtesy of Popperfoto, and Otto Kuijk and Bart van Veen, authors of *Soekarno Tabeh* (Becht, Amsterdam)

CHAPTER I

Youth: Raden Sukarno

Facts about Sukarno's earliest years are scarce. He was born on 6 June 1901 in the bustling harbour city of Surabaja in East Java, the son of *raden* Sukemi Sosrodihardjo, a Javanese schoolteacher, and Ida Njoman Rai, a Balinese woman. Very little is known about the life of *raden* Sukemi, who in existing literature is dismissed in a few paragraphs.

This scarcity of information has led to a great deal of speculation by friend and foe alike about Sukarno's family origins. Particularly, in Central and East Java where Sukarno drew most of his political support, stories abound about his supposed descent from Javanese royalty. One of these legends, which was current in the princely city of Solo (Surakarta) in Central Java, runs as follows:

A son of Paku Buwono X of the house of Surakarta was called Soekarno. The court's soothsayer had prophesied that when a baby boy called Soekarno would be born, this child would liberate Surakarta, and the whole of Indonesia from Dutch domination. . . . This prophecy was widely known in the palace before Soekarno was born. . . . One of Paku Buwono's wives who was pregnant persuaded the Sultan to have the child adopted if it was a boy. She argued that the child should not fall into the hands of the Dutch, who if they came to know about the prophecy would undoubtedly kill it. The real reason for this request, however, was that this wife wanted to make sure that her son would succeed to the throne. And although the Sultan understood what the woman was really after, he granted the request because he realized that it was the fate of the child to liberate the Indonesian people from the Dutch and to bring them to prosperity. When the baby was born and it was a son, the Sultan immediately looked for a loyal and trustworthy courtier. He found a handsome nobleman who was discreet and who had travelled outside Surakarta and Java. He entrusted the baby to this nobleman and ordered him to leave the court. The baby was given a magic heirloom which indicated his royal birth. The nobleman left the court with the new born baby and lived like a commoner wandering to East Java where he finally settled in Djombang. Giving up his noble title he earned his living as a teacher and came to be generally recognized as Soekarno's father. Both he and his wife kept the secret and nobody ever found out that Soekarno was actually the son of Paku Buwono X. The magic heirloom indicating his royal origin was given to Soekarno who as our president carries it with him wherever he goes . . .[1]

Far less flattering are the various legends current since 1945 in anti-Sukarno circles claiming that he was the illegitimate offspring of a Dutch planter and an Indonesian country girl. One Indonesian author relates the following story from a 'document' he read in East Java:

Towards the end of the nineteenth century, the vast plantations in the district of Kediri in East Java belonged to a Dutch firm. One day, the powerful head of this firm travelled from Holland to Indonesia and visited his possessions in Kediri. He was received, of course, with great hospitality. And as was the custom of the time this included the provision of a pretty bed-mate, because the nights in the highlands were chilly and the maidens of Kediri were lovely. After he left again for the cold country in Europe, the bed-mate was discovered to be pregnant. She gave birth to a boy. . . . The boy grew up, got a good education in Surabaja and in time worked in the plantations of his father, the big boss in Holland. It seems that this boy became a handsome man, an 'Indo' as they called him in Java, who was a Don Juan in his own right. . . . One day, he discovered a beautiful village girl . . . She got pregnant in time . . . Suddenly he became ill, very ill. And just at that time the girl gave birth to a child, a boy. He considered this boy as his son. His illness got worse and he became very weak. On his deathbed he called for a woman whom he knew very well and he persuaded this woman to promise him that she would take care of the baby and would give the boy a good upbringing. . . . According to this 'document' the baby was Soekarno, the mother was Sarinah, the idol of Soekarno's youth. Sarinah went to live with the family of *raden* Sukemi Sosrodihardjo. This 'document' might be a fake, might be a fabrication, but the man who let me read it said that he had it from his father, who knew the family Sosro well enough . . .[2]

In the absence of birth registration statistics and any other verifiable evidence in Indonesia it is impossible to confirm these stories.

Unfortunately Sukarno's own public revelations about his origins have done little to clarify the situation, as he was obviously far more concerned with achieving certain political effects demanded by the occasion than with sticking to historical facts.

During the Japanese occupation of Indonesia when the new colonial masters pursued a policy of conciliation towards Islam in order to gain the support of Indonesian Muslims for the Japanese cause, Sukarno apparently felt that it was good politics to claim descent from the Sultans of Demak, one of the earliest Islamized principalities in Java.[3] But in his autobiography published in 1965, Sukarno considered it more useful to select the kings of Kediri as his forefathers, while he claimed that his mother belonged to the Balinese nobility and was related to the princely house of Singaradja.[4] However, according to well-informed Balinese sources, Sukarno's mother was not of noble blood, but was a *sudra*, a lower caste person.

On many other occasions, when there was a need to identify himself with the masses, Sukarno stressed his common origin and the great poverty he had suffered as a child.

It is possible, however, to cut through some of the mystical haze in which Sukarno and others have enshrined his youth, and to pin-point with some accuracy the socio-economic class to which his parents belonged. The noble title *raden*[5] held by Sukarno's father did not automatically ensure high social status in Java. Of equal if not more importance was the type of position held. Government employment carried—as it still does today—a high social premium. The most prestigious sector of the colonial civil service open to Indonesians at the time was the *Inlands Bestuur* (Native Local Government Service),[6] in which the middle and top positions were monopolized by the higher nobility (*prijaji*).[7] The fact that *raden* Sukemi held the far less prestigious position of schoolteacher would place him among the numerous ranks of the lower nobility or in Western terms the lower middle class.

Raden Sukemi is believed to have attended a teachers' training school at Probolinggo in East Java; and his first posting after graduation was in Bali where he taught at an elementary school in Singaradja. In Hindu Bali he married a local girl, who because of her marriage to a foreigner was ostracized by her own people. At that time inter-ethnic marriages were still severely frowned upon and the ideal of one Indonesian nation, language and culture—for which Sukarno fought most of his life—was still unheard of. At the beginning of the twentieth century *raden* Sukemi was transferred to East Java, where he taught successively in Surabaja, Modjokerto and Blitar.

Sukarno's claim that he suffered extreme poverty in his youth must be considered as one of the many instances in his autobiography where he lets his fertile imagination run amok. In fact, twenty-five guilders per month, which Sukarno dismisses as a poor man's salary, provided his family with an income which was considerably higher than the Javanese working classes could enjoy at the time; and it would have afforded *raden* Sukemi and his family a fairly comfortable life in Javanese terms.[8]

Sukarno's early education was on traditional Javanese lines. His grandfather at Tulung Agung where he stayed for a few years taught him the rules of behaviour of the Javanese nobleman (*ksatryah*).[9] This training was continued by his father, who although having received a Dutch education had remained attached to Javanese tradition and was a member of the Theosophical Society.[10]

It is significant that in his youth Sukarno did not attend a Muslim religious school, but instead was brought up on the precepts of *kedjawen*: a basically tolerant, syncretic, mystical and pantheistic view of life, which draws its main inspiration from a mixture of the original Javanese animist beliefs, Hinduism, Buddhism, and Islam, and which is practised by the majority of Javanese; it is complete anathema to the smaller group of Javanese—*santri*—who adhere more closely to the tenets of the Islamic Law. In his autobiography Sukarno relates an incident which provides an interesting example of this early education:

Father, however, was a strict school master. . . . The rare times I was naughty he punished me harshly. Like the morning I climbed the jambu tree in our yard and knocked down a bird's nest. Father was livid, 'I thought I taught you to love animals', he thundered. I shook with fright. 'Yes, Father, you did'. 'You will please be so good as to explain the meaning of the phrase- "Tat Twan Asi, Tat Twam Asi".' 'It means "He is I and I am he; you are I and I am you".' 'And were you not taught this had a special significance?' 'Yes, Father, it means God is in all of us . . .'[11]

This Javanistic upbringing left an indelible mark on Sukarno who remained strongly mystically inclined and even during his presidency often asked advice of mystical teachers and soothsayers before making an important decision. Moreover, his later political philosophy was distinctly eclectic and he remained constantly opposed to the legalism and the theocratic tendencies of the more orthodox Indonesian Muslims.

When still very young Sukarno was allowed to attend the *wajang* (shadow play) performances, which usually last from late evening until early morning. It was here that he saw the Mahabharata and Ramayana epics recreated on the screen by the *dalang* (puppet master). Very popular in Java at the time was the Bharata Juddha, the last part of the Mahabharata, which depicts the final battle for the kingdom of Ngastina between the *pandawas,* such as Bima and Gatotkatja, and the *korawas,* such as Karna and Sangkuni. Many Javanese at the time attempted to escape the frustrations of colonial rule in the dreamworld of the *wajang* which they came to regard as a reality. In particular the Bharata Juddha came to be seen as the struggle for independence in which the national shame suffered at the hands of the Dutch would be expiated by the final victory of the *pandawas* over the foreign usurpers.

It was this version of the Bharata Juddha that Sukarno became familiar with during his childhood. And the scorn, hatred, and ridicule heaped upon the *korawas*—the Dutch—by the puppet master at these performances never seems to have left Sukarno throughout his life. Like any young boy in any part of the world Sukarno tried to identify himself with some of the heroes. In fact he was named after Karna, one of the *korawas,* a nobleman *par excellence,* who portrayed courage, honesty and a strong sense of duty. Sukarno in his autobiography relates the following about the namegiving:

... My name at birth was Kusno. I started life as an unhealthy child. I had malaria, dysentery, anything and everything. Father thought, 'His name is not good. We must give him another so that he may start fresh.' Father was a devotee of Mahabharata, the ancient Hindu classics. I had not yet reached puberty when Father said, 'We shall name you Karna. Karna is one of the greatest heroes in Mahabharata. . . . Grasping my shoulders tightly, Father looked deep into my eyes. 'It has always been my prayer', he declared, 'for my son to be a patriot and great hero of his people. You shall be a second Karna . . . .'[12]

This version is not fully acceptable in certain Javanese circles where there is some speculation as to why *raden* Sukemi took the unusual step of naming his son after one of the *korawas*, while it was customary to call Javanese boys after one of the *pandawas*. One explanation which has been put forward is that *raden* Sukemi's selection of Karna was a reflection on Sukarno's illegitimacy. In the Mahabharata story Karna was the illegitimate son of Bataru Surya, the Sun God, and Dewi Kunti Nalibrata.

Whatever importance one might want to attach to this explanation, it is interesting that Sukarno very seldom identified himself in public with his own namesake, but preferred to model himself on one of the *pandawas*. Bima, the powerful and uncompromising fighter, seems to have made a particularly deep impression on him. Sukarno's first newspaper articles appear under the pseudonym of Bima; and in his later writings and speeches he often alludes to this *wajang* figure.

The expectations nurtured in the Bharata Juddha about the eventual defeat of colonialism were even more strongly evident in the various prophecies current since the end of the seventeenth century about the coming of the *Ratu Adil*, the Just King, who would drive out the Dutch and inaugurate a millennium of prosperity and happiness for all. Undoubtedly Sukarno's childhood view of the world would have been moulded by these messianic beliefs. The most popular were the prophecies attributed to Djojobojo, who ruled the East Javanese kingdom of Kediri during the eleventh century. One of the latest versions of the Djojobojo legend current during the 1930s has been recorded by Van der Kroef as follows:

> According to this Java would first be ruled by the whites. Then the apocalypse would set in, characterized by the 'rule of the yellow skinned ones', who would govern Java until the padi (rice) had ripened on the fields seven times. The whites would then return for three rainy monsoons, after which Java would be free . . .[13]

The impact of these millenarian beliefs never seems to have been entirely erased from Sukarno's mind. This is evident from the strongly chiliastic content of the solutions he proposed to the major political and economic problems of the Indonesian republic when he became President.

Sukarno's early Javanistic upbringing was followed by a thorough Western education. He began his formal Western-style education at the village school at Tulung Agung, where he stayed with his grandparents who filled his head with the age-old stories from the *wajang* and spoiled him a great deal. His grandparents—at least so Sukarno tells us—believed he had supernatural powers and he was made to lick the bodies of sick villagers who, to his own amazement, were often cured quickly. His grandmother believed that Sukarno had the makings of a saint. The result was that he did not do very well at school. This changed somewhat when he moved back to his own home in Modjokerto where he attended his father's vernacular elementary school, although at home he is said to have been very spoiled particularly by his mother.

From his earliest years Sukarno appears to have possessed a tremendous ego. He tried to push himself to the foreground and dominated his friends, which earned him the nickname *djago* (fighting cock). When Sukarno wanted to play football everybody had to play and when he started a stamp collection it became the rage of the village. However, it was in the European primary school, which he entered when he was eleven, where 'bully' Sukarno met his match with the often rough and prankish Eurasian and Dutch pupils. Highly sensitive to jokes made at his expense and upset by the slightest signs of racial discrimination, the *djago* of the village became quiet and withdrawn, and this made him even more the subject of attention by the students. He was highly indignant when he was not selected to play soccer for the school, although as one Dutch commentator drily remarks:[14] Sukarno does not say if he really could play the game well enough. Even towards the end of his life Sukarno was still very bitter about these humiliating experiences of his schooldays: 'Dutch children never played with native children. It just was not done. They were the good, the pure, the snow white Westerners and they looked down on me because I was the native or inlander.'[15]

Sukarno suffered even more when after completing European primary school in 1915 he went to Surabaja to attend the Dutch High School—H.B.S. There were three hundred European boys at the school and only twenty Indonesians. The fist fights with Dutch boys and the teasings he received were unbearable cruelties for the hypersensitive Sukarno. Apparently he tried to get even by attempting to make love to Dutch girls:

It was the only way I knew to exert some form of superiority over the white race and make them bend to my will. That is always the aim, isn't it? For a brown skinned man to overpower the white man? It's some sort of goal to attain. Overpowering a white girl and making her want me became a matter of pride. A handsome

7

boy always has steady girl friends. I had many. They even adored my irregular teeth. But I admit I deliberately went after the white ones . . .[16]

There is a story told by Sukarno about the Dutch girl Mien Hessels with whom he fell so desperately in love that he went to see her father to ask for permission to marry her:

And there I stood, shaking, in front of the father of my ivory princess, a towering six-footer who stared straight at me like I was vermin on the ground. 'Sir', I said, 'if you please, I would like the hand of your daughter in marriage . . . Please'. 'You? A dirty native like you' spat Mr Hessels. 'How dare you even come near my daughter. Out, you filthy animal. Get out! . . .'[17]

A number of Indonesians as well as Dutchmen who passed through the same education system have argued that Sukarno's description of race relations in Dutch-language schools in pre-war Indonesia is far too biased; and they also feel that the story about Mien Hessels was probably invented by Sukarno in order to impress upon his audiences why he hated the Dutch so much. An Indonesian nationalist, Dr Abu Hanifah, who also attended Dutch schools, writes:

I was treated the same way as any other student in the school. I knew them all, most of them were my friends, boys and girls. I was a member of the Boy Scouts, I was invited to their birthday parties, I was the same as anybody else with the exception that my skin was light brown. However, I never could summon the courage to get closer to the Dutch girls, even though they seemed very lovely and all that. It might be that I was too much involved in school fights, playing soccer, going on picnics, in brief, having fun with my Dutch friends. . . . Dutch colonials were not too friendly to the natives but they were not as bad as the English colonials in India. Eurasians, the illegitimate offspring of Indonesian women and Dutch men, could have the best chances in the world. Some of them became even Ministers of State and professors in Holland . . .[18]

The vitriolic diatribes in Sukarno's speeches against everything Dutch and the warped picture of Dutch rule presented by him to foreign visitors in the post-war period, were undoubtedly necessary to radicalize the feelings of the indigenous masses and to justify the cause of Indonesian freedom to the outside world. Similar devices were employed by other Indonesian leaders. But in the case of Sukarno there seems to have been a deeper psychological reason underlying his attitudes to the Dutch and for that matter anybody, whatever the colour of his skin, who stood in his way.

At school he was considered by many of his co-pupils as shy and distinctly odd because he did not take part in normal school life outside the classroom. Part of the explanation might be that he was as yet unable to adjust himself to a situation where because of his Western education he was uprooted to a certain extent from his own civilization and culturally and spiritually felt himself suspended in mid-air. It is more likely, however, that it was Sukarno himself, with his stubbornness, his super-ego, his unbelievable vanity, who was responsible for any unhappiness that he might have suffered rather than anything else. Unlike the village days, there was very little opportunity in the Dutch schools for Sukarno to play the leading role which he seems to have believed was his natural prerogative, so he simply retired into a world of his own—as so many Javanese had done before him—and dreamt about the great deeds which fate had destined him to perform. This capacity for day dreaming and thinking up fantastic and world-shattering schemes remained with Sukarno until the bitter end. Apparently, he was unable to force himself across the racial dividing line to find out what the other side was really like. And in spite of his thorough Western education he never seems to have really been able—or what is perhaps nearer to the truth—wanted to grasp what Western civilization was about. Until the end Sukarno stuck stubbornly to his first impressions of European civilization which were based on books and on the watered-down and largely artificial version he had encountered in the Netherlands East Indies. To him the West stood for capitalism, imperialism, national degradation and economic exploitation. Unlike many other Western-educated Indonesians he could not appreciate Western music—he only liked the waltz—or literature, although he was more impressed by the plastic arts, especially if they portrayed the female body.

It must be added, however, that while his Indonesian schoolmates joined the Dutch students in the normal schoolboy pranks and pastimes out of school hours, Sukarno, in addition to day dreaming, also tried to grapple with a more practical solution to the unbearable frustrations he had to suffer. He eventually found the answer in the annihilation of the colonial system. Reading a great deal of political history—mainly Western—and listening avidly to the political discussions and disputes that took place in the house of Tjokroaminoto, an important nationalist leader with whom he boarded in Surabaya, Sukarno gradually turned into a radical nationalist. One of the sons of Tjokroaminoto—Anwar—who was about ten years younger than Sukarno, describes him as a *huilebalk* (cry-baby) liable to throw tantrums whenever he did not get his own way. He was also terribly spoiled by Mrs Tjokroaminoto as he was by most women in his life. However, even at that time he could also if necessary be very charming. It was these qualities of charm and joviality, which he could turn on at the drop of a hat, that often stood him in good stead during some of the most dangerous and critical moments in his political career. But beneath this charm, this back-slapping friendliness, there was the iron will of a ruthless go-getter. Sukarno's self-centredness and tremendous vanity attracted very few true friends throughout his life. It is paradoxical that one of the very few real friends he ever had was a Dutchman, Emile van Konijnenburg, later Director of the K.L.M., who even during the darkest days of the West Irian dispute kept close contact with him.

Later when Sukarno began to be known in the nationalist movement and achieved his early success as a charismatic speaker, he lost his shyness and became far more confident in his dealings with his opponents the Dutch, whose domineering behaviour and punctuality he loathed although secretly he seems to have envied them these qualities. And although Sukarno would have loudly denied it, some of the mannerisms of the Dutch colonial seem to have rubbed off on him. He was no longer a shy little Javanese boy, who would hide his feelings under a somewhat enigmatic smile, controlling his emotions as a civilized Javanese was supposed to do. In the early 1920s Sukarno had undergone a complete metamorphosis; he was cocky, arrogant, always perfectly dressed in the Western manner and reputedly obsessed with cleanliness. These typically Dutch traits remained with him throughout his life; later during his presidential years he would become livid with rage if an official was not properly attired in suit and tie and if he happened to find a speck of dust in any of the Palace rooms. By his own admission, he always prayed and swore in Dutch, which shows how deeply the Dutch language had imprinted itself on his subconscious.

In addition to his tremendous ego Sukarno was endowed with an intelligence which was far above average. He passed out of the Dutch High School in Surabaya with flying colours. This was no mean feat for an Indonesian boy whose knowledge of Dutch must have been at least initially defective. Moreover, unlike their American or Australian counterparts, Dutch secondary schools such as the H.B.S., Lyceum and Gymnasium demanded extremely high standards from students, based as they were on the French *lycée* with its notoriously difficult baccalaureate examination. In addition to mathematics, chemistry, physics, history and a host of minor subjects, Sukarno also had to study in considerable depth English, French and German, which explains his linguistic virtuosity in his later speeches and public performances.

In 1921 Sukarno left Surabaya for the West Javanese city of Bandung, the 'Paris of Java', where he enrolled at the newly established University of Technology to study architecture.

As with so many facets of Sukarno's life there is some controversy as to how *raden* Sukemi, who only earned a moderate wage as a schoolteacher, managed to finance his son not only through the costly Dutch High School, but also at the vastly more expensive university. Some say that Tjokroaminoto, the *Sarikat Islam* (Islamic Association) leader and Sukarno's political mentor, paid for his education. Others, who are less charitable, again conjure up a repentant Dutch father or grandfather in Holland who tried to do the right thing. However, it seems very unlikely that his supposed planter father would have allowed his son to board in the house of Tjokroaminoto, the 'uncrowned king of Java' and the most important nationalist leader at the time. More credible is the story reported by the Dutch Communist leader Paul de Groot, who in his memoirs relates that while he was in Moscow in the 1930s he was told by Musso, the Indonesian Communist leader, that both he and Sukarno had been adopted and educated by an 'Ethical' Dutchman.[19] It was not unheard of for Dutch colonial families to adopt Indonesian children and give them a Dutch education. This would also make it easier to explain why Sukarno—who takes the fact that he was Dutch-educated as a matter of course—as the son of a lower-middle-class Indonesian was permitted in the first place to enter the various highly selective European schools which were normally the preserve of Dutch and upper-class Indonesian children.

Sukarno was an able university student, although by his own admission he was weak in some areas of mathematics. On his graduation in 1926 Professor Wolff Schoenmaker offered him a tutorship in architecture,[20] which says a great deal for his ability particularly considering the heavy colonial prejudice against him. Sukarno refused the offer, because politics already held a much greater attraction for him than an academic career or private business as an architect. Later he often proudly claimed that he built a nation rather than material structures.

CHAPTER II

Nationalist Leader: Bung Karno

INDONESIAN nationalism in the sense of the desire to create a united, independent state of Indonesia, out of the scattered and culturally variegated peoples and islands of the East Indies archipelago, is a twentieth-century phenomenon.

The earliest signs of this national awakening became apparent soon after Sukarno's birth, when in 1908 the students of the Medical School—STOVIA—in Djakarta founded the first modern national organization in Indonesia called Budi Utomo—High Endeavour. The emphasis of Budi Utomo on cultural problems and education could not satisfy some of the more radically inclined Western-educated Indonesian intellectuals. The result was that in 1912 another organization, the *Indische Partij* (Party of the Indies) was founded, which demanded immediate independence and attempted —although with little success—to combine all the racial groups in the Indies in the struggle against Dutch colonialism. Neither Budi Utomo nor the Party of the Indies were able to draw a mass following.

In the Indonesian Islamic world there were also stirrings for renewal and reform at this time. A number of Islamic teachers (*ulamas*) influenced by modernist teachings in the Middle East began to agitate against the medieval thinking and attitudes of Indonesian Islam and set up modern Muslim schools, which in addition to religion also taught the normal Western curricula subjects. In 1912 the Islamic Association was founded which within a few years attracted millions of followers from all walks of life who attempted to find solace for the frustrations of colonial rule in the new organization. Many of the peasants saw in H. O. S. Tjokroaminoto, the charismatic Islamic Association leader, the embodiment of the long expected 'Just King'. Initially moderate in its programme and willing to cooperate with the colonial government's policy of indigenous economic development, the Islamic Association had by 1918 grown far more radical owing to the infiltration of Dutch and Indonesian Communists into its ranks. A serious split occurred in the organization which resulted in the ousting of the Communists, who in 1921 set up their own *Partai Kommunis Indonesia* (P.K.I.).

The P.K.I. grew rapidly, drawing away most of the members from the Islamic Association, which soon declined into political insignificance. In the years 1921–25 the P.K.I. became increasingly revolutionary in its activities. Strikes in industry and on the plantations increased continuously, culminating in Communist-inspired rebellions in West Java and West Sumatra in 1926–27. These uprisings were quickly suppressed by the colonial army and the police force; more than 18,000 people were arrested of whom four were condemned to death and executed, and 4,500 sent to prison. The colonial government, which hitherto had been fairly lenient and had allowed a number of revolutionaries to go into exile in the Netherlands or other overseas countries, now adopted a much harsher line and 1,308 people who had been involved in the uprisings were sent to the Tanah Merah prisoner camp at the Upper Digul river in West Irian. This suppressive policy and the greater vigilance of the *Politieke Inlichtingen Dienst* (Political Intelligence Service) effectively crushed the P.K.I. until the end of Dutch rule. As Ruth McVey has so aptly put it:

> The P.K.I. had been the last of the older generation of Indonesian political movements to play an active role; the others . . . had either given up entirely or retired . . . from the struggle against Dutch rule. The removal of the Communists from the political scene caused the new generation, which had hitherto been gathering in the background, suddenly to occupy the centre of the stage. These were the secular nationalists, who saw their anti-Dutch efforts directly in terms of striving for an Indonesian nation state rather than in the international framework of Islam or Communism or in the political and cultural nationalism of the regional movements . . .[1]

One of the outstanding leaders of this new generation of nationalists was Sukarno.

The first feelings of nationalism were probably instilled in Sukarno by his father, whose acquaintance with Tjokroaminoto and membership of the Theosophical Society influenced him towards nationalism. There is no doubt, however, that Sukarno's ideological position and his ideas about political tactics began to take shape in the period 1916–21 when he attended the Dutch High School in Surabaja. There he boarded in Tjokroaminoto's house, which at the time was the main centre of political discussion and agitation in the Indies, having as frequent visitors such leaders as the Communists: Semaun, Tan Malaka, Sneevliet, Baars; and the Socialist Douwes Dekker, who all tried to persuade Tjokroaminoto to lead the Islamic Association in a more revolutionary direction. In addition to listening carefully to the often hot-headed debates in Tjokroaminoto's house, Sukarno furthered his political education by attending seminars on Marxism conducted by the Dutch socialist C. Hartogh, who taught German at the High School, and who considered Sukarno to be the most intelligent participant and was amazed at his fantastic capacity to memorize facts. Sukarno also spent many hours in the library of the Theosophical Society to which he had access because of his father's membership. It was there that he debated in his mind with some of the great political figures in history:

> Mentally I talked with Thomas Jefferson, with whom I feel friendly and close because he told me all about the Declaration of Independence he wrote in 1776. I discussed George Washington's problems with him. I relived Paul Revere's ride. I deliberately looked for mistakes in the life of Abraham Lincoln so I could argue the points with him. . . . In the world of my mind, I also communed with Prime Minister Gladstone as well as Sidney and Beatrice Webb; I came face to face with Mazzini, Cavour and Garribaldi of Italy; Austria's Otto Bauer and Adler; Karl Marx, Friedrich Engels, and Lenin, and I chatted with Jean-Jacques Rousseau, Aristide Briand and Jean Jaures, the grandest orator in French history. I drank in these glories. I lived their lives. I actually was Voltaire. I was the great fighter of the French revolution, Danton. A thousand times, I myself, in my black room saved France singlehanded. I became emotionally involved with these statesmen . . .[2]

Sukarno first came to public attention while he was a member of *Jong Java* (Young Java), the youth organization of Budi Utomo. The non-political nature of Young Java, which was almost entirely concerned with educational problems and the strengthening and revitalization of Javanese civilization, would have been particularly galling to the more radical-minded Sukarno. His attempts to lead the organization in a more revolutionary direction, and his arrogant and stubborn behaviour during various meetings, caused a furore in Young Java where he came to be named Bima, the uncompromising warrior of the *wajang*.

In 1921 Sukarno wrote a number of articles for *Oetoesan Hindia*, the Islamic Association newspaper. These early writings show a distinct Marxist influence, but Tjokroaminoto's hold on the young Sukarno appears to have been still strong enough to make him side with his mentor in the dispute between the moderate and Communist factions within the Islamic Association. Sukarno condemned the Communists for breaking up the unity of the Islamic Association movement and argued that the time was not yet ripe for revolution. The people had to be educated first, and self-government along the lines envisaged by the colonial government would have to be achieved before a successful attack could be made on capitalism and imperialism:

> Once the right conditions have been created and a parliament with true representatives of the people is in existence, also then the Islamic Association must continue to work and agitate in order to reinforce democracy and Islam in the Indies and to destroy capitalism. What is the use of self-government if it is controlled by the supporters of capitalism and imperialism?[3]

The gradual approach in achieving independence and the syncretic position with regard to nationalism, Islam and Communism taken here by Sukarno reflects the influence of Tjokroaminoto, who first introduced him to practical politics. Sukarno often accompanied Tjokroaminoto to public meetings and while listening intently to the fiery and charismatic Islamic Association leader his own oratorial talents must undoubtedly have been considerably sharpened:

> I became the tail of Tjokroaminoto. Wherever he went I followed . . . and I just sat and observed. He had great authority over the people. Nonetheless, as I watched time after time I became aware he never raised or lowered his tone, never cracked jokes, his speeches were dull. I never read one of those cheap books on how to be a public speaker nor did I practice in front of a mirror. It isn't that I wasn't vain enough for a mirror, but because I had none. My mirror was Tjokroaminoto. I watched him throw his voice, I saw his gesture, I observed and applied.[4]

Soon, however, Sukarno no longer sat and watched, but was able to test his own speaking talents at smaller meetings in the villages where he was allowed to fill in more and more for Tjokroaminoto who saw that his serious and avid young student had the makings of a great popular leader. It was at these meetings in the humble villages and *kampongs* around Surabaja that Sukarno first realized his tremendous speaking abilities and charismatic power which brought his listeners under his spell.

Sukarno himself admitted that Tjokroaminoto was the most important influence in his early political life and that he felt very close to him. Shortly before Sukarno departed for Bandung to take up his university studies he sealed his close friendship with Tjokro by marrying his eldest daughter, Siti Utari. He was then twenty and she was sixteen. Intellectually she was not in his class and apparently Sukarno was not really in love with her, but—so he writes in his memoirs—he was motivated by feelings of gratitude to the great master, who after his wife's sudden death was made to feel a little happier when he saw his eldest child married to his favourite pupil. Undoubtedly he had reason to be grateful to Tjokroaminoto, but it would have been very much out of character if at least in the back of his mind Sukarno had not weighed the possible political advantages of marrying into the family of the most powerful and widely known political leader in the country at the time.

It was then in Surabaja that Sukarno served his apprenticeship as a public speaker and where he was introduced to nationalist politics under the guidance of Tjokroaminoto, who was basically a political moderate, always prepared to reach a compromise with the various factions in the nationalist movements as well as with the colonial government, providing it served his main objective which was the unification of all anti-colonial forces in the country. This quest for unity also rubbed off on the young Sukarno with whom it eventually became a complete obsession—something to be achieved even at the cost of denying the basic human rights to his people as well as ruining the national economy.

Whatever moderate political tendencies Sukarno may have had initially, they soon disappeared after his arrival in Bandung where he fell under the spell of such first generation radical nationalists as Dr Tjipto Mangunkusumo, E. F. Douwes Dekker and Suwardi Surianingrat, the triumvirate of the Party of the Indies, who after their return from exile in the Netherlands established a new radical party, the *Nationaal Indische Partij* (NIP).[5] 'Freedom now' once more became the slogan and the party worked hard to establish a united front of all the parties and groups in the country which were striving for self-government or independence. In 1923 the NIP issued a manifesto, signed by *seventeen* Indonesian political parties and organizations, calling on all nationalists to bury the hatchet and unite themselves in the struggle against colonialism. The manifesto pointed out that promises made in 1918 by the 'ethical' Governor-General van Limburg Stirum about the speedy introduction of true self-government had not been honoured by the Dutch government and it was clear that the colonial power could no longer be depended upon to introduce the political, economic and social changes which were so urgently needed and desired by the people.

Meetings discussing the manifesto were held all over Java, and Sukarno in his memoirs claims that at the meeting in Bandung he made an important speech:

I was just a youngster. I was listening. But suddenly I wanted to say something desperately. I couldn't control myself; they were all speaking nonsense. As usual they were begging. They weren't demanding. . . . I want to speak my piece, I yelled. Go ahead, the chairman yelled back. There were PID Dutch secret police, all over the place. Right in front of me stood one big, scowling red-faced policeman. The supreme power—the white man. He alone could stop me. He singlehanded could disband the meeting. . . . 'Why does a volcano like Mount Kelud explode? He explodes because the hole in the crater becomes stopped up. . . . It will be the same with our nationalist movement if the Dutch keep stopping our mouths and we are not allowed to give vent to our emotions. . . . One day there will come an explosion with us too. And when we erupt, the Hague will go sky high. . . . What good are tens of thousands of us massing together if all we do is produce petitions. . . . Until now we have never been the attackers. Ours is a movement not of pressure but of pleading. Let us today resort to a policy of self-reliance. Let us stop begging. Instead, let us shout, 'Mr Imperialist, this is what we DEMAND of you'.[6]

No doubt Sukarno here renders very well, although probably in more colourful terms, what the radical leaders at this meeting must have said, but it is generally agreed by contemporaries that he himself never uttered these words and was really a silent participant. It is known that only party leaders made speeches at this particular meeting and Sukarno at that time was certainly not yet important enough to have been asked or allowed to speak. So, again, as on so many occasions in his autobiography, the story is apocryphal and further illustrates how the great dreamer Sukarno with his fertile imagination could make himself believe that he was recording what had actually happened, and that the beginning of the non-cooperative nationalist movement of which later he was one of the major exponents could not possibly have occurred without him, Sukarno, in the leading role.

The reference Sukarno makes in this quotation to the Dutch policeman who could disband the meeting is rather interesting in that at the time of writing—which was in 1964—Sukarno himself certainly did have and did use his power to stop any meeting he wanted. But he just glosses over this fact because his early ideas about liberal democracy had long since been set aside as unworkable in the Indonesian context; or perhaps he had always, although unconsciously, wanted to replace the colonial power by his own, and could not see anything basically wrong with autocratic rule *per se*.

The greatest single influence on Sukarno during his Bandung period seems to have been Dr Tjipto Mangunkusumo who turned him into a convinced radical nationalist. In some ways this close relationship between Tjipto and Sukarno is not surprising; both were highly intelligent men and extremely sensitive to the reality of the colonial situation, an injustice which they took as a personal insult. Sukarno was soon to follow in the footsteps of Tjipto, the relentless and uncompromising fighter, who soon after his return from exile in Holland was placed under house arrest in Bandung and in 1927 was again exiled, this time to the East Indonesian island of Banda-Neira where he remained until just before the Japanese invasion. Here the similarity ends, however. Unlike Sukarno, Tjipto's belief in democracy remained until the end of his life and in his view traditional Javanese civilization which was basically feudal in character had to be obliterated. He considered that Western education and its subsequent social and cultural dislocation was indispensable in creating a revolutionary atmosphere. From the beginning Tjipto had disagreed with the emphasis put by Budi Utomo on the reinvigoration of the traditional Javanese civilization. As he had put it in a 1916 debate: 'The psyche of the Javanese people has been changed to such an extent that a change of language, or more cynically a killing of the language has become urgent. Only in this way will it be possible to build another language on its ruins and also another civilization.'[7]

Moreover, below his often cynical exterior Tjipto had a more strongly developed sense of humanity, intellectual honesty and gallantry than Sukarno. Both men repeatedly professed a deep concern for the poor peasant who eked out his existence without hope of any improvement in the villages and the overcrowded *kampongs* of the city in which he lived. During an outbreak of the plague in 1910 Tjipto's devoted and unstinting services to the people of Java were recognized by the colonial government who awarded him the Star of the Order of Oranje-nassau. Sukarno, who always identified his suffering with that of the peasant, rode to prominence on the back of the masses but in the process did very little for them in practical economic terms. He also seems to have lacked the great courage of Tjipto and many of his co-fighters have often accused him of cowardice in times of physical danger. Also the gallantry of Tjipto, who was genuinely shocked at the German invasion of Holland and the rape of Rotterdam and publicly offered his sympathy to the Dutch people in their hour of need, was entirely foreign to Sukarno.

In terms of character Sukarno was perhaps more akin to his other master in radical politics, E. F. Douwes Dekker, who was less scrupulous than Tjipto in the means he used to achieve his goal. Unlike Tjipto he was apparently unwilling to risk another term of exile or imprisonment. And severely hampered in his political activities by the constant surveillance of the Dutch intelligence service and also deeply worried about the internal division in the nationalist movement, Douwes Dekker from the early 1920s onwards grudgingly withdrew from public political life and threw himself with great energy into national education. In 1922 he established a school society in Bandung, later named the Ksatryan Institute, which in addition to a number of primary schools also maintained a training school for journalists, businessmen, and teachers. The main purpose of the Institute, as its name implies, was to train students in the qualities of the nobleman, such as self-reliance, courage and independence of spirit. Emphasis was placed on teaching economics and commercial subjects in order to help the creation of an Indonesian middle class of independent entrepreneurs. Great stress was placed in the curriculum on the development of character and personal initiative: 'Training which is solely directed at obtaining employment only creates half developed people. Our school diploma does not open the gate to government employment. But rather we desire to help to develop the knowledge, the understanding and especially the courage to be independent.'[8]

Sukarno at one stage taught history and mathematics in one of Douwes Dekker's schools and as he describes it in his memoirs, the Dutch school inspector on one of his regular visits was not exactly enamoured of the way Sukarno conducted his history lesson, which most of the time consisted of denunciations of colonialism and imperialism. His teaching career was apparently cut short by the local authorities who invoked an ordinance issued in 1923 which empowered them to suspend for a period of up to two years teachers in private schools who were considered political agitators.

In the years 1922 and 1923 Tjokroaminoto, Sukarno's father-in-law, suffered a serious setback to his prestige as a national leader. The Communists who had lost their bid to take control of the Islamic Association spread stories about Tjokro's illegal use of party funds and other corruptive practices which came to be widely believed in nationalist circles. To make matters worse the colonial authorities sentenced Tjokroaminoto to a six-month prison term not because of political activities but on a charge of perjury. Sukarno, as befitted a good son-in-law, interrupted his studies and returned to Surabaja with his wife Utari where he took up a job as a clerk with the railways department in order to support Tjokro's family.

On his return to Bandung he openly defended Tjokroaminoto against unpleasant accusations brought against him at the Communist party congress by the agitator Hadji Misbach whom he forced to retract his allegations and tender a public apology. But although Sukarno faithfully performed the duties which were expected of him as a member of Tjokroaminoto's family—failure to do so would have made him appear despicable in the eyes of the extremely kinship-conscious Javanese—he had already distanced himself from his father-in-law in political terms to the point of no-return. And when Tjokroaminoto accepted the offer of a seat in the *Volksraad*, Sukarno, the uncompromising radical, broke completely with him:

> Tjokro's ideology grew narrower and narrower to me. His vision of independence for our fatherland was viewed strictly through the microscopic lense of the Islamic religion. I no longer went to him for teaching. Neither were his friends considered my tutors any more. Though still a younger man, I was no longer a receiver. I was now already a leader. I had followers. I had a reputation. I had become Tjok's political equal. We had no sudden breakup over this. It was more like a slow bit by bit estrangement. Although Tjok and I pulled wide apart politically, we remained closeknit personally.[9]

According to some Indonesians Sukarno's concern with his political reputation might also have played a role in his decision at this time to divorce Tjokro's daughter, Utari. According to Sukarno he had never consummated the marriage and had treated Utari as his sister rather than his bedmate. This story, however, has caused a great deal of Homeric laughter among those Indonesians who knew Sukarno during his Bandung time and who remember his tremendous sexual appetite.

After he had sent Utari back to Surabaja, Sukarno married Inggit, his landlady, who as he admits himself had aroused his passion immediately upon his arrival in Bandung. Inggit was ten years older than Sukarno; she was beautiful, mature, motherly, and well versed in the ways of love. The novelist Suwarsih Djojopuspito who knew Inggit well at the time describes her as follows:

The oval face, the flowing lines of her nose and chin, the thick knot of hair resting on a sleek and still perfect neck, gave her a look of youthfulness which contrasted with the occasional furrow in her face and the tiredness of her eyes. She was a charming conversationalist and hostess, a real woman who found her greatest pleasure in pleasing others, in particular her husband. She spoke the peculiarly melodious Sundanese language in a clear voice gently and elegantly gesticulating which reminded one of the flowing movements of a dancer.[10]

But also Sukarno was a very handsome man who had a great attraction for women. Suwarsih Djojopuspito was deeply impressed meeting him for the first time.

Soelastri—the author's pseudonym in the novel—greeted him shyly, because Karno's fascinating personality made her feel small . . . she was captivated by his scintillating, dark, searching eyes, the firm mouth which made his forceful personality stand out even more strongly. 'Karno' she thought, and remembered the envelope in which she had kept his and Hatta's photo. Hadn't she been actually and consciously in love with him? At the time she had thought it was hero-worship, and a girlish veneration of romantic figures.[11]

For the first year or so of their marriage Inggit was apparently able to satisfy the demands of her fiery young husband, but after that Sukarno, who was known among his comrades to have more than just a roving eye for beautiful women, came home late at night with increasing frequency—ostensibly from 'political meetings'.

Another interesting description of Inggit and Sukarno is found in the memoirs of Abu Hanifah:

The first time I saw her, I must confess I was very impressed. I met her when I, together with Amir Sjarifuddin, was travelling by train from Bandung to Djakarta. Amir was one of my best friends in my student days. We had the same tastes and we both loved music, art and all the good things in life, such as fine food and good company . . . Amir and I got quickly acquainted with two lovely young girls who were accompanied by their mother. At one stage when I was asking the mother where she was travelling to, and Amir, who had been educated at High School in Holland, was telling tall stories about Europe, we suddenly heard a voice calling Amir from the front of the carriage. We looked up and saw Soekarno sitting next to a pretty young woman, beckoning us. 'Hey folks', he said loudly, 'please come over here for a moment.' We were a little reluctant to go . . . he was from the crowd in Bandung and we were from Djakarta. . . . We didn't feel that he was as important as people in Bandung thought he was. And besides, there were these nice girls we liked to talk to very much, and we felt he disturbed us. But then Soekarno came over to us and standing in front of us looked at the girls. He greeted the mother politely, smiled at the girls, and led the way to his seat. 'Inggit', he said to the woman, 'may I introduce my young friends. One day they will be famous people, and it will be useful to know them.' We were five years younger than Soekarno at that time but I still resented what I felt was his condescending manner. I did not have much time, however, to think about this because Inggit stood up with a smile, and gave us a hand. Indeed, Inggit was very attractive and had the ripened beauty of a woman in her early thirties. She wore a very dark red rose in her blue black hair, and she really looked smashing. Amir was speechless, and I was also impressed, but she was too old for our taste . . . Inggit did not seem too impressed with us, and compared with Soekarno, we were just badly dressed youngsters. He dressed in shantung silk, snow white shirt and dark blue tie. His black shoes were shining and he wore his *pitji*—small black cap—rakishly on his head. Our clothes were a little wrinkled, we had no ties, only sports shirts and our hair was ruffled. I didn't like the setting so after a little while I excused myself and went back to my seat.

Soekarno said with a loud laugh: 'I cannot blame you for preferring the company of the girls above ours. We are old people. Say, don't you think one of the girls is a real beauty.' Inggit frowned, Soekarno smiled at her soothingly. The man is incorrigible, I thought. Even then Soekarno was already known for his love escapades.[12]

Sukarno also headed the Bandung branch of the Taman Siswa organization, a cultural-nationalist movement exhibiting strong nativistic tendencies, which had been founded in 1921 in Jogjakarta by the radical nationalist Suwardi Suryaningrat, better known as Ki Hadjar Dewantoro, a name adopted in 1928, meaning 'teacher and intermediary of the gods'. Dewantoro strongly condemned the common practice of Western-educated Indonesians imitating the Dutch even to the smallest details. He argued that there should be no wholesale imitation of foreign cultures, but that foreign elements should be carefully selected and nationalized. The motto therefore adopted at the founding of the Taman Siswa was, 'Return to your inner self'. The Taman Siswa schools did not follow the Dutch influenced curriculum of the state schools, but emphasized the study of indigenous art forms such as the dance and the *wajang*, and in the history lessons the periods of former Indonesian grandeur and glory.

Dewantoro like so many other major figures in the nationalist movement at the time was deeply concerned about the serious internal divisions in the ranks of those who struggled against colonialism, and he tried to solve this problem in the age-old and well-tried Javanese way by taking the sting out of these ideological differences.

Pupils as well as teachers in Taman Siswa schools were forbidden to join any specific religious or political organization, because it was felt that religion and politics tended to take up the whole of the personality, which often caused serious division in the family, the nation and the world at large. Before a person should be allowed to choose a particular political or religious direction he should be an adolescent. Furthermore—and this was the sole *raison d'être* of the Taman Siswa movement—before making a choice an individual should first have been impregnated with a philosophy of life, which although allowing for freedom of action and expression, should have endowed him with a love and respect for the ways of life and convictions of others. As Mangunsarkoro, another important Taman Siswa leader, pointed out, this did not mean that the movement was non-religious or non-political, but rather than adhering to a particular institutionalized religion its principles were based on a religious code of ethics which was a synthesis of the old *kedjawen* and modern humanism. This meant that all religious faiths could be assimilated in the Taman Siswa way of life:

> After all every religion can be considered as a revelation of God's will. The perfection of man is the purpose of every religion. Thus, he who dedicates his life to it lives in accordance with the will of God, and therefore feels one with Him.[13]

The influence of the movement's philosophy on Sukarno's political ideology as well as methodology is unmistakable. In any case precepts such as harmony, unity and religious tolerance would have come naturally to Sukarno with his Javanistic background. Mohammad Said, the Taman Siswa leader in Djakarta, some years ago described the connection between Sukarno and the Taman Siswa as follows: 'Do you see this *sirih* leaf? You will notice that one side is rough and the other is smooth, but when you bite it, it tastes the same.'[14]

Sukarno, of course, is represented by the rough (*kasar*) side of the leaf but his later ideal of harmonizing all the various political and religious forces of the country into a type of mystical union stems from the same source. It seems, therefore, that some Western scholars are incorrect in classifying Sukarno as a secular nationalist. It is true that Sukarno has always advocated a separation of religion and state, but this aversion to theocracy does not necessarily stem from a Western secular-liberal position but flows rather from his traditionalist Javanese religious views. And although Javanese religion, *agama djawa*, is not institutionalized, it is nevertheless a religion. This point was well taken by Ki Hadjar Dewantoro in a speech made to the Colonial Education Congress in The Hague in 1916 when he described himself:

> . . . as somebody who is only Mohammedan by conviction. That is somebody without a particular religion . . . I have noticed that there is a general misconception concerning my religious position; and on the request of some of my compatriots, who are present here, I would like to point out, that it is incorrect to say . . . that we have lost our bearings. . . . We certainly see a light which recedes deeply into ancient Javanese history. We had a religion in ancient times. This was followed by another one etc., and it is perhaps just because of this changing of religion that the Javanese

are not very fanatical religiously. We prefer to take over various
doctrines from other religions. . . . The most important thing, of
course, is to lead a truly moral life in as far as this is possible,
and that in our opinion is true religion. And although (*kedjawen*)
is not recognized as one of the official religions it is unjust to deny
its existence. It would thus be totally untrue to say that we stand
here as Godless people. Far from it.[15]

Statements then such as the one by Palmier who described Sukarno
as a pious Muslim[16] are entirely meaningless unless they are shown
in the proper Javanese context. Sukarno has said himself, 'Despite
our country being predominantly Muslim, my concepts were not
rooted solely in the Islamic God. Even as I took hesitant steps down
the kindergarten path of belief, I did not see the Almighty as a
personal God.[17]

Suwarsih Djojopuspito records the following discussion between
her husband and herself about Sukarno's religious position.

He is pious, and likes to read religious books. 'Yes', Sudarmo
added, 'he also often burns incense on Thursday evenings.
Moreover, he treats his *kris* with great piety. Sometimes he fasts
on Mondays or Thursdays.' What? Are you sure about that?
'Yes, one day he did not come to dinner using the excuse that he
did not feel hungry. But his wife said in a whisper 'He's fasting.'
This religious trait in him is rather peculiar, particularly when
you hear him say repeatedly in his speeches: 'Even if you burn
a whole *picul* of incense it will not make Indonesia free'. But
perhaps none of us are completely free from mysticism, although
we would strongly deny it . . .' She thought 'Yes, we are modern,
and yet we reserve in a corner of our heart a space where we will
burn incense in desperate moments.'[18]

From his own writings Sukarno comes to the fore as the sole
architect and instigator of a new radical, nationalist movement
which emerges after the abortive rebellions of 1926–27. He almost
entirely ignores the very important role played in this new departure
in nationalist politics by a number of Indonesian university students
in Holland, who in 1922 had transformed an earlier largely social
organization of Indonesian students into a nationalist activist society,
the *Perhimpunan Indonesia* (Indonesian Association). The historical
significance of the Indonesian Association cannot be easily overstated

because many of its prominent members, such as Mohammad Hatta, Dr Sutomo, Sutan Sjahrir, and Ali Sastroamidjojo, exerted a profound influence on the pre-war nationalist movement as well as on the political scene in independent Indonesia.

This new generation of nationalist leaders influenced by Marxist anti-colonial ideas as well as the non-cooperation movement in India, emphasized self-reliance and self-help as the only feasible way to obtain Indonesian independence. In its programme of action issued in 1923 the Indonesian Association stressed that every Indonesian should strive for a free and democratic government without relying on support from outsiders. Moreover, the various nationalist regional organizations which had emerged in imitation of Budi Utomo were condemned for causing unnecessary division and instead urged that all efforts were to be directed at establishing a national Indonesian unity. In 1925 another important platform was added which emphatically stated that Indonesian freedom could only be obtained by conscious, self-assured and self-reliant mass action.

The ideas of the Indonesian Association reached the Indies initially through its journal *Indonesia Merdeka* which was smuggled in either by Indonesian sailors serving on Dutch ships, or sent through the mail wrapped in Dutch newspapers or other ostensibly innocuous material. Sukarno was one of the avid readers of *Indonesia Merdeka*. A little later a number of students returning from Holland set up various study clubs to put the programme of the Indonesian Association into practice. The first of these was established in July 1924 in Surabaja by Dr Sutomo, who concentrated his efforts almost entirely on inculcating a greater sense of economic self-help and activity in Indonesians, and established a national Indonesian bank, various advisory services, schools and cooperatives. More directly politically-orientated were the clubs set up in 1925 by Mr Singgih and Mr Susanto in Jogjakarta, Solo, and Semarang. In the same year similar organizations were established in Djakarta, Bogor and Bandung. The most important of these proved to be the Bandung Study Club, of which Sukarno was one of the founders.

Unlike the Surabaja organization which used non-cooperation as a tactical weapon, the Bandung group was unequivocally opposed to cooperation with the colonial government whatever the circumstances and when in 1926 the Indonesian Association in Holland advocated the establishment of an Indonesian national people's party in order to disseminate its ideas among the masses, it was the radical nationalists who followed suit and established, on 4 July 1927, the *Perserikatan Nasional Indonesia* (National Indonesian Union). The founding committee consisted of Sartono, Iskaq, Samsi Sastrawidagdo, Budiarto and Sunario, all former members of the Indonesian Association, and Sukarno and Anwari both from the Bandung Study Club, and Sujadi an employee of the Department of Finance in Djakarta, and the official representatives of the Indonesian Association in the colony, and J. Tilaar who worked in a Djakarta bank.[19] At the First National Congress in 1928 in Surabaja, the party's name was changed to *Partai Nasional Indonesia* (P.N.I.), the Indonesian Nationalist Party. Sukarno became its first chairman.

The P.N.I. stood for the complete independence of Indonesia and the party programme stressed that non-cooperation, national unity, and self-reliance were the only means by which this ideal could be realized more speedily. Also the geographical limits of the new Indonesia were clearly defined for the first time as comprising all the territories under the control of the Netherlands East Indies government stretching from Sabang, a small island at the northern point of Sumatra, to Merauke in West New Guinea.

In 1928 Mohammad Hatta wrote in *Indonesia Merdeka* that with the establishment of the P.N.I. the major objective of the Indonesian Association had been achieved and that from then onwards it was up to this new party to put into practice the theoretical principles which had been formulated by the students in Holland. Hatta was happy to see that: 'True to the principle of the Indonesian Association the flag of the P.N.I. carries the slogan: National Independence Through Our Own Strength and Ability.'[20]

But although it is clear that the Indonesian Association played an extremely important role in getting the non-cooperative radical movement off the ground, it was Sukarno who was able to give this movement and in particular the P.N.I. the imprint of his own ideas which were not always in accordance with the views and philosophies of other prominent and more Western-orientated leaders such as Hatta and Sjahrir.

Why was it that Sukarno, who was by no means the most intelligent or most brilliant among the radical intellectuals at that time, came to the fore and assumed the leadership of the P.N.I.? Part of the answer is that Sukarno, unlike many of the others who had spent many years away from the home country studying in Holland, had an intimate knowledge of the Indonesian political scene. From his High School days in Surabaja he had grown up at the centre of the nationalist movement. Then, of course, Sukarno's personal charm, his joviality, his powers of persuasion, and his unbending will to succeed greatly helped him when he was lobbying for votes to support his candidature.

Furthermore, his fame as a fiery, flamboyant speaker who could hold the masses entranced was spreading, and his contemporaries admit that he was undoubtedly the most powerful political orator in the country at the time. As the P.N.I. was planned as a party of the masses Sukarno was the obvious choice to instigate and radicalize the feelings of the people. His competitors such as Hatta and Sjahrir were completely unsuited in the role of charismatic demagogue.

Mohammad Hatta was born in Bukittinggi in the region of Minangkabau (West Sumatra) on 12 August 1902. His parents were well-to-do traders. After passing through the Dutch language school system, he went to the Netherlands in 1921 where he studied at the economic faculty of the university of Rotterdam from which he graduated with a Ph.D. in 1932. The long duration of Hatta's university studies was caused by his switch in mid-stream in 1926 from theoretical economics to political economy.

Although never fanatical, Hatta always remained attached to the religion of his youth, Islam. He was a disciplined thinker and unlike other nationalist leaders from Minangkabau he was an unimpressive orator; he was dry, humourless and too analytical to be able to captivate the masses. In fact, he was almost the complete opposite of Sukarno who later complained: 'Hatta gave always the impression of the rain. If I was in a real good mood and full of ideas and then happened to encounter Hatta, then I felt I was suddenly surprised by a rain shower and got wet all over the body. My good mood was gone and also my ideas.'[21]

Achmad Subardjo Djojoadisurjo, who played a very prominent role in the Indonesian Association and who has known both Sukarno and Hatta intimately and for a long time, makes the following cutting comparison about the two leaders:

Hatta's personality was marked by an exacting nature and a strong sense of self-discipline which flowed from his puritan Islamic outlook. He could not easily conceal his disapproval of the bohemian way of conduct of many members of the Indonesian Association who were neglecting their patriotic duties as well as their university studies ... Hatta had a practical sense of organization. He was a man of action, but he didn't want to move without having made a plan first. ... Hatta and Sukarno differed not only in character and temperament but also in their intellectual and cultural backgrounds. ... Hatta's approach to a problem was rational rather than psychological. He had been trained to use certain methods of approach in tackling a problem when he was studying at the Faculty of Economics in Rotterdam, one of the influential centres of economic thinking in Western Europe. . . . Sukarno had a different personality. His training as an architect at the technical faculty in Bandung had made him conversant with the exact sciences which had undoubtedly given him a sharp sense of realism. But unlike those who had spent many years in Western countries for higher education and general experience . . . Sukarno's world had been largely determined by the cultural heritage of Bali and Java which is a syncretism of Hinduism, Buddhism, Islam and animism. He received much inspiration from the essential teaching of Islam and from the code of behaviour of the heroic and symbolic figures from the Hindu epics Maha-bharata and Ramayana. . . . His attractive personality and his strong personal magnetism had made him a born leader of the masses, but he was above all self-possessed, and this quality enabled him to face the most difficult situations and critical, dangerous moments with amazing calmness, and a quiet inner poise and self-assurance. These qualities enabled him to disconcert his most vehement political opponents when they confronted him face to face.[22]

Another very important leader at the time who was closely akin to Hatta's way of thinking, was Sutan Sjahrir, another Minangkabau, a convinced Socialist and a strong believer in parliamentary democracy, who stressed the need for a complete Westernization of Indonesia. Sjahrir strongly opposed Sukarno's Javanistic outlook and the attempts of the Budi Utomo and the Taman Siswa in reinvigorating the traditional civilization. He wrote in his memoirs:

Here for centuries there has been no intellectual, no cultural life, no progress any more. There are the much-praised Eastern art forms—but what else are these than the rudiments of a feudal culture, which for us, the people of the twentieth century, are impossible to fall back on. The *wajang*, all the simple symbolism and mysticism—which is parallel to the allegory and mediaeval wisdom in Europe, what can they still offer us intellectually and culturally? Almost nothing. Our intellectual needs are twentieth-century. Our problems, our outlook are twentieth-century . . . To me the West means effervescence, surging life, the dynamic.

It is Faust whom I love and I am convinced, that only the West, in this dynamic sense, can liberate the East from its slavery.[23]

But Sukarno had already solved in his own mind the problem of unity in the nationalist movement before the establishment of the P.N.I. It was a typically Javanistic solution and in the same way as Ki Hadjar Dewantoro advocated the creation of a unitary Indonesian culture out of the various regional cultures without having to eliminate the latter, Sukarno, in a number of articles in the journal *Indonesia Muda* in 1926, attempted to convince his readers that it was both possible and feasible to unite the three major streams of thought in Indonesia: Islam, Marxism, and nationalism, into a harmonious whole, without having to suppress any of the ideologies as long as they did not disturb the harmonious order of the whole. Sukarno argued that after all these three major groups were striving for the same objective: the freedom of Indonesia and the destruction of imperialism and capitalism. To the objections usually made by nationalists that Islam was an international movement Sukarno replied:

> Many nationalists among us forget that the nationalist struggle and the cause of Islam in Indonesia—yes, in the whole of Asia— have the same beginnings . . . both originate in a condemnation of the West or more explicitly of capitalism and imperialism . . . many of our nationalists forget that Muslims, wherever they are in the Islamic world, have in accordance with their faith a duty to work for the well being of the people and the country they live in.

Sukarno also condemned the Indonesian nationalists who refused to cooperate with Marxists because they adhered to an internationally oriented ideology. He wrote that the nationalist seemed to forget that:

> The origin of the Marxist struggle in Indonesia or Asia is basically the same as the struggle for freedom. He forgets that the aim of this struggle often fits in well with the aims of the Marxists. He forgets that to oppose the Marxists means the same thing as to reject a sympathetic friend and to make another enemy. He forgets and does not understand the motives underlying the attitudes of his brothers in other Asian countries, such as the great Sun Yat Sen, the great nationalist leader, who wholeheartedly

cooperates with the Marxists, although he realizes that the Marxist system cannot yet be established in China, because conditions there are not yet ripe for the establishment of this Marxist system.

As to the clash between Islam and Marxism Sukarno referred Muslims to the great Islamic reformers, Al-Afhaghani and Moham-mad Abduh, both of whom had struggled against Western imperial-ism in all its forms. He also pointed to Tjokroaminoto who had shown that many socialist tenets could be found in the teachings of Islam:

Although we know that Islamic socialism has not the same origins as Marxism, because Islamic socialism is spiritual in nature and Marxism is based on materialism . . . Muslims should not forget that the Marxist view of history (the materialists' view of history) often acts as a road sign pointing to the economic and political problems of the world which are difficult and compli-cated. They must not forget that this method of historical material-ism explains the facts of the past but also what will happen in the future which will be of great use to them. Muslims should not forget that capitalism the enemy of Marxism, is also the enemy of Islam. Because surplus value, as the Marxist term it, it really nothing else than what is called usury in Islam. . . . Muslims, who are fanatics and who are opposed to the Marxist struggle, do not know the laws of their own religion. Such Muslims do not know, that, similar to Marxism, true Islam forbids the piling up of money in the capitalist way, that is it forbids the hoarding of wealth for one's now use.[24]

And then in an endeavour to put the religious qualms of Muslims completely at rest Sukarno rode roughshod over both Marx and Lenin and blandly castrated the Marxist theory of materialism of its atheistic content. He argued that there was an essential difference between philosophical and historical materialism. The first was highly speculative and could either be rejected or accepted like any other philosophical theory. Historical materialism, however, was based on undeniable factual evidence and should therefore be acceptable to any logically thinking person. According to Sukarno, anti-Marxists in Europe, in particular the Christian churches, had purposely denied the existence of this essential difference between these two aspects of Marxism:

In their anti-Marxist propaganda they constantly interchange these concepts and they never tired of accusing the Marxists of believing that thinking was solely a product of the brain in the same way as saliva originates from the mouth and gall comes from the liver. . . . That was the reason why the Marxists in Europe hated the churches and opposed religion. This hostility and this hate intensified whenever the churches made use of religion to protect capitalism, to defend the rulers' class, or to conduct an emphatically reactionary policy.[25]

Addressing himself again to the Marxists, Sukarno pointed out that religion in Indonesia unlike Europe did not support the capitalist regimes; and Islam should not be seen as the religion of the poor and the oppressed. It should therefore not be too difficult for Indonesian Marxists to come to terms with their Muslim brethren and cooperate in their common struggle against colonialism and imperialism.

Sukarno's attempt to anaesthetize the obvious differences between Marxism, Islam, and nationalism was not only a case of political tactics, but also reflected his own ideological position. As he wrote in his autobiography:

The year 1926 was my year of three-dimensional maturisation. . . . Politically Bung Karno was a nationalist. Theologically Bung Karno was a theist. But Bung Karno had become a triple-headed believer. Ideologically he was now a socialist. I repeat that. I became a socialist. Not a Communist. I did not become a Communist. I did not even become a camouflaged Communist. I have never become a Communist. There are still people who think socialism is equivalent to Communism. On hearing the word socialist they cannot sleep. They jump and yell, 'Aha, I knew it! That Sukarno fellow is a Communist!' No I am not. I am a socialist. I am a leftist. Leftists are those who desire to change the existing capitalist, imperialist order. The desire to spread social justice is leftist. It is not necessarily Communistic. Leftists are even at odds with the Communists. Leftophobia, disease of dreading leftist ideas, is a sickness I dread as much as Islamophobia. Nationalism without social justice is nothingism. How can a miserably poor country such as ours have anything but a socialist trend?[26]

In reaching this 'three-dimensional maturisation', however, Sukarno

in line with the Taman Siswa motto had 'returned to his inner self';
and he found the solution to the problem of national unity in the
cosmological Hindu-Javanese world where everything was allocated
its right place in the cosmos without disturbing the harmony of the
whole. The following quotation from Sukarno's *Indonesia Muda*
article of 1926 clearly shows the influence of traditional Javanese
thinking and it could have been taken almost word for word from
the writings of Ki Hadjar Dewantoro, the Taman Siswa leader:

We do not hope that the nationalists will change sides and become
Muslims or Marxists, but what we desire is harmony, and unity
between these three factions. . . . The true nationalist who loves
his country bases his thinking on a knowledge of the structure of
world economics and history and his nationalist feelings do not
emerge merely as the arrogant reaction of a backward people.
The nationalist should not be chauvinistic, he must reject all
narrow-minded views. True nationalism is not merely a copy or
an imitation of Western nationalism, but it should flow from a
feeling of love for the world and humanity. A nationalist who
accepts this kind of nationalism as a divine revelation and practices
it as a religious devotion has escaped from narrow-minded
thinking.[27]

Sukarno plunged himself with great energy and enthusiasm into the
formidable task of achieving a mystical union of all the anti-colonial
forces in the country. The conciliatory overtures which Sukarno
had been making for some time to his old master Tjokroaminoto and
other prominent Muslim leaders paid off, and he was invited to
attend the Islamic Association Congress at Pekalongan in September
1927 to explain his plans. Sukarno played his cards carefully and
emphasized to the delegates that he was opposed to the fusion of
the existing political parties and other national groupings. He argued
that a unitary organization comprising the whole of the Indonesian
people with its multifarious culture and social structure was not only
physically impossible, but also highly undesirable because uniformity
would take away the freedom of the individual and of the groups and
would destroy spontaneity and originality:

The motto therefore should be federation, federation which must
leave intact the personality, the individuality, the character of the
cooperating parties. The ties which are necessary to combine the
parties should be loosely constructed. . . . They should be like the

ties binding together the various parts of the British Empire, which are loose in order to be strong. The agreement which is to be reached between the Indonesian parties cannot be on the basis of ideological principles, because this would imply that the parties who joined would submit themselves to outside discipline. And this would mean that the parties concerned would have to sacrifice some of their independence and freedom of movement. A union which does not impose its own ideology . . . is inconceivable. Yet such a union is possible, if one is satisfied with incidental cooperation and the need for this is felt urgently and unanimously. For example, cooperation in the case of the right to hold public meetings, the treatment of plantation workers, mass arrests . . . cooperation with respect to the student martyrs in Holland . . . we Indonesians should be ashamed that over and over again we are defeated when we attack . . . and that until now we have not been able to infuse strength in our movement.[28]

Sukarno was so successful in enthusing the delegates at this Muslim conference that they pledged their support for a national federation and charged him to work out a more detailed plan of action. Sukarno immediately set about contacting the other political groups and he was able to convene a meeting on 17 December 1927 where the delegates of the various major nationalist organizations agreed to the formation of an anti-colonial federation, which on the suggestion of Sukarno came to be called the *Permufakatan Perhimpunan Politik Kebangsaan Indonesia* (P.P.P.K.I.), which literally means the unanimous consensus of the political organizations of the Indonesian people.

The deliberate selection of the word *Permufakatan* is highly significant and refers to the age-old system of problem-solving and decision-making used in the villages of most of the Indonesian archipelago, where after the full deliberation of all the parties involved and mutual compromise (*musjawarah*) a final unanimous decision (*mufakat*) is reached which is binding on the whole community. Sukarno rejected Western parliamentary democracy because it was based on the tyranny of the majority. He argued that in using the traditional *mufakat* system—which he called 'a return to one's self'—true unity of purpose and action could be achieved because it would provide every party and every group, however small, with the opportunity to make its viewpoint heard and to directly influence the decision-making process.

While Sukarno's syncretic solution to the problem of nationalism,

Marxism, and Islam—which foreshadowed his later doctrine of NASAKOM[29]—was not new and would have come easily to any Javanese with a *kedjawen* background, the transplantation of the method of *musjawarah* and *mufakat* from the village to the national level can be regarded as Sukarno's first original contribution to Indonesian political thought.

Unlike the earlier radical concentrations of 1918 and 1923 European socialists were not admitted to the P.P.P.K.I. and membership was restricted to indigenous organizations. This policy can be seen partly as a reflection of the P.N.I. principle of self-reliance, but it also resulted from a feeling of betrayal by European socialists, who at the Congress of the Second Internationale had taken a 'soft' line over colonialism and had only been prepared to grant the Indonesians self-government on the grounds that they were not ripe yet for independence.

Both Sukarno and Hatta, who was then the chairman of the Indonesian Association in Holland, fiercely denounced this decision. Sukarno argued that the European socialists apparently stood on the same side as the capitalists, who also held that Indonesia was not yet ripe for independence. A clear demarcation should henceforth be made between *sini* and *sana*, between those who were genuine fighters for Indonesian freedom and those who supported colonialism. Sukarno argued that in order to gain strength, to create a national will, which would result in national action, a 'brown national front' was needed. Out of the confrontation between the 'brown' and the 'white' front—as Marx had prophesied—there would be born the antithesis: freedom and prosperity for the oppressed.

Critics who pointed out that so far the P.N.I. and Sukarno had done a great deal of talking but had achieved very little in the way of improvements in the social and economic condition of the people were dismissed by Sukarno on the grounds that the first objective should always be: 'An independent Indonesia in the quickest way possible. This entails that we do not strive for independence by means of improving miserable living conditions in our country, but we must strive for independence *in order to* improve these living conditions.'[30]

The P.P.P.K.I., however, was too restricted in its activities by the *mufakat* principle to perform the great national deeds Sukarno had hoped for, and only a few general and rather lame declarations were made.

Sukarno's call for unity, however, had more success in the national youth movement. Attempts made at the first Indonesian Youth

Congress, held in May 1926 in Djakarta to fuse the various youth groups into one, had broken down because of the intransigence of the Muslim organizations, who demanded that Islam should be given a privileged status in an independent Indonesia. Far more important was the second Indonesian Youth Congress held in 1928 at which it was unanimously decided to work for the creation of one country, one language, and one people.

In his autobiography Sukarno writes: 'On October 28, Sukarno officially proclaimed the solemn pledge: "One nation, one flag, one language".'[31] This is hotly denied by those who were present at the time. Sukarno and other political leaders were present but did not actually proclaim the youth oath although it is admitted that Sukarno had undoubtedly strongly influenced the various youth leaders. It was also at this youth congress that the Indonesian anthem, *Indonesia Raja*, was performed for the first time.

But it was not until the beginning of January 1931 that the various separate Indonesian youth organizations decided to fuse into one large national group, which came to be called *Indonesia Muda*. It is significant that one of the major Muslim youth organizations, the *Jong-Islamietenbond* (Union of Young Muslims), refused to join because it claimed that the new organization was too secular in its outlook.

Sukarno, during the years 1928 and 1929, became increasingly vehement in his speeches, arousing the messianic expectations of the people to a high pitch. Presenting himself as Bima, the hero of the *wajang*, he called upon his listeners to identify themselves with the forces of the right, the *pandawas*, in order to struggle as in the Bharatha Juddha against the *korawas*, the usurpers of the kingdom of Ngastina. His performance roused the masses to ecstasy wherever he went, and it is said that one Indonesian journalist who was sent to report on one of Sukarno's speeches was so taken in that he apparently believed that he was already free.[32]

Not all Indonesians, however, were impressed and in particular many Western-oriented intellectuals, including many students, disagreed with his thinking as well as with his approach. Abu Hanifah, who was a student at the time in Djakarta, writes:

> Undoubtedly Soekarno was a great orator. I saw him at his best, which was before he became President of the Republic of Indonesia, bewitching whole gatherings with his speeches. . . . He couldn't enchant us, the angry young men, because we did not find him either serious or sincere enough. But in front of the common people he was in his element.[33]

Once, during a meeting of Djakarta students, Sukarno suffered the worst humiliation which can overcome a speaker: he was shouted down so that it was impossible for him to continue his speech. The students, in imitation of the campaign of Gandhi in India, were fanatical followers of the *swadeshi* movement. But Sukarno was opposed to *swadeshi* not so much perhaps in principle, but as he once put it, he was loath to appear in public in a sackcloth. Abu Hanifah describes this incident as follows:

> There were good speakers who inflamed our spirits. And then it was the turn of Soekarno. He appeared on the podium and everybody became speechless. He looked to us like someone who had just stepped out from a fashion show or formal reception. When he began to speak everybody remained quiet for a few moments then suddenly from the back of the hall there came the first shrill whistles and loud remarks. . . . Then a group of students started shouting: 'Let him come down, he doesn't belong here. He is *anti-swadeshi*, down with him.' The tumult became worse and the committee sent Soekarno a note: Please go back to your chair. We will fix the misunderstanding. And so Soekarno had to come down from the speaker's platform. It was his first defeat as a leading speaker and he was furious.[34]

In 1929 Sukarno appears cocksure, arrogant, secure in his belief that the end of colonialism was near. While stories among the masses did their rounds again about the coming of the Just King and about the prophecies of Djojobojo, Sukarno, as Dahm points out, believed strongly in another Djojobojo, that is the prophecies of Marx about the eventual breakdown of imperialism and colonialism. In his writings at the time, Sukarno prophesied the coming of a Pacific war between Japan on one side and the United States and England on the other. And he asserted that Japan would be the key to Indonesian independence.[35]

Sukarno in his speeches and writings exhorted his people to unite, because, he argued, the powers of colonialism were already receding. But the Dutch colonial government apparently thought differently and proved the opposite when on 29 December 1929 it arrested Sukarno and a few other stalwarts of the P.N.I. and sent them to gaol to await trial on the charge of conspiracy to overthrow the colonial government.

As usual in his autobiography Sukarno romanticizes the events of the night of his arrest:

Outside, with rifles at the ready, stood fifty policemen, blockading the house, the complex, and the street leading up to it. Three motor cars were lined up. The middle one was a special vehicle in which we dangerous criminals were escorted to the police station. In the car were hustled Gatot and the taxi driver, who was totally innocent and whose sole crime was that he loved his country too much. Suhada was released subsequently but, meanwhile, they booked him because he too looked like a desperado to them. A few years later he died. His final request was, 'Please, I wish to have a photo of Bung Karno placed on my chest.' That wish granted he folded his gnarled hands over his picture and passed away peacefully.[36]

But during an interview with two Dutch journalists in 1967 the same chauffeur revealed:

How does he get it into his head to say that I am dead? After the arrest in 1929 the Dutch sentenced me to eight months in prison and they impounded my 1924 model Chevrolet. I met Sukarno for the first time again in 1956 in Bandung. He was then President and promised me expressly that he would give me my own car in order to replace the only one which I have ever owned. But he did not keep his promise.[37]

While in gaol Sukarno seems to have lost his staunch faith in the new Djojobojo and he tried to find solace again in the stories of the *wajang*.

During the initial stages of the trial, which caused a tremendous sensation in Indonesia as well as in Holland, Sukarno was very subdued and did not play the great hero of the masses at all. He admitted that he was a leading figure in the P.N.I. but he emphasized the theoretical aspects of his revolutionary beliefs and denied that he had ever called on his followers to forcefully overthrow the colonial regime. When pressed by his interrogators, Sukarno admitted that the P.N.I. was revolutionary, but this, he argued, did not necessarily mean that the party was a threat to public peace and order. Sukarno stressed that in fact the P.N.I. was against the use of force. Gradually, Sukarno's answers became more poignant and belligerent. For example:

The President of the Court: Are you satisfied with the policies of the present government?

38

Sukarno: On the contrary! The P.N.I. is completely opposed to imperialism and capitalism. This system must be destroyed by the actions of the masses as is stated in the P.N.I. programme. But before tackling capitalism the P.N.I. first wants to attack imperialism.

The President: How does imperialism show itself in the Netherlands Indies?

Sukarno: In the large sugar and tobacco plantations, etc.

The President: In your opinion, is Dutch power here possible without imperialism?

Sukarno: Without imperialism Dutch power here would not be able to exist . . .

The President: It is always the same over and over again. The government is always depicted as a potentate, as an enemy. You have done the same thing, haven't you?

Sukarno: I have never said that.

The President: The spirit of bitterness and hostility towards the Netherlands Indies government is the only tangible result of your activities. From all the evidence it appears that everything is directed towards inculcating hate. Do you really believe, Mr Sukarno, that in this way you can achieve your objective in a peaceful way?

Sukarno: No, not in this way, but I am convinced that the P.N.I. is opposed to the use of force and that the party has a different purpose in mind . . .

The President: Why did you have secret files from the police archives in your possession?

Sukarno: They were given to me to read. I did not know they were stolen.

The President: Why did you keep them?

Sukarno: There was no sense in giving them back, because after reading them it became clear how badly the police was informed! These documents were useless to them . . .[38]

The climax of the trial was Sukarno's defence oration which later was published under the title *Indonesia Menggugat* (Indonesia Accuses).

In this speech, Sukarno, running through almost the whole history of imperialism and capitalism, quoting widely from Marx, Lenin, Kautsky, Schumpeter and also from Sun Yat Sen, particularly used Dutch critics of colonial policy in the Indies, such as van Kol, Kuyper, and the socialist Van Gelderen to illustrate the perniciousness and injustice of the system. He argued that as the capitalists controlled the colonial government and its agencies and also the Press, little help for the plight of the indigenous people could be expected from them. The destruction of the colonial system was therefore not only the logical answer, but would definitely occur in line with the laws of history:

> Indonesia *will* be free! We are absolutely convinced that Indonesia will break away from Holland. And this will no longer depend on whether either Indonesians or Netherlanders want to be just and do the right thing. The history of the world and mankind does not provide one instance where a people remains under foreign domination for ever. On the contrary, it points over and over again to the fact that every people always succeeds in liberating itself. Thus if the Indonesian people, the P.N.I. and all of us strive to put an end to foreign domination, and call out for independence, then they only fulfill the historical role which of necessity must be correct. But as to the manner in which our chains shall be broken, that is entirely in the hands of the imperialists. It is not we, the Indonesian people, but the imperialists who will have the last word.[39]

Sukarno then tried to put the blame for the revolutionary tendencies in Indonesian society on the Dutch themselves in order to show his judges that he and his comrades were only the tools selected by fate to accomplish the inevitable predetermined historical process; and certainly in terms of the traditional Javanese view of the world there could be no question of guilt. On the contrary, it was the duty of every Javanese to live and act in accordance with the demands of the forces of nature, the cosmos.

The Bandung court, however, had no qualms about finding Sukarno guilty, and although its decision was challenged by some prominent Dutch legal scholars, Sukarno was condemned to a four year prison sentence.

The widely publicized trial instantly made Sukarno into a national hero. He was talked about even in the remotest Indonesian villages. The trial did more than a thousand of his speeches could have done, it suddenly made him the most popular nationalist leader.

Sukarno was sent to the new prison Sukamiskin in Bandung, where as in the days before the trial he tried to find solace in religion. This time apparently he became interested in Islam and Christianity. He seems to have made a careful study of both these religions, but in his usual style he only made certain of their tenets 'his own' regarding the remainder as unsuitable for his purposes:

> In my dungeon I undertook the study of all religions to see if I were truly one of the 'false and lost'. If they were better for me then I wanted them. With Pastor van Lith I commenced the study of Christianity. I particularly cherished its Sermon on the Mount. Jesus' inspiration imbued the early martyrs so they walked to their deaths singing psalms of praise to him because they knew 'We leave this kingdom, but we will enter the kingdom of Heaven'. I clung to that. I read and re-read the bible, the Old Testament and the New became dear friends to me. I renewed their acquaintances often. Then I read the Koran. And it was only after absorbing the thoughts of Mohammed that I stopped looking to books on sociology for answers to how and why things are. I found all my answers in the words of the Prophet. I felt totally satisfied.[40]

Even while in prison, Sukarno was able to stir up a furore in public life. A letter dated 17 May 1931, smuggled from the prison, appeared in an Indonesian newspaper and caused an uproar in Indonesia as well as in Holland. Sukarno complained in this letter that he was treated as a criminal; his head had been shaved clean, he was forced to wear blue prison clothes and the physical work he was required to do in the prison book-binding shop was so heavy that in the evening he was too tired even to read. Sukarno wrote that he was becoming lethargic and that physically he was gradually going downhill.[41]

The reaction in Indonesia and Holland was tremendous. Various members of the *Volksraad* including van Mook, who later was so often unjustly accused by Sukarno of all kinds of misdeeds against humanity, pressed in a fiery speech for a more humane and gallant treatment of political prisoners who after all were not criminals.

In the Dutch parliament similar demands were made, and the Dutch trade union leader Moltemaker, who during a tour of the Indies visited Sukarno twice in Sukamiskin prison, promised in an emotional speech on 30 August 1931 that the S.D.A.P., the Dutch socialist party, would force the Dutch government to release Sukarno from prison. This promise was partly fulfilled the next day when Queen Wilhelmina on the occasion of her birthday reduced Sukarno's prison term by three months. In December 1931 Governor-General de Graeff, who is dismissed in Sukarno's memoirs[42] as an arch reactionary despite the fact that he tried with great patience and against overwhelming odds to reduce the power of Dutch capitalism and its impact on colonial policy, decided as a conciliatory gesture to the Indonesian nationalists to release Sukarno from prison two years before the end of his term.

How much Sukarno had been the soul of the radical nationalist movement had become abundantly clear when within a few weeks of his forced disappearance from the Indonesian political scene, the P.P.P.K.I. and its built-in dynamic force, the P.N.I., came tumbling down like a house of cards.

Both organizations seemed to be lamed by the arrest and trial of the radical nationalist leaders; and the various protest meetings that were staged were rather tame and unimpressive.

The P.N.I. which had now been officially declared a forbidden organization was disbanded by Sartono, the acting chairman, on 24 April 1931, a week after the verdict against Sukarno had been confirmed by the authorities in Batavia. On 30 April 1931 a new party, the Partai Indonesia or Partindo was founded. The party had the same programme as the old P.N.I. and declared that the Indonesian people should continue to try to unify themselves irrespective of race and religion in order to gain sufficient power in the struggle for freedom.

The P.P.P.K.I., which from the beginning had been no more than a pseudo-unitary organization, was even more ineffective now that it was without its leading spirit Sukarno; and *mufakat* even on unimportant issues was no longer possible, because of the growing hostility between the Islamic and nationalist groups. While Sukarno had been able to hush up the various controversies that had arisen between the Islamic group and the nationalists such as national education, the establishment of a national Indonesian bank, and child marriage, in his absence hostility between the two sides reached such a high pitch that in December 1930 the Islamic Association left the federation.

The policies of Sukarno and the P.N.I. were now severely criticized by a number of more Western-orientated nationalists. In particular, Mohammad Hatta, the president of the Indonesian Association in Holland, was disgusted with the direction the movement had taken. In 1930 in an article entitled 'The crisis in the P.P.P.K.I.' he openly took issue with Sukarno's principle of *mufakat*:

Our happiness about the founding of the P.P.P.K.I. as a type of political concentration was mainly based on our hope that this body would develop into a representative body of the Indonesian people, a true Indonesian national parliament. Both popular parties, the P.N.I. and P.S.I., have the power to let the P.P.P.K.I. evolve in this natural manner. . . . Two years have since passed and instead of a consolidation of national power ideological confusion on the national level has increased and is reaching a crisis point. What are the reasons?

Hitting at Sukarno's Javanistic solution to achieve national unity, Hatta continued:

A superficial observer of the Indonesian nationalist movement, or a dreamer about a unitary policy could perhaps be amazed and ask us on what grounds we could speak about a crisis in the P.P.P.K.I.

Hatta agreed that the unification of the youth movements and greater acceptance of the idea of national unity also among the older generation were an undeniable fact, but they could not camouflage two other facts, namely an ideological crisis and a manifestation of powerlessness:

Ideological confusion has resulted since many members of the P.P.P.K.I. began to believe that the ideal of national unity should be realized in terms of politics. There is a strong tendency to create the P.P.P.K.I. into an organ of supreme power rather than a national parliament, in which the voice of the people is heard and in which differences of opinion do not have to be suppressed. The truth of the saying that *Du choc des opinions jaillit la verité* seems to have been forgotten. . . . It is the tragedy of this mistaken ideal of unity that criticism is often seen as an attempt to disturb unity. But in this way, the mutual understanding and greater tolerance one is seeking cannot be achieved. On the contrary bitterness will increase unnecessarily. Eventually, the P.P.P.K.I., while giving an outside appearance of strength, will be weak on the inside. Of greater importance from a political point of view is the apparent existence of a feeling of powerlessness in the P.P.P.K.I. which is apparent from its inability to declare its solidarity when its left-wing, the P.N.I., was attacked. The P.P.P.K.I. only seems to be able to stage mock battles. . . . But when on 29 December 1929 the P.N.I. was strongly attacked, all the P.P.P.K.I. could do was to show its powerlessness. Admittedly shortly after a protest meeting was held in Batavia—and probably also in other places—where declarations of solidarity were given. But these seem to have only been words and one has not heard anything any more about protest actions by the P.P.P.K.I.[43]

Hatta's arguments appear to have been impressive enough for the P.P.P.K.I. to decide at its meeting in May 1931 to abandon the principle of *mufakat* and to adopt instead a Western type voting system.

Hatta was even more deeply perturbed about the disbandment of the P.N.I. In a letter published in July 1931 in the Indonesian press, he dismissed Sartono's action as high-handed and premature, and he argued that although the P.N.I. was involved in the trial of its leaders the colonial government would have refrained from outlawing the party out of fear of widespread popular disturbances. In view of the severity of Dutch repressive measures in the colony and the fact that Hatta had actually been away for more than ten years, this contention was perhaps somewhat out of touch with reality. More fundamental, however, and showing an entirely different frame of mind to Sukarno's thinking was Hatta's criticism that the P.N.I. had been disbanded arbitrarily and without reference to the wishes of the rank-and-file. And in a very sharp attack on the style of leadership developed by Sukarno, Hatta wrote: 'The people are used as a mat to wipe one's feet on. They are considered necessary to applaud after listening to a leader's fierce speech. The people are not taught how to take care of its responsibilities and duties.'[44]

According to Hatta it was useless arousing the people into a great frenzy without guiding them into constructive thinking. Instead the people should be educated first in economics and politics in order to become aware of their rights. Non-cooperation, so Hatta argued, was an educational method and not, as Sukarno had perceived it, a thing-in-itself. Moreover, it was highly dangerous to leave the fate of the nation in the hands of a single man, as was obviously clear after Sukarno's arrest when the movement had fallen completely flat. Instead, emphasis should be placed on the training of cadres who would be able to create the people into the vast countervailing power that Sukarno had always desired.[45]

Hatta's letter caused a serious division in the nationalist camp. This has carried through to the present day. Unlike Sukarno, who had only experienced Western civilization in the watered-down form he had encountered in the colony, and in whom traditional Javanese civilization had remained deeply embedded, most of the Hatta group originated from the islands outside Java. Many of them had also been to the Netherlands where they had spent a considerable time as students, and where they had experienced Western civilization, including parliamentary democracy, at its source. They objected to Sukarno's rather facile denunciation of Western culture and they were also opposed to his *nativistic* approach in solving the problems of the Indonesian people.

It was Sutan Sjahrir who in December 1931 founded the rival nationalist party, the P.N.I. Significantly the letters P.N.I. stood for *Pendidikan Nasional Indonesia* (the National Education of Indonesia). The new party condemned the tactics of Sukarno, and emphasized the great need to train cadres to diffuse a truly revolutionary spirit among the people. The new party then incorporated the ideals of Hatta, who became its chairman on his return from Holland in 1932.

When Sukarno was released from prison he was confronted with a P.P.P.K.I. in a state of advanced decline and a serious split in the nationalist camp. But he immediately showed that he was his old self and to the large crowd that gathered to meet him he explained in a fiery speech that his return could be compared to a *kris* which had been kept for three years and had now become sharper on both sides: 'I will fight. Give me a weapon, that is the unity of the masses. I shall fight for a free Indonesia as long as there is a drop of blood flowing in my veins.'[46]

The next day he went with Inggit to Surabaja to attend the *Indonesian Raja* (Greater Indonesia) Congress which had been postponed until he was released. It was obviously clear that the masses had not forgotten him and the trip to Surabaja turned out to be a triumph, a real hero's welcome. At every station where the train stopped crowds of jubilant Indonesians were standing and waving. The national Indonesian newspapers presented special Sukarno editions. He was kissed and hugged, and buried under garlands of flowers. At the station at Surabaja a crowd of more than 6,000 people awaited the great leader, the martyr of the people. At the Congress he again reaffirmed his intention of struggling to the death for Indonesian freedom. Comparing himself to the *wajang* figure, Kokrosono with his magic weapon *nanggala*, Sukarno, although saddened by the split that had occurred in the nationalists ranks, promised his listeners that he would bring unity again. However, it proved impossible for Sukarno, despite his charismatic power, to convert Hatta and Sjahrir.

In addition to the formation of cadres the P.N.I. was more orthodox Marxist in its policies; and it considered a mystical union of all classes in the indigenous society as impossible. Hatta argued that Sukarno's method would not be able to achieve *persatuan* (unity) but only *persatean*. *Sate* is skewered roasted pieces of meat. According to Hatta, a stick of *sate* could consist of all kinds of meat, but concepts such as nation, bourgeoisie, and nobility could never be chained together into one compatible arrangement. These highly divergent groups could only be united if they were all prepared to abandon their principles which they could hardly be expected to do. The only sensible way to achieve freedom therefore was to organize the proletarian masses and to wage a class struggle against both foreign capitalism and the indigenous nobility and bourgeoisie.[47]

After eight months of intensive lobbying Sukarno still hadn't succeeded in healing the breach. Unwilling to give up his own political views, Sukarno then decided to join the Partindo.

But even if Sukarno had been convinced by the arguments of the Hatta-Sjahrir group, he would never have been willing to admit this because among the intellectuals, among his peers, he would not have been allowed to play the dominant role which he believed fate had destined him to perform. And if not fate, then certainly his vanity forced him to take the different and more palatable course of arousing the masses and mirroring his power and his greatness in them.

Sukarno's answer to the insistence of the P.N.I. on the class struggle was the concept of *marhaenism*. According to Sukarno Marxist theory did not fully fit the Indonesian situation. The number of people who only had their labour to sell (proletarians) was too small to build a revolution on. Indonesia was basically an agrarian country with teeming millions of poor peasants, who owned some tools, some land, and a small house. These people—the *marhaens*—were to be the backbone of the struggle for independence and the revolution. Sukarno relates the following story as to how he came to use the term *marhaen*.

Pedalling around aimlessly on my cycle—thinking—I found myself in the southern part of Bandung, a compact agricultural area where you see many farmers in their little fields, each of which is less than a third of a hectare. My attention for some reason was captured by a peasant hoeing his property. He was alone. His clothes were shabby. This typical scene struck me as symbolic of my people. I stood there awhile contemplating it silently. We Indonesians being a warm, friendly sort, I approached him. In the regional Sundanese I asked 'Who is the owner of this lot on which you are now working?' He said to me

'Why I am, sir'. I said, 'Tell me, does anyone own this with you?'
'Oh, no, sir, I own it all by myself'. . . . I then asked this young
farmer his name. And he told me, Marhaen. Marhaen is a
common name like Smith or Jones. At that moment the light of
inspiration flooded my brain. I would use that name for all
Indonesians with the same miserable lot. From then on I would
call my people *marhaenists*.[48]

For Sukarno, then, *marhaenism* meant the magic formula which would
unite all groups and classes in Indonesian society, because they were
all exploited, into a mass movement to fight for independence.

Sukarno argued that independence should be achieved first and
that then the establishment of a just and prosperous society would
almost automatically come about, providing the proletariat—the
factory workers and plantation coolies—assumed and retained the
leading role in the struggle. Sukarno wrote:

Generally the peasants still are half-feudal in their thinking, they
live in a mystical dreamworld indulging in fancies. They are not
as modern and rational as the proletariat that lives in the hurly
burly twentieth century. They still revere the feudal nobility a
great deal, they believe in the coming of the Ratu Adil or Heru
Tjokro, incarnations from heaven, a paradise on earth in which
there will be prosperity and justice. . . . In everything they (the
peasants) are backwards and old-fashioned. . . . They have an
old-fashioned social structure. Their methods of production have
not changed. . . . In short, their whole social economic life is
still old-fashioned—and also their ideology is obviously old-
fashioned. . . .

On the other hand the proletarians as a class are the product
of capitalism and imperialism. They know about factories, they
know about machines, about electricity and the capitalistic
production process and about all the modern things of the
twentieth century. They also hold the fate of capitalism more
directly in their hands, they can have a greater direct impact in
fighting capitalism. It would therefore be logical that they would
be in the front line fighting capitalism and imperialism . . . that
they would be shock troops. . . . Marx has said that in the struggle
of the peasants and the workers, the latter must become 'the
revolutionary shock troops'. . . . The peasants must be the
comrades of the workers, they must be united and harmoniously
associated with the workers. . . . In this united struggle the workers

must 'become the standard-bearers of the social revolution' . . .
because according to Marx as a class they are a 'social necessity
and the eventual victory of the ideology is a historical necessity—
a necessary historical event, a certain historical event'.[49]

After the 'golden bridge' of independence had been achieved, the
final objectives of the *marhaenist* struggle would be to establish a true
political as well as economic democracy, a true social democracy.
Social democracy meant a state of affairs, where all political,
cultural and economic life was controlled by the people. All large
business concerns and means of production were to become the
property of the state.

Indonesian nationalism, the struggle for freedom, should therefore
not be of the bourgeois kind or the feudal kind, but it should be
deeply impregnated with the peoples' spirit (*volksgeist*). This social
nationalism as Sukarno called it, was to be opposed to every type
of capitalism and imperialism, and it was to be pervaded by a strong
feeling of justice and humanity.[50]

Sukarno, however, was not given a great deal of time to propound
his theories, because on 1 August 1933 he was arrested again
and in February 1934 he was exiled for an indefinite period to the
island of Flores in eastern Indonesia. Hatta and Sjahrir and a
number of other prominent nationalist leaders were arrested soon
afterwards and many of them were sent to the infamous Tanah
Merah camp in West Irian.

When Sukarno was unable to convince the Dutch police that he
was not planning an immediate revolution, he did a complete
volte-face, and as a token of his sincerity offered to cooperate with the
colonial government and take a seat in the Bandung City Council
or even in the *Volksraad*. As further proof of his 'conversion' Sukarno
wrote a letter to the Partindo leadership asking to resign from the
party. He added that he was retiring from politics because he no
longer agreed with the principles of the party and the direction
that the radical movement had taken.

When the news of Sukarno's 'conversion' leaked out in the
national Indonesian Press it caused a furore, the vibrations of which
took a long time to die down. With this one move Sukarno destroyed
a great deal of the prestige and trust he had gained among many of
the Indonesian nationalists. Among people who had previously
almost venerated him as a god there were some who now turned
their hate on him, pulling his portrait down from the walls and
mutilating it. Some Partindo leaders demanded that Sukarno

should not be allowed to resign, but that his name should be struck dishonourably from the party's register. The reasons for this drastic decision by Sukarno will probably never be fully known.

It has been argued that Sukarno took this decision in deference to his wife, who beseeched him to give up his radical non-cooperative stance. Others again argued it was purely a tactical move on the part of Sukarno who attempted in this way to save the Partindo from further persecution by the Dutch. There is also the story that it was on the advice of Husni Tahmrin, the radical cooperative nationalist, that Sukarno took this momentous step. Tahmrin apparently argued that Sukarno would be far more useful as a free cooperative nationalist than as a captive non-cooperator in Flores which was far away from the centre of Indonesian political activity.

Another and a more likely explanation is that Sukarno at the time was suffering from a severe mental depression and was psychologically unstable, something which is noticeable at various stages in his career when he was up against tremendous odds. Undoubtedly his future as a great national leader must have looked rather bleak to him at the time. In addition to being hampered by the Dutch colonial power, Sukarno had also been thwarted by both the Western-orientated Indonesian intellectuals and many of the Islamic leaders in his plans to set up a mass Indonesian organization, and he had singularly failed to bring about the 'mystical union' he had dreamt about for so long.

This would have been sufficient to discourage any man, but it would undoubtedly have hit even harder a man like Sukarno, with his highly emotional makeup, who was liable to change from a state of high elation to a fit of deep depression in a split second. His failure as a politician together with the spectre of being exiled for an unspecified period to a remote island was probably enough to bring the hypersensitive Sukarno close to a mental breakdown.

It is known that Sukarno was already in a mood of mental depression before his arrest. He confessed to one of his friends, Sanusi Pane, a well-known journalist and writer, that he had serious doubts about the innate ability of the Indonesian people ever to regain their freedom, and create something of world-shattering importance. He told Sanusi Pane: 'I would have the moral courage to work together with the Dutch if I could be persuaded that it would be useful.' And during a walk with Sanusi Pane in the hill-town of Lembang near Bandung, Sukarno exclaimed:

Where are the great works of art we have produced? Where are our gigantic statues of Buddha, our Angkor Vats, our Mahabharatas, our Homers, our Dantes, our cathedrals, our peaking temples? We were and we are a weak people! . . . The Indian, Chinese and Western cultures are three dimensional; ours is two dimensional. We do nothing else than copy. We are not able to produce something original. It will still take a long time before the national movement will amount to something, before we are worthy of freedom.[51]

Dr Tjipto Mungunkusumo, his mentor during the early Bandung days, was of the opinion that Sukarno had suffered a mental breakdown. He wrote:

When Baron de Graeff had Soekarno released from Soekamiskin —the prison of Bandung—he was receiving psychiatric treatment. I know for certain that his genuine friends advised him strongly to seek refuge in Europe or anywhere else where he would be away from his normal surroundings and could enjoy some spiritual rest. But, of course, an overseas trip, which was no luxury for the man, was not liked by his so-called best friends. The movement could not miss him, not even for a day or a night. If the popular leader went on an overseas trip, that would be taken as an example of cowardice. All these were arguments of so-called patriots, who when it comes to the point prefer to have sacrifices made to the fatherland by others rather than by themselves. During the first month after the Soekamiskin period Soekarno's actions were marked by serious nervous tension which caused me a great deal of anxiety. He was honoured with incense, flower and hallelujahs. It was as if the people were intent on applauding him away from Java, away from his country. All this filled us, who were more realistic, with disgust. I haven't followed Soekarno any longer, because I felt that his activities were not based on truth, which is the only basis on which a movement can and may be founded.[52]

Sukarno disappeared from Java on 15 February 1934, almost unnoticed. There were only a few people to see him off at the Surabaja wharf, from where he took ship to Flores.

The exiling of the radical nationalist leaders and their successors, as well as the imprisonment in 1934 of the leaders of the Indonesian

Islamic Association and the Permi in Minangkabau caused the death blow to the radical, non-cooperative national movement. Also the radical youth organizations were lamed when the colonial government forbade them to hold public meetings.

The national federation P.P.P.K.I. died a natural death in 1935, and the Partindo as well as the P.N.I. followed suit in 1936.

In the meantime the two moderate nationalist parties, Budi Utomo and the P.B.I. of Dr Sutomo, had fused themselves into a new party, the Parindra, which strove for national independence and the social-economic improvement of the people on the basis of cooperation with the colonial government.

Also the radical wing began to reorientate itself. Already in 1934 the Partindo had decided that non-cooperation should no longer be a strict principle, but should only be used as a tactical measure on suitable occasions. The Indonesian Association in Holland was the first national organization which completely changed course and decided in 1936 that circumstances had changed and that for the time being non-cooperation would be harmful to the nationalist movement. According to the Indonesian students in Holland the growing strength of fascism in Germany, Italy and Japan was a serious threat to Holland, as well as Indonesia, which could expect a great deal more from a democratic country such as the Netherlands than from autocratic Japan. Radical nationalists in Indonesia followed suit and in May 1937 founded a new nationalist party called *Gerakan Rakjat Indonesia* (Gerindo), which had the same programme as the old Partindo, but with the important exception that it was willing to cooperate with the Dutch and take seats in the various representative councils. The Gerindo, in which younger generation national leaders, such as Amir Sjarifuddin, played an important role, was strongly anti-fascist and anti-Japanese.

The Islamic movement had fared little better than the nationalists and was also suffering from a great deal of internal strife and division. A number of smaller groups separated from the Islamic Association. In 1938 a splinter party, the Party of Indonesia, was founded which strove to convince the people that Islam was the most perfect religion and that Allah had promised that the Islamic community would rule the world. In 1940 another group of Muslims who demanded an Islamic theocratic state separated from the Islamic Association. They were led by Kartosuwirjo, who later during the revolution became the leader of the terrorist Darul Islam. Similarly in Atjeh, North Sumatra, a number of theocratic Islamic teachers united themselves in the *Persatuan Ulama Seluruh* under the leadership of Daud Beureuh, who in the early fifties revolted against the 'godless Indonesian republic'.

During the late 1930s it became widely felt in both Muslim and nationalist circles that internal division was damaging to their respective causes. It was the Mohammadyah movement, which hitherto had stayed out of politics, which in 1937 took the initiative in founding the M.I.A.I., the Great Council of Indonesian Muslims, which was joined by the Nahdatul Ulama, and the Islamic Association. As stated in its programme, the M.I.A.I. was founded to unite Muslims to defend the honour of their faith seriously threatened by the colonial government, which was apparently opposed to the Islamic Law and since the mid-1920s had officially recognized and propagated the *adat* law.

In May 1939 the nationalists also federated again and established the *Gabungan Politik Indonesia* (Indonesian Political Union), which was joined by the Parindra, Gerindo, and the P.S.I.I. Also the various national youth organizations united themselves again and in December established a central council. The Muslims, however, set up their own united youth organization in February 1940.

The conciliatory moves of the Indonesian nationalists since the mid-1930s were not reciprocated by the Dutch government. After almost two years of 'consideration' they rejected a petition by the moderate nationalist Sutardjo, signed by other Indonesian members of the *Volksraad*, to call an imperial conference where both parties on the basis of equality were to construct a plan for gradual political reforms which would enable Indonesian to gain independence in a period of ten years within the framework of a Netherlands Commonwealth.

The Dutch, in spite of the obvious threat of Japan, were apparently cocksure about the impregnable defence shield which the U.S.A. and Britain would provide.

Also the demands of Gapi for a true Indonesian parliament were dismissed by the Dutch government in February 1940 on the grounds that Indonesia was not yet ripe for self-government, let alone independence. In February 1941 the Indonesian nationalists tried another approach and suggested that Holland and Indonesia should form a federation in which each partner would have its own head of state, government, and parliament. This suggestion was again ignored by the Dutch government, which at the time was in exile in London, on the grounds that discussion should be postponed until after the war.

During his period of exile on the remote island of Flores, Sukarno seems to have spent a great deal of his time on perfecting and deepening his political philosophy. He continued the study of Islam as well as Christianity, partly perhaps to find solace in his great misfortune, but also as is obvious from his writings, to become more familiar with these religions in order to show the Muslims as well as the Christians the error of their ways and to fit them more easily into his own nationalist ideology. In his 'Letters from Endeh' to Hadji Hassan, a well-known Islamic scholar in Bandung, Sukarno simplified the Islamic religion to such an extent that the final product would have been unrecognizable to many devout followers of the prophet.

Sukarno was extremely unhappy in Flores. He was lonely. He missed the vast crowds of Java, the shouting, the wild ecstasy of the masses, the great exhilaration of being at the centre of things. In Flores, Dutch as well as Indonesian officials had been ordered to stay away from Sukarno. Also many of the Islamic traders in the predominantly Roman Catholic Flores kept apart from Sukarno out of fear of punitive measures by the Dutch authorities. The only people with whom Sukarno came into close contact were some of the Roman Catholic missionaries on the island. Sukarno had free access to the library and the recreation hall of the Roman Catholic Mission. He hired the Parish Hall in Endeh to stage a number of plays together with some of the local people. Sukarno talked a great deal with the missionaries, mainly Dutchmen, and gained a much deeper insight into Roman Catholicism and into what the missionaries were trying to do in furthering the economic and social development of the local people.

But all this could not satisfy Sukarno for long. Psychologically he started to go rapidly downhill. He became listless and moody; his depressions became worse and he began to suffer from severe attacks of malaria which also weakened him physically.

It was because of his sickness that the Batavian government decided, in February 1938, to transfer Sukarno and his family to the town of Bengkulu on the west Sumatran coast. The fact that Bengkulu was a strictly traditional Islamic town, provided a challenge to Sukarno. Almost immediately upon his arrival he began to attack traditional orthodox Islam which he dismissed as inane and stupefying. And, misquoting as usual from well-known Islamic scholars, Sukarno argued that Islam would only expect to flourish again if greater respect was given to freedom of spirit, knowledge, and nationalism.

He joined the modernist Islamic organization Mohammadijah

and he lectured to Mohammadijah teachers. In his usually impetuous and high-handed manner Sukarno tried to cut through centuries of Islamic tradition: at one prayer meeting, for example, he tore away the curtain that traditionally separates the men from the women. Sukarno's behaviour caused a great deal of adverse comment from orthodox Muslims in Bengkulu as well as in other parts of Sumatra and Java.

Sukarno also caused another stir when he began to intersperse his politico-religious polemics with a love affair with a fifteen-year-old girl, called Fatmawati, the daughter of Hadji Hassan Din, the local head of the Mohammadijah.

Sukarno was lonely and desperately wanted children. Inggit was already fifty-three years old and barren. To take a second wife was not unusual in Indonesia, as Muslims are allowed to have four wives. But when the news leaked out it caused a storm of protest from many modern Indonesians, in particular from the militant womens' organizations who were strongly opposed to polygamy. Friends, although in sympathy with his physical needs, strongly counselled Sukarno against taking a second wife, because it might damage his prestige and image as a national leader. It was Inggit's stubborn refusal, however, to agree to a divorce and to make way for a younger and prettier playmate which forced Sukarno to shelve his new marital adventures for a few years.

Sukarno's attempt in his autobiography[53] to whitewash his romance with Fatmawati has caused some derisive replies from other Indonesians. For example:

In his autobiography Sukarno is a real hypocrite when he remarks, 'To me she was just a pretty child' and further on, 'to stop the aching loneliness'. And then he said 'What I felt for her was fatherly affection'. When I read this part of the book to a couple of friends they all exploded into loud laughter. Imagine, Sukarno trying to stop his so-called 'aching loneliness' with a 'fatherly feeling' towards a pretty girl. One of my friends said rather crudely: 'What he really felt was an ache in his loins.'[54]

During the last years of his exile in Bengkulu a strong note of self-satisfaction can be detected in Sukarno; with the outbreak of war in Europe and the rapidly approaching Pacific war he felt that his prophesy of the collapse of imperialist capitalism, out of which a free Indonesia would be born, was closer to fulfilment.

The news of the attack by Nazi Germany on Holland in May

1940 and the rape of Rotterdam which caused many staunch Indonesian nationalists, including Dr Tjipto Mangunkusumo, to openly show their sympathy with the Dutch people, was received by Sukarno with stony silence. Not one word of sympathy was heard. And when in the spring of 1941 Dr G. F. Pijper, the government adviser to the *Volksraad*, came to visit Sukarno in Bengkulu to ask him to write pro-Dutch articles in return for his freedom, he refused indignantly. A year later, however, Sukarno the staunch non-cooperator piped an entirely different tune, when he almost threw himself at the new Japanese masters, offering his services. In spite of his years of exile, his psychological ups and downs, and the consternation he had caused in the nationalist movement by his 'conversion' in 1933, his stock as a nationalist leader in Java apparently still stood very high at the outbreak of the Pacific war. Amir Sjariffudin wrote in a letter to a friend in 1939 about Sukarno:

They have not forgotten him here in Djakarta. His name is still good, but you see, because he is absent he has no influence any more on the course of things. The trend of our policy has changed its tactics. He might not have approved of this if he were here in Djakarta. Poor fellow, Sukarno. You remember of course . . . that in fact we . . . were never very nice to him. At that time we envied him a little because he was really getting somewhere, he was such a good orator, but his thoughts and deeds were not sympathetic to us. I believe he knew it too. There was not much love lost between us and him. However, I still believe that he is still one of our top leaders. I personally don't think that he liked us too much.[55]

CHAPTER III

Under the Heels of Nippon

THE Japanese occupation constitutes an important watershed in modern Indonesian history. It acted as an important lever in the achievement of Indonesian independence and it provided Sukarno with opportunities of achieving his ambitions which otherwise might not have been realized.

In less than three months after the treacherous attack on Pearl Harbour of 8 December 1941, the Japanese in a lightning strike southwards occupied most of South-East Asia. Singapore, the bulwark behind which the Dutch had felt themselves safe, fell on 15 February 1942 and the Dutch Commander-in-Chief, General Ter Poorten, surrendered his forces to the Japanese on 8 March 1942. The Netherlands Indies was no more.

Contrary to popular Indonesian hopes the Japanese soon proved themselevs to be far stricter and more cruel masters than the Dutch had ever been. It is clear from the available documents that the Japanese had no intention of complying with the demands of Indonesian nationalists for a greater degree of self-government and independence. It was only towards the very end of the war that the Japanese changed their tune and, more as an afterthought and also perhaps to leave a time bomb behind for the Allied forces, indicated to the Indonesian leaders that Japan would no longer stand in the way of Indonesian independence.

Japanese policy, however, towards the Indonesian independence movement was by no means homogeneous; considerable differences of opinion existed within the armed forces, as well as between the military and certain sections of the Japanese government, as to how much leeway should be given to the demands of indigenous nationalists.

In the months immediately preceding the attack on Pearl Harbour various conferences were held in Japan to determine an outline of

56

policy to be followed in the occupied territories. The Japanese Ministry of Foreign Affairs advocated that the more developed parts of Indonesia, such as Java and Sumatra, should be granted independence within the framework of the Japanese empire, while the remainder of the archipelago should become a Japanese colony.[1] This proposal was strongly opposed by the military who argued that direct occupation of the whole of the Indies was necessary to ensure the safe and uninterrupted supply of raw materials vital to the war effort. The generals were supported by some of the civilian authorities who took the view that in maintaining the political *status quo* of the Netherland Indies the Japanese government would have an important lever at its disposal in case of peace negotiations with the Allies.[2]

The military apparently got their way and at a conference attended by representatives of the Japanese government and the imperial staff held on 20 November 1941 it was decided to follow a conservative policy in the occupied areas and to ignore the demands of local independence movements at least for the duration of the war.[3] The main concern of the Japanese was obviously the economic exploitation of South-East Asia and the occupying authorities were instructed that:

> Emphasis shall be placed on the acquisition of resources, particularly those essential to the prosecution of the war . . . the emphasis on resource development shall be on petroleum, and all matters necessary for this purpose shall be provided, including the priority allocation of funds, equipment and the like. . . . Economic hardships imposed upon native livelihood as a result of the acquisition of resources vital to national defence and for the self-sufficiency of occupation troops must be endured; and pacification measures against the natives shall stop at a point consistent with these objectives.[4]

The Japanese Navy was on the whole more moderate in its views towards indigenous nationalism. Most of its top-ranking officers originated from the upper classes; many of them had spent considerable periods abroad and had become internationally oriented. The majority of Army officers had a far more limited cultural horizon and were less flexible in their thinking, although there were notable exceptions to the rule. However, the 'tough liners' in the armed forces seem to have been victorious all along the line; with the result that the more politically sophisticated Navy was put in charge of the less advanced areas of Indonesia such as Borneo and the Eastern Islands, while the Army was to control the more nationalistically conscious areas of Java and Sumatra.

The 16th Japanese Army, which occupied Java, was under the command of Lieut.-Gen. Immamura Hitoshi, who had been in England for some time as military attaché and had fought in the China campaign. He was more cosmopolitan in his outlook than most of his fellow officers and apparently wanted to pursue a 'soft line' policy in Java. Immamura argued that as Japan had already shown its superiority by defeating the Allies it would be politically unwise as well as against the rules of the Japanese warriors' code[5] to follow the high-handed, arrogant, and repressive policy which was advocated by many of the younger officers of his command. Instead, during the first few months of the occupation Immamura concentrated his efforts on bringing civilian life back to normal and staged a propaganda campaign emphasizing the need for Japanese-Indonesian friendship and cooperation. He also insisted that the Dutch civilian authorities should retain their positions for the time being and that prisoners of war were to be treated in accordance with the Geneva Convention.[6]

On the other hand Indonesian hopes for early independence were quickly smashed by Immamura's persistent refusal to discuss the question which in line with the earlier policy decision of November 1941 was to be postponed until after the conclusion of the war.

Japanese propaganda in pre-war days as well as during the initial weeks of the occupation had given many Indonesians the impression that Nippon would be far more accommodating to their political aspirations than the Dutch had been. This was partly the reason why the Japanese troops were welcomed by the majority of the Indonesian population as liberators. There was no panic, no obvious fear, and Dutch propaganda about Japanese atrocities seems to have had little effect. Moreover, many Indonesians, and in particular the Javanese, took the Japanese invasion calmly because they firmly believed that the Japanese victory was the realization of the first part of the prophecies of the legendary king Djojobojo, who had predicted that the Dutch usurpers would finally be forced to surrender to the 'forces coming from the islands of Tembini, the members of which are yellow-skinned, short-legged, and they will occupy Java but only for the life-time of the maize-plant.'[7]

The Japanese who for years had been carefully studying the

internal political situation in Indonesia made good use of these popular messianic beliefs and just before the attack on Java, Japanese planes released thousands of leaflets stating that the Japanese army would come to occupy Java in order to make the prophecies of Djojobojo come true.

Japanese promises and the fact that Indonesians in Java were initially allowed to display the red and white national flag and sing the national anthem appear to have lured a number of nationalists into believing that self-government if not independence was just around the corner. Not only did some of the pre-war cooperative parties want to offer their services to the Japanese, but also some of the non-cooperators. The most conspicuous convert among the latter was perhaps the Partai Sarekat Islam Indonesia, which apparently argued that it could increase its strength and influence by jumping on the Japanese bandwagon.[8] Also some of the Gerindo leaders seem to have been impressed by Japanese propaganda and Mohammad Yamin is reported to have urged a large mass meeting of students to send a deputation to the Japanese on their arrival requesting immediate freedom for Indonesia from their brother Asian victors over colonialism.[9]

Soon after their entry into Djakarta the Japanese made it officially known that they wanted to come into contact with prominent Indonesian leaders, and there was great excitement in nationalist circles and various newspapers printed lists of possible Indonesian ministerial candidates. Sukarno, who at that time was still in Sumatra, was mentioned as a possibility for the Ministry of Propaganda and the Press, Minister without Portfolio, and Vice-Premier.[10]

Nationalist hopes were raised to an even higher pitch when on 13 March 1942 the newspaper *Tjahaja Timur* reported a statement by Abikusno Tjokrosujoso, a leader of the Islamic Association, claiming that the Japanese authorities had decided to set up a civilian government and that he had been charged with the task of forming a cabinet.[11]

Abikusno's statement seems to have been the sign for the Japanese to begin to deflate the Indonesian hope of immediate political concessions. The Army-controlled newspaper *Kan Po*, on 14 March 1942, dismissed Abikusno's story as untrue.[12] Three days later Sukardjo Wirjopranoto, the leader of the Parindra, was summoned to Japanese headquarters in Djakarta and told that political speculation had to stop.[13] The final blow fell on 20 March when regulation No. 3 of the military government in Java forbade, for the time being, all discussion, activities, suggestions, and propaganda concerning the future political and constitutional development of the colony. To add insult to injury, regulation No. 4, which was issued the same day, prohibited the use of the Indonesian national flag and the national anthem.[14]

As it turned out, the Japanese proved to be even more repressive than the Dutch, who had at least allowed the existence of moderate political parties and limited participation in government. Now all political parties were forbidden. By the end of March 1942 the Japanese apparently felt that their veiled promises of greater political freedom had served their purpose of keeping the bulk of the population from siding with the Allies; and that now with the Dutch defeated and most of them behind bars they could show their true colours and begin to exploit the material and human resources of the archipelago on a scale which even surpassed the legendary voracity of the Dutch during the notorious *Kultuurstelsel*[15] of the nineteenth century.

In addition to the repression of political activity, the Japanese initially cold-shouldered the overtures of the radical nationalists and Muslims, and instead concentrated their efforts on the pre-war cooperators, in particular the Parindra, a party largely patronized by the politically moderate *prijaji* (nobility). Apart from wanting to retain the existing socio-political *status quo* as far as possible, the Japanese during the first year of their occupation were desperately short of experienced civilian personnel and were therefore forced to cultivate the cooperation of the *prijaji* who constituted the largest corps of skilled administrators in the colony. For some of the nobility the removal of the Dutch meant an immediate elevation in status and initially Indonesians held such important positions as Governor and Vice-Governor of West Java, Mayor and Resident. However, only a few Indonesians were allowed to continue in these positions when greater numbers of Japanese personnel arrived in Java later in the year.[16]

Another reason for the prominent place held by the Parindra in Japanese planning at the beginning of the occupation was that some time before the war some members of the party who had become completely disillusioned with the intransigent attitude of the Dutch towards their demands for a greater degree of self-government had offered their services to the Japanese, in the hope of a better deal. The most prominent members of the Parindra party who stayed in Japan before the war were R. Soedjono and Madjid Oesman, and they made contact with extremist right-wing figures such as Toyama

Misuru, the leader of the Kokoryakai (Black Dragon Society), Taniguchi, and Shimizu Hitoshi. While still in Japan this group worked out a plan to establish a Parindra-led popular movement which was to guide the Indonesian people into cooperating with Japan.[17]

Soedjono, a Dutch-educated lawyer who had worked as a teacher of Indonesian languages and as a radio commentator in Tokyo, returned to Java as a Japanese Army officer to advise the High Command on the indigenous situation. Shimizu Hitoshi was sent to Java to head the Sendenbu, the powerful Japanese propaganda bureau. It was largely under Shimizu's direction that the *Gerakan Tiga A* (the Three A Movement)—the *A* standing for Japan the Light, Protector, and Leader of Asia—was set up, which was to be a national front replacing the former political parties and combining all forces in Indonesian society in support of the Japanese cause. The new organization, which was to be 'a spiritual movement of popular enlightenment', was inaugurated on 29 April 1942 and on the suggestion of Shimizu, a certain Sjamsuddin, the editor of the Parindra newspaper *Berita Umum* and a second-grade political leader, was appointed chairman.[18]

The initial popular enthusiasm for the Three A Movement soon dwindled into sullen, token support, when the people began to realize the real intentions of the Japanese. Moreover, Sjamsuddin and the predominantly *prijaji* leadership appear to have been far more interested in advancing their personal interests and prestige than in supporting the Japanese effort, and corruption in the civil service was reported to have become widespread. But perhaps the most important reason for the failure of the Three A Movement to arouse the interest of the people in supporting the war effort was the equivocal attitude towards the organization of the occupation forces themselves. Apparently, the spectre of an urban élite leading and guiding the growing rural unrest caused by the Japanese exploitation of the peasantry, forced the military government to restrict the Three A Movement to the cities; and the Japanese secret police are reported to have suppressed with considerable force branches of the movement in the West Javanese countryside.[19]

The first experiment in Japanese-Indonesian 'cooperation' in Java, the centre of the Indonesian political scene, took place without Sukarno having any say or playing any role in it. Sukarno rather belatedly returned to Java in the beginning of July 1942. This happened not, as some have suggested,[20] because the Japanese authorities in Djakarta did not know about his whereabouts earlier, but rather because they were not particularly interested in his services during the earlier months of the occupation.

When the Japanese landed at Palembang in South-East Sumatra, the Dutch authorities moved Sukarno and his family from Bengkulu to the port of Padang on the central-west coast of the island, from where he was supposedly to have been evacuated to Australia.[21] Whatever the colonial government might have had in store for him, Sukarno was left behind in Padang when the Dutch, surprised by the lightning speed of the Japanese advance, left the city in panic. Sukarno's version of his activities during the days immediately before the arrival of the Japanese and the first week of the occupation seems somewhat coloured. Taking into account his tremendous vanity and his unshakable belief in his holy mission to free his country, he probably could not help himself when in 1965 he reminisced:

> As I walked the streets I realized my poor, weak, subservient, undefended brothers needed to be rallied. There was nobody in charge. Nobody but Sukarno. Right actions are simply efforts to fulfil the service of God. I knew the time had come once more to go forth and answer the call. I assumed leadership immediately.[22]

When he wrote this, Sukarno probably forgot that at the time in question he was not in Java but in Central Sumatra among the fierce and outspoken Minangkabaus, who were not by and large poor, weak, or subservient, and had shown throughout their history that they could take care of their own affairs, as the Dutch colonial governments could well testify.[23] Over whom then was Sukarno assuming the leadership? Certainly not the majority of Minang-kabaus, who had produced most of the nationally prominent opponents of Sukarno, such as Hatta, Sjahrir, Natsir, and Tan Malakka, and who at no time showed a sufficient liking for him to readily submit to his commands.

Even less credible is Sukarno's version of his first meetings with the Japanese authorities. According to his autobiography Sukarno within a few days of the arrival of the Japanese in Padang was contacted by an officer, a member of the Propaganda Bureau, who told him that the Japanese were aware of his great fame as a nationalist leader and wanted to pay their respects to him. Somewhat later Sukarno was politely 'requested' to travel to headquarters in Bukittinggi, where the commander, Colonel Fujiyma, asked him to cooperate with the occupation army:

The Japanese needed me and I knew it. But I also needed them to make my country ready for revolution. This was like a game of volleyball. Except that the stakes were freedom. Colonel Fujiyama had first serve. Now it was my turn. Allah, I prayed silently, show me the way. 'Well', I said, 'now I know what you want, I presume you know what I want'. 'No, Mr Sukarno, I do not. What would the Indonesians really like?' 'To be free.' 'As a patriot who loves his people and longs for their liberty, you must realize independent Indonesia can be established only in cooperation with Japan', he retaliated. 'Yes', I nodded, 'it has become clear and bright to me that our lifeline lies in Japan . . . Will your government help me to liberate Indonesia?' 'If you promise total cooperation during our occupation, we will grant our unconditional promise to establish the freedom of your homeland.' 'Can I be guaranteed that during the whole period I work for you, it will be permissible for me to work for my people in the full knowledge that my ultimate aim is someday . . . somehow . . . to release them from the yoke of both Dutch and Japanese domination?' 'It is guaranteed. The Japanese government will put no obstacles in your way.'[24]

Sukarno's categorical statement that the Japanese could not do without his services seems entirely unrealistic under the circumstances. The situation was such that if Sukarno had not been willing to cooperate and had instead turned against the Japanese, he would undoubtedly have been shot as had happened to other Indonesian intellectuals who had dared to oppose the new colonial masters. And it is very doubtful whether the execution of Sukarno would have caused a large-scale uprising at that time, particularly in Sumatra. Undoubtedly Sukarno's further assertion that he could not achieve anything without the Japanese is far more realistic.

But it is the last part of this supposed conversation with Colonel Fujiyama which has a strong flavour of the unreal about it. It is known that the 25th Army which occupied Sumatra and Malaya acted very much the role of the haughty conqueror, treating the indigenous people as well as Europeans harshly, openly flaunting the rules of the Geneva Convention. Furthermore, the Japanese were of the opinion that nationalism was still comparatively weak in Sumatra and that the indigenous population was not yet ripe for self-government. So, organizations such as the Three A Movement and its various successors which had been set up in Java, were not considered necessary in Sumatra. It was only towards the end of

1943 that a number of advisory councils were set up in Sumatra which were designed to streamline the Japanese economic exploitation of the island. The members of these councils were all Indonesians who had been appointed by the military government. The discussion of political matters was forbidden until September 1944 when Tokyo announced that within the foreseeable future Indonesia would be granted its independence. But even then it was with considerable reluctance that the local Japanese commander complied with the order to allow Indonesians to prepare themselves for independence and to set up a Central Advisory Council similar to the one established in Java eighteen months earlier.[25]

It is also a known fact that the 25th Army was very critical of the 'soft line' policy adopted by the 16th Army in Java; and it seems therefore rather incongruous to see General Immamura, who was more accommodating to Indonesian demands, steadfastly refusing to commit himself on the question of independence, while the hard-liner Fujiyama is supposed to have readily guaranteed Indonesian freedom to Sukarno.

The important role which Sukarno assigned to himself in his autobiography during the first months of the Japanese occupation was probably no more than a figment of his fertile imagination. Characteristically, Sukarno always had to be at the centre of things, and for him to admit that for the first five months of the Japanese regime he was in the political backwoods and that his actions were of no consequence whatsoever in the making of nationally important events, would have militated against his tremendous vanity and been unfitting to the memory of the Great Leader of the Revolution.

What is more likely to have happened is that the Japanese considered Sukarno—whose revolutionary record they were well aware of—politically dangerous, and wanting to keep him under close surveillance appointed him to a relatively unimportant advisory post. This impression is reinforced by Sukarno's own glowing reports[26] of how he was successful in regulating rice supplies in Padang and in procuring prostitutes for the Japanese soldiers, activities which cannot exactly be described as particularly glorious and of great importance to the nation. Something similar happened to Mohammad Hatta, the other prominent radical nationalist leader. Just before the outbreak of the Pacific war the Dutch had brought both Hatta and Sjahrir back to Java from exile in the remote island of Banda-Neira in Eastern Indonesia. The Japanese within a few days of their arrival contacted Hatta, demanded his cooperation, and then appointed him to a sideline job as head of an advisory bureau to Army headquarters.[27]

Also the comparative readiness with which Singapore agreed to the 16th Army's request to have Sukarno transferred to Java, as well as its warning to Immamura that he was dealing with a dangerous nationalist who would bite the hand of friendship extended to him, suggests that the 25th Army rather than finding Sukarno indispensable was apparently glad to get rid of a possible troublemaker.[28] Another indication that at this stage Sukarno figured very little in Japanese plans, is the fact that he was not considered worthy of being flown back by plane to Java; instead he and his family had to risk their lives for four days in rough seas on an old ramshackle motor-launch.[29]

Why then did Immamura ask for the return of Sukarno to Java? According to Mohammad Hatta,[30] the Japanese authorities in Java had been interested in contacting Sukarno from the beginning of the occupation. But to conclude, as H. J. Benda has done, that 'this shows that the new rulers had counted on enlisting the co-operation of the most important and most colourful leader of Indonesian nationalism from the very outset . . .'[31] does not seem warranted in view of the early policy of the Japanese towards Indonesian nationalists. If Immamura had been so keen to ensure Sukarno's services from the beginning he would certainly have gone further out of his way to find the Indonesian leader than he actually did.

It seems more realistic to see the return of Sukarno to Java in the context of a tactical change in Japanese policy. The obvious failure of the Three A Movement, as well as growing discontent in the country with the new rulers, made it clear to Immamura and his advisors that a different approach was needed; that to ensure more effective cooperation of the population for the war effort without recourse to brute force, it would be necessary to reach beyond the moderate nationalists and the *prijaji* and try and tap the support of the more radical leaders among the nationalists as well as the Muslims. Immamura could also have been influenced in this direction by the arguments of Count Kodama, the advisor to the military government and a representative of the Ministry of Foreign Affairs, which from the beginning had advocated limited political independence for Java and Sumatra and had stressed the need for the closest possible cooperation with the more prominent radical nationalist leaders.[32]

Sukarno arrived in Djakarta on 9 July 1942 after an absence of more than eight years. His return was heralded by the Indonesian Press as an event of great national importance. That same evening Sukarno, Sjahrir, and Hatta met to discuss the tactics that were to be followed with regard to the Japanese. It was agreed that as the Japanese obviously wanted to make use of Sukarno's charismatic hold over the people, he should ostensibly cooperate with the new colonial masters hoping in this way to obtain political concessions. It was also decided that Hatta should follow the same course of action. In any case Hatta was already in Japanese service and it would have undoubtedly been dangerous for him to extricate himself at that stage. Sjahrir, who so far had kept himself in the background was delegated to set up an anti-Japanese underground movement which was to ensure that the true goals of Indonesian nationalism were kept alive among the people. Furthermore, the three leaders agreed to maintain the closest possible liaison.[33]

The anti-Japanese feeling of Sjahrir and Hatta is beyond question. Both leaders were committed to a Western type of parliamentary democracy and as convinced socialists they were principally opposed to fascism. During the whole of the occupation Hatta made it clear in his speeches that for tactical reasons he had been forced to cooperate and whenever he could he stayed in the background quietly working for the nationalist cause and all through the war keeping in close contact with Sjahrir's underground workers.

Sukarno's position vis-à-vis the Japanese is by no means so clear-cut and he certainly gives the impression of being willing rather than being forced to comply with the wishes of the new colonial masters. This caused the Allies—in particular the Dutch—and also some Indonesian leaders to brand him as a quisling, while there were many more Indonesians who accused him of being over-compliant.

Sukarno was never fully able to live down these accusations and until the end of his life he was very reluctant to comment publicly about this rather painful episode. It apparently took Cindy Adams, Sukarno's pretty American confidante, months before she could get him to talk about his experiences during the Japanese occupation.[34] And even then the 'autobiography' unfortunately does very little to dispel any lingering doubts which the historian might have about Sukarno's real intentions at the time.

Dutch allegations that Sukarno and other Indonesian leaders who cooperated with the Japanese were traitors, although perhaps correct from a technical point of view, must be dismissed as unrealistic under the circumstances. The military debacle of the Allies and the unwillingness of the Dutch colonial government to train large numbers of Indonesians to help in the defence of their country left the indigenous population completely at the mercy of the new colonial rulers. Many Indonesian leaders, cooperators as well as non-cooperators, left in the lurch by the Dutch military defeat, considered that whatever right Holland might have had to rule Indonesia had now been completely forfeited.

The possibilities open to the Indonesian leaders were therefore limited. They could either openly cooperate in the hope of furthering the nationalist cause; or stay out of public life and remain inactive; or engage in underground activities against the Japanese.

For Sukarno to stay quietly in the background would have been completely out of character. Neither was he the type to conduct an underground resistance movement. He was squeamish and could not stand the sight of blood and is known to have been very fearful of his life in times of physical danger, which perhaps unfairly has brought accusations of cowardice against him from some Indonesians.

It is true that whilst Sukarno displayed great courage in his conviction before the war and was willing to go to jail and into exile thereby sacrificing a relatively bright and prosperous career, he was never in any great physical danger. And although the political prisoners' camp set up by the Dutch at Tanah Merah in West Irian was in many ways an inhumane institution, Sukarno was never sent there; and while in exile he was permitted a fairly liberal living allowance by the Dutch colonial government, which at that time was not in the habit of physically torturing or executing its political opponents.[35]

During the Japanese occupation there was no *Volksraad*, where Indonesian members protected by parliamentary privilege could publicly criticize the colonial government with impunity. Also the Indonesian Press was muzzled far more severely than it had been in the Dutch time. Nor was it possible for Indonesians to play the role of the loyal opposition. Any open criticism or opposition to the Japanese military government meant imprisonment, torture and usually death.

Bereft of arms and modern military know-how, the vast majority of Indonesian leaders were unwilling to commit suicide and either elected to cooperate with the Japanese, hoping to be able to steer the situation to their country's advantage, or stayed in the background.

However, there are important differences in the basic attitude of

Sukarno towards Japan and that of many other intellectuals, in particular the Social Democrats. While the latter were principally opposed to fascism and before the war had frequently condemned Germany and Italy, as well as Japan, and had serious qualms of conscience about cooperating with the Japanese, Sukarno does not seem to have been in any way inhibited by such considerations.

Since the end of the 1920s Sukarno had advocated the principle of Asian solidarity in the struggle against colonialism and prophesied the outbreak of a war between Japan and the other major capitalist-imperialist powers in the Pacific, the U.S.A. and Britain, and had continuously stressed that Japan would be the key to Indonesian freedom.

Sukarno, although obviously at a loss as to how to reconcile Asian solidarity and the fact that Japan itself was an imperialist power, seems to give the impression in his pre-war writings that he considered Asian imperialism less dangerous than the Western variety. He also believed for a long time that it was Japan which would be attacked, making the Western powers the villains. Sukarno's thinking at this time might perhaps have been somewhat akin to that of his teacher Tjokroaminoto who during the early 1920s made a distinction between the 'sinful' capitalism of the West and legitimate indigenous capitalism.[36]

But all this does not fully explain the complete metamorphosis in Sukarno from the Marxist-tinged non-cooperator of pre-war days into the Japanese cooperator par excellence. The deeper reasons for this drastic change in attitude can perhaps be found in Sukarno's own political philosophy and his ideas about government which showed some affinity to the Japanese model. Undoubtedly, Japans' rejection of Western-style democracy, its condemnation of Western degeneration, the call to regenerate the spirit of Asia, and the slogan 'Asia for the Asians' were grist for Sukarno's mill. Admittedly, Sukarno was far too eclectic and unruly a person and thinker to be easily fitted into any of the major recognized ideological compartments. However, Sukarno's condemnation of Western democracy and Western values; his emphasis on strong personal leadership; his advocacy of the use of *musjawah* and *mufakat* which in essence were a native Indonesian version of the corporate state; and his strong indigenous feelings which resulted in his emphasis on the need for regeneration of Indonesian culture: all these factors put him closest to the fascist camp, not the Japanese kind of fascism, because Sukarno was not a military nor bloodthirsty type of man by nature, but his love for uniforms, his grandiose plans, his oratorical style, gave him a close resemblance to one of the greatest European swashbucklers of all time, Mussolini. Therefore ideologically Sukarno could go at least part of the way with the Japanese, a thing which had been impossible for him to do with the Dutch. The Dutch blueprint for Indonesian political development—however vague it might have been—undoubtedly envisaged a Western democratic system of government. Apart from the fact that if the Dutch had remained in power the realization of Indonesian freedom would probably not have occurred in his lifetime, Sukarno was opposed in principle to Western democracy and the Western individualistic ethos. Moreover, in the parliamentary democracy, there was no place for a man of his talents; and without the opportunity to display his charismatic and demagogic qualities he could never have reached the top.

And then, of course, there is the fact that Sukarno considered the Japanese decision to bring him back to Java as an indication that they needed him and that he would therefore be able to obtain concessions in return for his services. In this Sukarno was far too optimistic and characteristically overestimated his importance in the scheme of things. This must have become painfully clear to him when during his first interview with Immamura, the Japanese general refused to commit himself on his government's plans for Indonesian self-government or independence, but promised that Indonesians would be allowed to participate on a larger scale in government administration. After the interview Immamura rather indifferently instructed Colonel Nakayama, the commander of Djakarta, to hold discussions with Sukarno but not to force him into cooperating with the Japanese. Immamura added: 'It all depends on the doctor himself; either the doctor would cooperate with the Japanese or assume the attitude of an onlooker. However, it is forbidden to attempt something against Japan.'[37] But during further meetings Immamura, like so many before and after him, was impressed by Sukarno and came to admire him. The general saw in Sukarno a man with an iron will who never lost sight of the great passion to gain freedom for his people. From his side Sukarno left no stone unturned to gain the friendship of Immamura, going as far as to commission a well-known Indonesian artist to paint the general's portrait which was accepted apparently with great pleasure by Immamura. But to Sukarno's great chagrin it still took a considerable time before the Japanese allowed him to play the major role in Indonesian affairs which he had assumed was his due. The Three A Movement was not officially discarded until November 1942 and its predominantly *prijaji* leadership was obviously unwilling to make place for Sukarno. And in the organization's propaganda organ, *Asia Raya*, Sukarno was taken to task for his grandiose airs.[38]

But Sukarno remained bent on playing a leading role and against the advice of Sjahrir and Hatta wanted to join the Three A Movement in order to change it into a true people's organization.[39] However, the Japanese kept Sukarno away from the central leadership of the Three A Movement. Instead he was appointed to head the organization's youth front, and in this capacity he was given the opportunity to influence the more radical youth leaders.[40]

A further disappointment to Sukarno's plans was the unwillingness of the Japanese to appoint Indonesians into major administrative positions. By August 1942 more Japanese officials had arrived and many Indonesians were ousted from the high posts which they had held from the early days of the occupation; and even the Indonesian Mayor of Batavia was replaced by a Japanese.[41]

It was also around this time that the Japanese attitude towards the demands of Indonesian nationalists began to harden. In Tokyo the colonial party, which advocated the direct annexation of the Indies to Japan, seemed to have won a decisive victory over its opponent, the Ministry of Foreign Affairs, which wanted to grant limited political freedom to Java and Sumatra. This considerably affected the situation in Java where Count Kodama, a member of the Foreign Affairs department and adviser to the Military government, initially exerted considerable influence on Immamura.

During a meeting on 1 September 1942 General Tojo, the Japanese Prime Minister, wanted to restrict the power of the Foreign Affairs ministry in South-East Asia to matters of protocol only. As a result, on 1 November 1942 a Ministry for Greater Asia was set up in which the South-East section of the Ministry of Foreign Affairs was incorporated. Also in November 1942 Count Kodama was repatriated to Japan. In April 1943 Colonel Nakayama was replaced by Colonel Yamamoto who took a more unrelenting stand towards the demands of Indonesian nationalists. In the same month General Immamura was appointed as Commander of the 8th Army in Rabaul, and he took up this position in June 1943.[42]

In the meantime the Japanese in Java were making preparations to replace the Three A Movement with a similar but more effective organization. As a first step the *Empat Serangkai* (Four Leaf Clover) was established with a committee consisting of Sukarno, Hatta, the Mohammadijah leader K. M. M. Mansur, and the Taman Siswa leader Ki Hadjar Dewantoro.

On 20 November 1942 the Four Leaf Clover was instructed to organize a new people's movement which initially was to be officially inaugurated on 8 December 1942, the anniversary of Pearl Harbour. When Sukarno had to announce on 8 December and again on 31 December that the establishment of the new organization was postponed, many Indonesian intellectuals were disappointed and complained that Sukarno and the other leaders had apparently been taken in too much by Japanese promises.

Stung by this criticism and also obviously annoyed at the equivocal attitude of his masters, Sukarno, in an article commemorating the fall of Singapore, wrote rather pointedly: 'Every form of colonization is destructive. Always, colonization lays waste and brings catastrophe to the land and people who are colonized. Their riches, their culture, their love of life, their character, all destroyed, all laid waste.' And although Sukarno quickly made it clear that by colonialism he meant British and Dutch colonialism to most Indonesians it was obvious that a condemnation of Japanese imperialism was also meant.[43]

This soft-pedalling of the promised new organization was un-doubtedly in part caused by the victory of the colonial hard-liners in Tokyo, which was referred to above. But another important reason was the intense rivalry in Java itself between the Senendan led by the hard-liner Shimizu and the Department of General Administration led by Mioshi and Nakayama who were in close agreement with Immamura's policies. It is reported that Shimizu, in an attempt to save his creation the Three A Movement, tried to put a spoke in the wheel of the Four Leaf Clover by setting up a rival group, the so-called *Golongan 7 S*.[44]

The Indonesians had to endure another serious blow to their expectations when at the end of January 1943 General Tojo promised in the Diet independence to the Philippines and Burma but not to Indonesia. Significantly Tojo did not use the term Indonesia but referred to the Southern Areas, mentioning Java, Sumatra, and Malaya as separate areas.

Tokyo's announcement caused considerable disillusionment and the intellectuals again accused Sukarno and other leaders of having become Japanese stooges. A report by an unnamed Indonesian written at the beginning of 1943 comments upon the situation as follows:

Regarding the people's party which is to be founded, the leaders attempt to gild the pill by telling the nationalist groups that because of the war situation they have no other choice but to follow the (Japanese) government. They consider it as their duty. The leaders try to be out of town as much as possible in order to avoid curious questioners. It is difficult for the nationalist movement to get used to the idea of having to cooperate with the government, because during the Dutch time they were always in the opposition. . . . The great masses because of the constant economic struggle appear to have no time to pay attention to the planned organization. They are completely indifferent and they have very little respect left for the leaders. It is feared that eventually the people itself may take its own measures. The symptoms are already apparent.[45]

Finally on 6 March the new organization was officially launched. It came to be called *Pusat Tenaga Rakjat* (Concentration of the People's Power) or in short PUTERA. The programme of the PUTERA was extremely vague. Its main purpose was to increase the people's sense of duty and responsibility, in terms of the Greater Asian Co-prosperity Sphere. The movement was to work towards the elimination of all Western influences in the country and it was to be prepared to take part in the defence of the new order. The people were also to be prepared to bear the economic hardships caused by the war and mutual respect and trust was to be strengthened by propagating the Japanese and Indonesian languages. Another important function of the PUTERA was to increase the self-confidence of the Indonesians and to further public health.

Sukarno's views about the PUTERA, however, were quite clear. He wanted to make it into a national front organization to incite, solidify, and consolidate the Indonesian nationalist spirit. So much is clear from his inaugural speech when having kowtowed to official Japanese policy he ended up by saying: 'Brothers, it is not just coincidence that we have named our movement PUTERA [the word *putera* in Indonesian means son—*bhumi putera* means indigenous]. You must all reply: "Yes, I am a PUTERA, a PUTERA of the new era, a PUTERA of the new struggle, a PUTERA of the new society, a PUTERA of Indonesia." '[46]

But again the Japanese prevented Sukarno from realizing his great ambition to set up a nationwide, comprehensive, mass organization and they squashed his and the other Indonesian leaders' hopes for early independence.

Requests for a Japanese promise of Indonesian independence similar to the one given to the Philippines and Burma, which were put by Sukarno and Hatta to Aoki, the minister in charge of the

Greater East Asian Affairs, who visited Java at the end of March 1943, received a noncommittal reply. Moreover, the new head of the General Affairs department, General Yamamoto, who arrived in Java in April to take over from Colonel Nakayama, made it abundantly clear that Tokyo was unwilling to comply with Indonesian's demands for independence. He forbade the PUTERA to set up branches in the countryside and he ordered Sukarno to guide the PUTERA movement in a more spiritual direction.[47] In a post-war statement Yamamoto declared:

I heard that the nationalists had organized the PUTERA movement in the expectation of making it the nucleus of their campaign for independence. . . . The 16th Army had no plans in that direction. . . . All the official speeches of the leaders were subjected to censorship by the Japanese military authorities. According to my knowledge the movement has not been very active. On the other hand, it provided the Japanese administration with the means to control the activities of the top nationalist leaders.[48]

Apart from the fact that Japan wanted the Indies with its rich resources of oil and rubber as a colony—an ambition which dated back to the First World War—the Japanese authorities in Java like their Dutch predecessors apparently considered that the Indonesians were not yet capable of running their own affairs. A report of 1942 by a high-ranking Japanese official in Java states that the demands of Indonesian nationalists went much too far. There were too few indigenous intellectuals and politicians and the population as a whole was politically immature and apathetic. This report also argued that the intellectuals were too far removed from the people and the various classes 'reacted to each other as oil to water'; and the officials of the PUTERA were only interested in self-aggrandizement, and seemed to spend most of the time competing with each other for higher wages. The report was also critical of Sukarno's abilities as a leader and complained that after four months the PUTERA leadership had as yet achieved very little.

The lower classes agree with Sukarno's leadership and his speeches are well received. But it is felt that he involves himself too much with details. A great leader is somebody who is concerned with general policy and speaks only about important matters. Too much chatter may well cause the people to become disinterested and to lose respect for the leaders. Great leaders such as Hitler and Mussolini do not only exert great influence, but they have also inculcated fear, respect and love in the people. According to the best of my knowledge I have never seen Sukarno having been properly greeted or given a sign of respect when he arrives for a speaking engagement. When the smaller leaders do not want to honour the great leader, then the masses will also not listen with respect to what he has to say. A great leader must know everything about his co-workers. He must have dossiers about well-known personalities which contain a description of their lives, details about their way of life, hobbies, character, etc. Moreover, a leader must have supporters, who can take care of the details.[49]

This Japanese report was correct in stating that Sukarno was not a cruel man and did not employ the fiendishly inhuman methods of Hitler and Mussolini. In other ways, however, this report was unrealistic; in criticizing Sukarno's style as a politician and as a speaker, the author of the report completely misses the reason why Sukarno was one of the very few leaders who was able to get across to the people. So far as the other complaint is concerned, Sukarno did not really need dossiers. He had a fantastic memory and this combined with a certain streak of vindictiveness in his character ensured that very few of his personal and political opponents ever got away unharmed either in the short or long term. However, the point about not having the respect of other leaders rings more true. Neither then nor later did Sukarno have the allegiance of most of the Indonesian intellectuals, in particular those who had their minds attuned to the West.

The report does show that Sukarno completely overestimated the importance he had to the Japanese. In fact Sukarno and the other leaders of the PUTERA who initially had been taken in by the genuine enough promises of Nakayama and Mioshi, were eventually duped by the new orders from Tokyo. However, it would be going too far to suggest with Dahm[50] that Sukarno had hoped for a real partnership with the Japanese on the basis of mutual respect and trust. This would make him too much of an idealistic simpleton. Despite his frequent romantic dreams and fantasies, Sukarno exhibited a strong sense of realism and political acumen throughout the course of his political life.

Momentarily the hopes of the Indonesian leaders were brightened when Premier Tojo declared on 17 July 1943 in the Japanese parliament that in the near future the people of Java would be given a greater opportunity to participate in the administration of the island. Sukarno fastened on Tojo's speech and construed it into a promise for independence, and as if to show his thankfulness in advance for this Japanese gift he began to identify himself more closely with Japan, intensifying in his speeches the hate campaign against the Allies. It is also significant that at this time Sukarno no longer consulted with Sjahrir and the underground. Was this perhaps to avoid any accusation of being in collusion with the Allies? Or was it perhaps that Sukarno was now convinced that the Japanese would win? The real motivation behind Sukarno's thinking at that particular time will probably never be known.

Premier Tojo, who unexpectedly visited Java in July 1943, was not taken in by Sukarno's welcoming speech in which the Indonesian leader attempted to elicit a promise for independence. Tojo made it clear that he had travelled to a colony and he did not use the term Indonesia or Indonesians but indigenous, making it obvious that he expected the people to expend all their strength in supporting the Japanese cause.

Tojo's promises were followed by the implementation of three new measures: the establishment of a central advisory council and regional advisory councils; the gradual transference of important administrative posts to Indonesians; and recognition of the authority of the self-governing sultans of Jogjakarta and Surakarta in their respective territories. This change in Japanese policy brought back at least a semblance of participation in government which had existed during the last decades of Dutch colonial rule.

The Central Advisory Council, however, although resembling the *Volksraad*, was by no means endowed with the same powers. The pre-war *Volksraad* had co-legislative powers and its members enjoyed parliamentary privilege. It functioned in many ways as a legitimate organ of criticism of Dutch colonial policy and practice, whereas the Central Advisory Council was meant solely as an advisory body to the Japanese military government and its members were not allowed to make any criticism of the colonial masters and their policies.

On the other hand, the transfer of important administrative positions with which the Dutch had made a hesitant beginning at the end of the 1930s, was effected on a much larger scale by the Japanese, and proved to be of immense value to the Indonesians during the early years of the revolution.

Another measure which proved to be of great importance to the Indonesian cause was the establishment by the Japanese of a corps of Indonesian auxiliary troops, the PETA or Defenders of the Fatherland. Sukarno's assertion that it was he who was responsible for the founding of the PETA has been effectively denied by Gatot

Mangupradja, Sukarno's old comrade-in-arms of the pre-war P.N.I. days in Bandung.[51]

1943 was probably one of the most exasperating years of Sukarno's life. He was hurt and deeply disappointed at the unbending attitude of the Japanese which put a complete stop to his aspirations and ambitions. To make matters worse his home life was in a shambles and he was suffering a great deal from malaria and kidney stones, a disease which was finally to kill him a quarter of a century later.

Sukarno's relationship with Inggit, which had been severely strained because of his affair with Fatmawati in Bengkulu, had become completely impossible since his return to Java. Inggit, who for some time had suspected—and with cause—that her husband was playing around with various secretaries and was a frequent visitor to geisha houses, finally put her foot down. One night when Sukarno returned home from one of his escapades Inggit made a scene and threw a cup at him, hitting him on the forehead. Finally Inggit agreed to a divorce and went back to her hometown of Bandung. Now the coast was clear for Sukarno to marry Fatmawati, and the Japanese, glad of an opportunity to do him a personal favour without having to make any political concessions, promptly brought the lady from Sumatra to Djakarta where the wedding took place on 22 August 1943. Sukarno was severely criticized for divorcing Inggit by the Indonesian women's organizations, and Fatmawati was only begrudgingly accepted in Djakarta circles. Sukarno and Fatmawati seem to have spent as much time as possible away from the gossip of Djakarta and they often spent the weekend in Sukabumi with Dr Abu Hanifah, who was then in charge of the local Catholic hospital and who later became a Masjumi leader and Minister for Education in the republic. Abu Hanifah describes Fatmawati at that time as follows:

My wife and I were very curious about the young wife of Soekarno. She was young alright and she had the prettiness of a wild flower. We found her, however, completely unsophisticated. She had no dress sense and her manners were faulty. The young bride had really only her youth, her prettiness and her smile. She was in fact only a beautiful village girl. Her social education and upbringing afterwards was Soekarno's work, she was really the product of Soekarno's imagination of how a first lady should be. That he afterwards became bored with his own creation is another question.

Although happily newly married Sukarno apparently could still not control his roving eye. Abu Hanifah writes:

> One beautiful warm day we were driving Soekarno and Fatmawati back to Djakarta. Every time we saw a pretty woman or girl on the street he would say 'Look how pretty that one is, I bet she is not yet 20', or 'What a mouth, what a bosom.' I told him smilingly if he wanted so badly to look at girls, why should he look that far because on his right and on his left were the prettiest girls in the world. Soekarno didn't appreciate the remark, he looked a little crestfallen. Fatmawati said with a teasing smile but seriously enough: 'Bung Abu, you know Bung Karno. He never knows what he really wants. He wants to have everything. Yesterday he married an older, experienced woman, today he marries me, an ignorant virgin, God knows what he wants tomorrow.'[52]

A further setback for Sukarno in 1943 was the omission of Indonesia from the Greater Asia conference held in Tokyo between 5 and 8 November at which China, the Philippines, Burma, Manchuria and Thailand were represented. Probably in order to soften the Indonesian leaders tremendous disappointment and annoyance, the Japanese military administration in Java convinced Tokyo of the need to award Sukarno, Hatta and Ki Bagus Hadikusumo a consolation prize and present them with a trip to Japan. The Indonesians arrived in Tokyo on 13 November where they were feted and received by the Emperor who handed out decorations. Sukarno was obviously thrilled when he was the only one considered worthy of being shaken hands with by the Emperor. The Indonesians toured the mighty Japanese industrial complexes and Sukarno, in particular, who had never before been outside Indonesia, seems to have been greatly impressed. There was a visit to Tojo during which the question of independence was brought up but with very little result and the Indonesian leaders had to return home emptyhanded.

In spite of Sukarno's frequent ostentatious manifestations of Indonesian-Japanese solidarity, his power was largely illusory. And by the end of 1943 there was little to show for his efforts to advance the Indonesian cause. And his personal ambition to become the great and undisputed leader in charge of a vast and nationalistic front had so far been thwarted by Japanese policies.

From the beginning the Japanese had been well aware of the security risks involved in the establishment of a single, national, Indonesian front; and taking recourse to the well-tried colonial remedy of 'divide and rule' the military government attempted to bottle up the various major political and ideological forces in the colony into separate organizations.

As the major objective of the Japanese in Java was to increase agricultural production at all costs, the greatest problem lay in the countryside. The Japanese, who had made a careful study of the Indonesian Islam, were undoubtedly aware of the long history of rural rebellions in Java led by Islamic teachers in times of economic hardship. The Dutch, in order to counteract the influence of Islam on the peasantry, had consistently pursued a policy of supporting and shoring up the position and power of the *adat* chiefs and the basically religiously syncretic *prijaji* and nobility. In contrast the Japanese, though by no means neglecting to obtain the support of the *prijaji*, adopted a policy of dealing directly with the Muslim leadership. In order to prevent the more sophisticated urban élite from creating possible rural unrest, organizations such as the Three A Movement and its successor, the PUTERA, were forbidden to set up branches in the countryside. The Japanese also tried—and with apparent success—to play on the divisions within the urban Muslim community and were able to prevent the pre-war, non-cooperative and militant P.S.I.I. from playing a leading role in the Muslim movement. The early offer of cooperation by leading P.S.I.I. figures such as Abikusno was ignored, and the Japanese gradually undermined the position of the P.S.I.I.-controlled pre-war Islamic federation, the M.I.A.I.

The first Japanese attempt to reduce the power of the M.I.A.I. by forcing this body to dissolve itself into the *Persiapan Persatuan Ummat Islam* (Preparation for the Unification of the Islamic Community), a subsidiary organization of the Three A Movement, was not successful. The Japanese therefore decided to take up contact directly with the rural Islamic teachers whom they tried to bind to the Japanese cause by instituting indoctrination courses—the so-called *latihan kijaji*—and by granting important concessions which tended to increase the status and power of the rural religious leaders vis-à-vis the *prijaji*.

In October 1943, the Japanese dissolved the M.I.A.I. and, in order to isolate the P.S.I.I. leaders even further, the essentially non-political Islamic organizations: the Nahatadul Ulama and the Muhammadyah were given legal status. At the same time the decree of March 1942 abolishing all political parties remained intact, leaving the leaders of the P.S.I.I. out on a limb, even further isolated from the centre of Islamic leadership.

The next step taken by the Japanese was the establishment on 23 November 1943 of the *Madjlis Suro Muslimin Indonesia* (Consultative Council of Indonesian Muslims) or in short MASJUMI. The MASJUMI could only be joined by legally recognized organizations which existed at the time: the Nahatadul Ulama and the Muhammadyah, as well as individual *ulama*. Thus, in the MASJUMI the Japanese tried to link the more moderate urban Islamic leadership with the grass-root Islam in the rural areas. The new organization was headed by the well-known and respected founder of the Nahatadul Ulama, Hasjim Asj'ari.

A further check to Sukarno's plans was the abolition on 1 March 1944 of the PUTERA, which left the nationalists without an organization of their own. According to Yamomoto, the PUTERA was abolished because:

> It had various defects, it was an exclusively Indonesian movement. Other races were not involved . . . the people became alienated from their own rulers which made it very difficult to indoctrinate the masses with Japanese political ideas. The common people did not show any appreciation about the fact that there was a war going on. They complained and were discontented. Therefore I felt that it was very urgent to establish an organization which was deeply rooted in the masses.[53]

As a result the PUTERA was replaced by a new organization called the Djawa Hokokai or the People's Service Association of Java. In creating the People's Service Association the Japanese were concerned solely to coordinate the activities of the whole of the Javanese population for the war effort. There was no longer any pretence of catering for Indonesian national aims. Unlike its predecessors the Three A Movement and the PUTERA, the central leadership of the People's Service Association was in Japanese hands, while Sukarno and the MASJUMI leader Hasjim Asj'ari were made advisers. The organization also included representatives of the Eurasian, Arab, and Chinese communities, and was therefore not specifically nationalist in character. Furthermore, People's Service Association branches were set up all over the island in which the *prijaji* came to play a predominant role. To penetrate even deeper into the villages, neighbour organizations (*Tomari Gumi*) were set up which were led by lower *prijaji* and village chiefs in order to press the people directly into greater productive effort.

On the other hand the MASJUMI, although it was fitted into

the People's Service Association structure, remained an independent and Indonesian-led organization, while the nationalist groups were now without any formal organization of their own.

Sukarno's chairmanship of the Central Advisory Council, and his post as the main adviser to the People's Service Association only provided him with a semblance of power. He could do nothing to alleviate the sufferings of the people who were starving in large numbers in many areas of Java. Also he could do nothing to stop the transportation of hundreds of thousands of labourers, all over Java, the archipelago and many parts of South-East Asia. Nobody could have blamed Sukarno then because he was powerless; but what many Indonesians have never been able to forgive him for is that in his speeches he actively encouraged many of his unsuspecting countrymen to volunteer as slave labourers and sent many of them to an almost certain death on the Burma railway or other parts of the archipelago.

Particularly galling to some Indonesians was an occurrence in early September 1944 when Sukarno and Shimizu and other white-collar workers pulled a propaganda stunt by volunteering as labourers (*romushas*). The *Soeara Asia* dutifully reported:

Soekarno wore shorts and an ordinary shirt and a panama hat. Mr Shimizu also wore shorts, a shirt and carried a *kain*[54] across his shoulder. He wore tennis shoes and had a *petji*[55] on his head. . . . Although the volunteers generally were not used to this kind of work, considerable progress was made, and they did not seem to get tired. This was due to the spirit of cooperation and a happy working atmosphere. Soekarno did his bit and together with the rest of them worked on a heap of stones. After completion of the work there was a social evening with performances by the cabaret of the Cultural Centre of Djakarta which had travelled with the volunteer *romushas*.[56]

This idyllic picture of Sukarno and associates happily dirtying their hands for the good of the fatherland must have looked to thousands of real labourers—if they could have seen it—a cruel and callous parody of their sufferings.

According to his autobiography, Sukarno when criticized by some of his countrymen at the time about his attitude towards the labourers is supposed to have justified himself by saying: 'There are casualties in every war. A Commander-in-Chief's job is to win the war even if it means losing a few battles on the way. If I must sacrifice thousands to save millions, I will. We are in a struggle for survival. As leader of this country I cannot afford the luxury of sensitivity.'[57]

This story sounds rather unconvincing. In the first place Sukarno had nothing to command as yet, and as one Indonesian critic has pointed out[58] he could well have left the job of selling his countrymen to someone else. Moreover, even if there had been no takers for the job, the Japanese like the Germans in Europe would certainly have taken other measures to secure a supply of forced labour.

Perhaps the kindest way to describe Sukarno's role in the Japanese occupation is to compare him with the rather pathetic figure of the Vichy leader Pétain, the national hero who, with honourable intentions and in order to get the best for his people in a desperate situation, cooperated with the new masters. But after this fateful step he was drawn ever more deeply and inextricably into the enemy's net, being eventually forced to carry out policies which not even by the wildest stretch of the imagination could be considered in the national interest.

But it seemed as if the gods finally took pity on Sukarno and decided to stop him from having to stoop even lower under the Japanese heel. It was exactly on that same day of 7 September 1944 when he was leading his volunteer labourers, that the news reached Java like a bolt out of the blue, about Premier Koiso's promise in the Japanese parliament for the future independence of the whole of Indonesia.

Sukarno was suddenly called back to Djakarta from his work camp in Banten and when Yamomoto told him the news he seemed to be stunned, and he sank down and wept openly.

The official announcement on 8 September 1944 allowing the display of the national red and white flag and the playing of the Indonesian national anthem was taken by many Indonesians as a sign that the Japanese finally meant business and would speedily grant Indonesia its freedom.

Tokyo, however, agreed to a request by the authorities in Java that a more gradual approach should be used and the military government in fact tried to soft pedal the issue of independence as long as possible, granting piecemeal concessions while at the same time attempting to guide the popular enthusiasm that had been engendered by the Koiso promise into channels that were more productive for the Japanese war effort. The real motives of the Japanese are clearly spelt out in a policy statement, dated 7 September 1944, in which the military authorities were forbidden to make any definite commitments about the date for independence, the geographical limits of Indonesia, or the future governmental structure. Moreover:

National consciousness must be aroused to the highest possible degree and must be used to strengthen our defences and the cooperation with the military government in order to create Japan and Java into an inseparable unit. No drastic changes are to be allowed in the political and economic structure created by the military government, although steps must be taken to increase the participation of Indonesians in government administration and their political education must be taken in hand. . . . The local population under the direction of the military government is allowed to investigate and study the possibilities for the realization of independence. . . . Although the insatiable nature of the Indonesians may sometimes cause us to become upset, we may not adopt a hostile attitude towards them, but we must lead them constantly in accordance with the prescribed policy. A so-called crawling attitude is forbidden. . . . Looking at the present situation and seeing the enthusiasm and festive excitement of the people we must not be tempted to draw the superficial conclusion that we have already reached our objective: that is the peoples' trust in Japan and a greater will to fight.[59]

For the next six months this policy was followed almost to the letter. The first important breakthrough for the nationalists occurred in September 1944 when, after repeated requests by Sukarno, the Japanese agreed to the establishment of a nationalist-led propaganda organization, the *Barisan Pelopor* (Pioneer Corps). As Benda puts it:

The nationalist élite was thus for the first time during the occupation given an organizational weapon of the first magnitude. It could now make a beginning at penetrating the Indonesian village, and at rallying to its cause the *Abangan* elements that for decades had resisted *Ulama* influence. Equally important, nationalist leaders could obtain a firm footing among the thousands of young Indonesians whom the Japanese Military administration had afforded the first political schooling and who, as a result, had outgrown the traditional allegiances of the Indonesian peasantry, *Abangan* as well as *santri* oriented.[60]

This gain by the nationalists, however, was counteracted to some extent again by the Japanese decision to agree to Muslim demands for their own military organization. On 4 December 1944 the Japanese allowed the MASJUMI to set up its own military forces, the *Hizbullah* (Army of Allah) which by the end of the occupation was able to put almost 30,000 troops into the field.

Towards the end of 1944 a number of Indonesians were appointed mayors in various towns and even more important Indonesians were appointed as Vice-Residents, and given top positions in the various government departments.[61]

The question of independence, however, was carefully avoided by the Japanese, and Sukarno did very little to put pressure on the military in this respect. The reason for this was not so much—as has been suggested—that Sukarno was pro-Japanese and believed until the end in a Japanese victory, but rather as Dahm has said that Sukarno was more anti-Western than anti-Japanese.

Sukarno and most other Indonesian leaders realized that the Japanese defeat was imminent. But unlike many of the younger generation and socialist leaders such as Sjahrir, who were strongly anti-Japanese and wanted to obtain freedom totally by their own efforts, Sukarno argued that it was better to have one bird in the hand than seven flying in the air. He therefore made frenzied efforts to arouse the people ostensibly to support the Japanese until the end. Moreover, Sukarno was apparently worried by the threats hurled against him by the Dutch radio from Australia that traitors would be taken care of after the war. Sukarno apparently reasoned that he would have a better chance to survive politically as well as physically if he was to confront the Allies as the head of an established free—although Japanese-sponsored—state of Indonesia. And according to a well-informed Indonesian source Sukarno at that time appears to have felt that even if the Allies removed him from office on their arrival, it was preferable to taste glory for a few months than not at all.

Speculating on the gradual deterioration of the Japanese military position, which would mean increasing concessions for the Indonesians, and like everybody else not expecting the sudden collapse of Japan after Hiroshima and Nagasaki, Sukarno's belief that Indonesia would be given independence some months before the end of the war was a distinct possibility.

Another important tactical reason for Sukarno's attempt to keep the lid on the growing anti-Japanese feeling among large sections of the population was the fear that too much pressure and certainly open rebellion would undoubtedly have caused harsh and ruthless retaliation by the Japanese. Sukarno and a number of other Indonesian nationalists argued that the lightly armed Indonesian forces such as PETA and the Army of Allah and the Pioneer Corps would certainly be annihilated in a clash with the Japanese, leaving Indonesia without any armed forces to get the revolution off the ground and fight the real enemy, the Allies, and in particular the Dutch.

So, in November 1944, Sukarno succeeded in pushing through the Central Advisory Council his concept of the *Pantja-Dharma*—the Five Duties—a pledge of loyalty to the Japanese which read:

1. In this life and death struggle, together with the other peoples of Greater East Asia, we stand united with Dai Nippon and are prepared for sacrifice because this is a struggle in defence of right and truth.
2. We are laying the foundations of an Indonesian state which will be independent, united, sovereign, just, and prosperous, it will give credit to Dai Nippon and it will live as faithful member within the circle of the Greater East Asian family.
3. We strive with unfeigned ardour for fame and greatness, as we guard and exalt our own civilization and culture, promote Asian culture, and bring its influence to bear on the cultures of the world.
4. We serve—in firm brotherhood with the other peoples of Greater East Asia—our own state and people with unshakable loyalty, in continual accountability before Almighty God.
5. We struggle with ardent longing towards lasting peace throughout the world, a peace founded on the brotherhood of all humanity and one that conforms to the ideal of the *Hakko Ichiu*.[62]

Sukarno's attempt to stop uprisings against the Japanese was not entirely successful. For example in February 1945 the PETA unit stationed at Blitar in East Java staged a rebellion against the Japanese which was quickly suppressed. Most of the Indonesian officers captured were executed. Sukarno's claim that he knew about the PETA rebellion in advance and had argued against it appears to be untrue.[63]

During the early months of 1945 the Japanese military situation in the Pacific and southern Asia started to deteriorate rapidly. American forces landed on Iwoshima on 19 February; Manila fell five days later. The Sulu Islands, to the north-east of Borneo, fell into American hands on 4 April, and Rangoon was captured by the British on 3 May. Allied air activity over the archipelago intensified and frequent bombing raids made it clear to the local population that the end of the war was near.

As a result the military government in Java decided to give in a little more to the Indonesian demands, and on 1 March 1945 the Japanese announced the establishment in the near future of a Committee to Investigate Indonesian Independence. As its title suggests, this committee was rather a reluctant gesture on the part of the Japanese and the fact that its first meeting did not take place until 28 May is a clear indication that the military authorities in Java tried to retard the issue of independence as long as possible. It is rather interesting that the Committee to Investigate Indonesian Independence was not headed by Sukarno, but by Dr Radjiman Wedioningrat, an old-time nationalist of the Budi Utomo days, and a spokesman for the more conservative elements in the Indonesian élite. The usual explanation for this is that Sukarno wanted to play a more active role in the committee and therefore was not interested in the chairmanship, and that Dr Radjiman was appointed by the Japanese on the suggestion of Sukarno and Hatta. Such a move by Sukarno seems to be somewhat out of character. There is some evidence which suggests that the Japanese, who knew his ability to arouse the masses, did not consider Sukarno the right person to lead cool and rational discussions about the future state of Indonesia and that they were therefore looking for a calmer, more reasonable and less emotional person. At least this is the impression given in a report by Yoshio Ichibangse, one of the Japanese representatives on the committee, who later reported:

The majority of the nationalists wanted immediate independence even if it was not yet complete. Sukarno expressed himself as follows: 'Independence is like marriage. Should one wait until one's income has risen to for example 500 guilders per month and until one has furnished a house? I say: No, marry first and then try together to build up a household. If you want another comparison: independence is like the construction of a bridge across a river. The virgin soils on the other side can be brought under cultivation later on.' It looked to me that Sukarno would even consider a break with Japan if it was unwilling to grant independence immediately. This was contrary to the opinion of the Japanese, which was shared by the more careful Indonesian leaders, that a state must have at its disposal sufficient power and the opportunities to generate a feeling of pride and fiery will in its sentiments. A state cannot only rest on the passions of the people, but must be founded on cool thinking and a soundly constructed basis . . .[64]

Sukarno continued his attempts to turn the growing hate of the people away from the Japanese and divert it to the Allies, and his hysterical outbursts, 'We will flatten America, and we will crush England', date from this time.

Sukarno was also anxious to convince the leaders of Indonesia that they should forget their individual, political and ideological differences, and form a united national front to stand firm against the coming onslaught of the Dutch colonialists. The formula for this national unity was to be the *Pantja-Sila* (Five Principles) of the Indonesian state, which Sukarno propounded in his famous speech to the Committee for the Preparation to Investigate Indonesian Independence on 1 June 1945. In his memoirs Sukarno reminisced:

Nationalists from throughout the archipelago, chosen by me and approved by the Japanese, attended the sittings with their own plans, rules, and painfully hair-splitting suggestions worked out in advance. No one coordinated with the other. The sophisticates of Java, the traders of Sumatra, the peasants from the outer islands, found no common ground. . . . Orthodox Muslims pushed for a state on an Islamic-theocratic basis. There were moderates who decided we were too immature to govern ourselves at all. There was a great twisting and turning and lack of cohesion. For three days there was solid disagreement concerning the basic principles of *Indonesia Merdeka*. I sat through the hubbub letting everybody say his piece. My hair stood on end listening to them expounding plans worked out to the smallest detail. They brought forth far too many ifs and conjectural problems. At this rate none of us would know *Merdeka* until we were in our graves. If the Japanese had liberated us that day we would have had to say, 'Wait a while, hold it a minute. We are not ready yet.' I had sixteen years to prepare what I wanted to say . . . I knew we couldn't found our nation on the constitution of the United States of America. Nor on the Communist manifesto. We couldn't borrow anybody's way of life, including Japan's *Tenno Koodoo Seishim*, Divinity of the Emperor. *Marhaenist* Indonesia corresponds to no other concept. Year after year I turned this over in my brain. . . . The night before I was to speak I walked out in my garden, alone. And I gazed up at the stars. And I marvelled at the perfection of creation. And I cried softly. I said to God, 'I am crying because tomorrow I shall experience a historic moment in my life and need your help. I know the thoughts I shall speak are not mine. You unfolded them to me. Yours is the only creative mind. You have guided every breath of my life. Please, please give me again your guidance and inspiration tomorrow.'[65]

In fact the next day, on 1 June 1945, Sukarno, divinely inspired or not, managed to electrify his listeners and have them accept his solution. His speech is perhaps one of the best examples ever of Sukarnoist thinking. Sukarno began his exposition by repeating the claims of some members of the Commission that Indonesia was not yet ready for independence:

I listened to Mr Soetardjo's speech several days ago when he replied to the question: What is it that is called independence? He said, If every individual is already independent at heart, that is already independence. If every single Indonesian of these 70 million must first be independent at heart before we are able to achieve political independence, I repeat once again, we shan't have *Indonesia Merdeka* until doomsday. It is *within that Indonesia Merdeka* that we shall make our people independent. Within that *Indonesia Merdeka* we shall make our people independent at heart.[66]

Sukarno then emphasized to the delegates that in addition to the existence of a people with their own territory, recognition by International Law depended also on the existence of a stable national government. And he argued that true freedom could only be achieved on the basis of the political philosophy which he had expounded since 1927 and which could be expressed in the five principles: nationalism, internationalism, *mufakat* or democracy, social well-being, belief in the one supreme God.

Sukarno further explained that Indonesian nationalism meant the establishment of a state, which should contain the territories that in the distant past had been part of the great empires of Sriwidjaja and Modjopahit. Such a nationalism, however, he warned, must be opposed to regionalism as well as the chauvinism of the 'Indonesia *über alles*' variety. And arguing in the same vein as the Taman Siswa leader, Ki Hadjar Dewantoro, Sukarno argued that Indonesian nationalism should be concentric with a feeling of belonging to the human race.

The third principle contained Sukarno's solution to the inherent Indonesian problem of political and ideological division. In the same way that he had argued in 1927, he put it to the delegates that unity could not be obtained on the basis of Western democracy, on the principle of 50 per cent plus one, but only on the basis of the traditional system of reaching unanimous agreement (*mufakat*) after full deliberation (*musjawarah*).

Sukarno further argued that political democracy alone was not enough, so he introduced a fourth principle of social democracy and social justice.

And finally coming to the fifth principle, the belief in the one supreme God, Sukarno argued that all people should have the right to confess their particular religion in the new Indonesia freely and without fear.

Sukarno then pointed out that he had selected the number five because he loved symbolism. The principles of Islam were five, the human hand had five fingers, and human beings had five senses. But, Sukarno continued, if some people did not particularly like the idea of having five principles, they could easily be reduced to three: social nationalism, social democracy, and belief in the one God:

> But perhaps not all of you like this '*Tri-sila*' and ask for one, one principle alone. Alright, I shall make them one, I shall gather them up again to become one. What is that one? As I said a while ago, we are establishing an Indonesian state which all of us must support. All for all. Not the Christians for Indonesia, not the Islamic group for Indonesia, not Hadikusumo for Indonesia, not van Eck for Indonesia, not Nitisenito for Indonesia, but the Indonesians for Indonesia—all for all. If I compress what was five into three, and what was three into one, then I have a genuine Indonesian term, *gotong-rojong*, mutual cooperation. The state of Indonesia, which we are to establish must be a *gotong-rojong* state.[67]

Sukarno wrote in his autobiography that he received a tremendous ovation and that the delegates accepted his philosophy of five principles by acclamation.[68] It is clear, however, that not all the delegates were entirely happy about the compromise suggested by Sukarno and they wanted a clear exposition of what the role of Islam would be in the new state of Indonesia. The Commission delegated Sukarno to head a smaller working committee and from its labours there evolved, on 22 June 1945, the Djakarta Charter, in which the Five Principles are prefaced by the Qur'anic verse: 'In the name of Allah, the forgiving'; and the fifth principle now read: 'The belief in God with the duty of the adherents of Islam to live according to the religious laws.'

The Committee for the Investigation of Indonesian Independence also concerned itself with devising an Indonesian Constitution. To speed up the proceedings on 11 July 1945 Sukarno was appointed as chairman of a special constitutional committee consisting of nineteen members. The actual preparations were left to the well-known lawyer Supomo who was able to submit a draft Constitution by 13 July to the full committee.

The draft Constitution envisaged the free Indonesia to be a unitary state and a republic. Three instruments of government were proposed: *Madjelis Permusjawaratan Rakjat* (People's Deliberation Council) or M.P.R.; *Dewan Perwakilan Rakjat* (People's Represent- ative Council) or D.P.R.; and a Presidency and a Vice-Presidency. Sovereignty was vested in the people and embodied in the M.P.R., which was to consist of members of parliament (D.P.R.), and repre- sentatives from the regions and racial minorities. The M.P.R. was to lay down broad principles of policy and was required to meet at least once every five years. The D.P.R., which was to meet at least once a year, had the right to initiate legislation and all statutes needed this body's approval. The President was vested with impor- tant discretionary powers. He was given the right to make statutes with the approval of the D.P.R., while legislation initiated by the D.P.R. required presidential approval. The President was to hold office for five years; was made the Supreme Commander of the armed forces; and was given the prerogatives of declaring wars, states of emergencies, and concluding peace. The President was to be assisted by ministers, who were directly responsible to him and not to parliament.

The emphasis on strong leadership, as exemplified by the great powers vested in the Presidency, and the emphasis on deliberation in the various representative bodies, shows the influence of Sukar- noist thinking on the Constitution.

The objections of supporters of a more liberal democratic system of government were drowned in the debates of the Independence Investigation Committee in which Javanistic inclined members held a majority.

Muslims expressed considerable concern about Article 29 of the draft Constitution, which provided for freedom of religion. Orthodox leaders pointed out that according to the Islamic Law,

Muslims could not change their religion with impunity, and that according to the more strict interpretations the offenders were to be punished by death. Article 29 was subsequently amended and in the new version Indonesians were guaranteed the freedom to adhere to a particular religious position and to carry out the duties and responsibilities accordingly. No mention was made of the right to change religion, although in fact this remained possible in principle. A further concession to Islam was the clause that the President must be a Muslim.

These rather meagre concessions which the Muslim representatives in the Radjiman Commission were able to obtain suggests two things: first, the political power of Islam had by no means increased during the Japanese occupation to the extent that is sometimes believed; and secondly, the Japanese policy of divide and rule had not fully succeeded. For the vast majority of orthodox Muslims the Indonesian national spirit proved to be strong enough to bury their differences with the nationalists temporarily, so as not to endanger the success of the greater good of national independence.

The continuous deterioration of the military situation in South-East Asia and the Pacific caused the Japanese to speed up the granting of Indonesian independence and on 7 August 1945 the Radjiman Commission was replaced by a Committee for the Preparation of Independence. This committee was headed by Sukarno and Hatta and consisted of twenty-seven members drawn from all parts of the country. Scenting victory Sukarno made his now well-known speech of 7 August in which he referred to the Djojobojo prophesies and told the Indonesian people that the country would be free before the maize would ripen.[69]

The next morning Sukarno, Hatta and Radjiman were suddenly summoned to Japanese headquarters in Djakarta and told that they would be flown to Vietnam to confer with Marshal Terauchi, the Commander-in-Chief of the South-East Asian area, about the question of Indonesian independence. Terauchi told the Indonesian leaders that independence was now a certainty and that they should speed up preparations. The date on which independence would be granted was apparently laid down by Terauchi as 24 August.

However, the holocaust at Nagasaki and Hiroshima, the sudden collapse of the Japanese war effort, and the mounting pressure of anti-Japanese forces, mainly students (*pemudas*), within the country, took Sukarno and Hatta by surprise and almost forced freedom on them.

CHAPTER IV

Revolutionary Leader

O N their return from Saigon on 14 August 1945 Sukarno and the other delegates were enthusiastically welcomed by thousands of Djakarta citizens at Kemajoran airport. In a speech of welcome, Koesoemo Oetoyo, the Vice-President of the Central Advisory Council, expressed the hope that the leaders had brought back with them the news which the people had been waiting for so long.

Sukarno's reply, however, was very restrained and evasive. Knowing the radical attitudes and feelings in particular of the students, he apparently feared that a direct report on Terauchi's instructions might trigger off a violent anti-Japanese explosion. Sukarno rather lamely told the crowd that: 'Sometime ago I said on the radio that Indonesia would be free before the maize plant would ripen. But now I can tell you: Indonesia will be free before the maize plant begins to flower.'[1]

While Sukarno's speech might have calmed the general population, Sjahrir and the students regarded this further example of complete submissiveness to Japanese orders as the last straw.

On the afternoon of that same 14 August, Sjahrir told Hatta about radio reports of a Japanese peace offer to the Allies; and he urged that the Japanese-sponsored preparation committee should be by-passed and that Sukarno should declare independence immediately in the name of the Indonesian people.[2]

Sjahrir's claim that he managed to have Sukarno agree to proclaim Indonesian independence on the evening of 15 August[3] is refuted by both Hatta[4] and Sukarno,[5] who apparently did not believe that the Japanese had surrendered. Unwilling to start off an untimely revolution which might be smothered immediately in streams of blood by the Japanese Army both leaders remained inactive. Communications both internal and external were defective at that time, and Sukarno and Hatta were by no means alone in doubting the rumours about the Japanese surrender:

All of us in Indonesia were convinced that Japan would fight till the end. Even the collapse of Hitler's power would be no reason for Japan just to quit everything and surrender. We were deeply impressed by Japanese propaganda that Japan was undefeatable. Their spirit was enormous. How could they surrender? Knowing their fanaticism and chauvinism and unbelievable faith in their God Emperor, it was really unthinkable that the war could be finished by just a couple of bombs. Only afterwards when the news came trickling in bit by bit, we began to realize that the destruction caused by the atom bombs was on a scale almost beyond human imagination.[6]

Before taking any action Sukarno decided first of all to get official clarification of the situation. On the morning of 15 August 1945 he and Hatta tried to get in touch with General Yamomoto, the head of the Japanese Military Administration. When the general could not be located, both leaders went to see Subardjo, the head of the Research Bureau of the Japanese Naval Liaison Office, which was under the command of Vice-Admiral Mayeda. But Subardjo was also still in the dark and made an appointment to see Mayeda in the afternoon. Mayeda proved to be unwilling to either deny or confirm the rumours about a Japanese surrender, and he could only promise the Indonesian leaders that he would inform them as soon as any official news was received.[7]

Sukarno and Hatta then realized that the time for action had come and that independence had to be proclaimed as quickly as possible, because the Japanese after their surrender might be ordered by the Allies to maintain the political *status quo*. It was decided to call a meeting of the Preparation Committee at ten o'clock the next morning at which members were to be urged to adopt the draft Constitution without delay so that the delegates from the remoter parts of the country could return home with full instructions before the Japanese could put a spoke in the wheel.

Sukarno, Hatta, and most of the other older leaders wanted an orderly transfer of power and tried to avoid an open clash with the Japanese. This was not to the taste of the students who wanted an immediate uprising.

On the afternoon of 15 August Hatta was visited by a few youth leaders; he rejected outright their plan for an uprising by the PETA and the students against the Japanese, which was to be preceded by a Declaration of Independence by Sukarno.[8]

In the evening of that same day Sukarno was also beseeched by some students, led by Wikana and Chairul Saleh, who tried to convince him that on that same evening he should announce on the radio that Indonesia had freed itself from the Japanese yoke. When Sukarno persistently refused Wikana threatened that he would start a bloody revolution the next day. Hatta who witnessed the scene, writes:

> On hearing this threat the blood rushed to Bung Karno's head. He rushed towards Wikana and said: 'Here is my neck. Drag me to that corner and take my life, now tonight. You don't have to wait until tomorrow.' Wikana appeared to have been frightened by Bung Karno's unexpected reaction, and said: 'We don't want to murder you. We only want to remind you that if by tonight the Independence of Indonesia is not declared, tomorrow the people will take action and they will murder whom they mistrust and consider as supporters of the Dutch such as the Ambonese for example.'[9]

After that there was dead silence for some time and then Wikana and his followers left to report to the other students who decided to take matters in their own hands.

The students who were bent on a bloody clash with the Japanese the next day apparently decided to abduct Sukarno and Hatta to a safe place where they could make the Proclamation of Independence without interference by the Japanese. At 4.00 p.m. on 16 August Sukarno and Hatta were kidnapped by some students led by Sukarni and brought to the PETA garrison of Rengasdengklok which was to the south-west of Djakarta.

Subsequent events, however, vindicated Sukarno's and Hatta's view that an anti-Japanese uprising at that stage would have been disastrous to the Indonesian cause. On 16 August nothing happened either in Djakarta or in the remainder of Java. The PETA units who according to Wikana were supposed to have risen *en masse* against the Japanese remained inactive. There was no attack by students in Djakarta, and the general population went about its business as usual. The plans for a student-led general uprising apparently proved to be no more than a figment of the romantic imagination of a few younger leaders such as Wikana, Chairul Saleh, and Sukarni.

In the meantime, on the morning of the 16th, Subardjo, when informed about Sukarno's and Hatta's disappearance, decided to get the backing of the Japanese Navy in having the two leaders released in case they might be captured by the Japanese Army authorities. After having informed Naval headquarters about the kidnapping, Subardjo went to see Mayeda at his house at the Nasau Boulevard. The admiral was greatly disturbed about Sukarno's and Hatta's disappearance, and promised Subardjo that he would do his utmost to discover the whereabouts of the two leaders.

Subardjo then went to the Naval headquarters where he knew that Wikana, his subordinate in the Naval Liaison Office, was holding a meeting with the students. He finally succeeded in convincing the young revolutionaries about the genuineness of Mayeda's assurance that the Japanese Navy was willing to back an Indonesian Declaration of Independence; and late in the afternoon Subardjo was allowed to visit Sukarno and Hatta at Rengasdengklok after he had guaranteed with his own life that independence would be proclaimed immediately.[10]

In the meantime, the kidnappers at Rengasdengklok were apparently at a loss as what to do with the two recalcitrant leaders. Sukarno wrote later:

> We waited there all day. They treated us well. They even sent for special milk for baby Guntur. There was no rush. Except, nothing happened. Not even in Djakarta. Periodically couriers arrived and departed. Whenever one returned I would ask, well, uh, has the big revolt started yet? Each time they would shake their heads sadly and mumble, no news yet from Djakarta.[11]

Subardjo reached Rengasdengklok at 6.00 p.m. and surprised Sukarno and Hatta in their pyjamas and quietly told them about Mayeda's confirmation of Japan's surrender; without any resistance from the students the three leaders journeyed back to Djakarta, which they reached safely about eleven o'clock that evening.

Somewhat later, Sukarno, Hatta, and Subardjo went to the house of Admiral Mayeda, the only place where they felt themselves safe to discuss the plans for the Declaration of Independence. Subardjo describes the meeting with Mayeda as follows:

> We saw Mayeda coming downstairs from his bedroom on the first floor. We exchanged greetings with the Rear-Admiral. He looked tired, apparently under the pressure of the heavy responsibilities he had to shoulder but he didn't lose his self-control and his usual dignified attitude. At a glance he took in the crowd assembled in

94

the front room. Uniformed students were standing behind Sukarno and Hatta. They were looking around suspiciously, as if they didn't trust matters one hundred per cent. I was told later . . . that in case we didn't appear they would have started the scheduled revolt at midnight. Sukarno said a few words, thanking the Rear-Admiral for his hospitality. . . . Mayeda answered that his house was available . . . and he assured us that as long as we remained under his roof, he would be responsible for our safety.[12]

Soon after, Sukarno, Hatta and Mayeda left the house to contact General Yamomoto who refused to receive them in the middle of the night. The three leaders then went to see General Nishimura, who was adamantly opposed to the Indonesian plan to proclaim independence immediately, pointing out that the Japanese had become mere agents of the Allies and could therefore not allow any change in the *status quo*. Sukarno, Hatta and Mayeda returned at about 2.30 a.m., accompanied by Colonel Myoshi, the political adviser of General Nishimura, and a member of the Foreign Affairs department, who had always been sympathetic to the claims of the Indonesian nationalists. In spite of the Army's opposition Mayeda stuck to his promise and did not interfere with the proceedings in his house.

Sukarni, and Nishizima, a Japanese Naval officer, had also left Mayeda's residence and had made a rather adventurous car ride through the city in order to dissuade the students and PETA units from revolting. They were almost arrested by a Japanese army patrol, which after telephoning Admiral Mayeda let them go on their way. Sukarni returned to Mayeda's house around 1.00 a.m.

The Indonesian leaders decided to proclaim Indonesian independence in spite of the Army's disapproval and proceeded to compose the wording of the Declaration. The text of the Proclamation had already been formulated in the Djakarta Charter of 22 June. Sukarno is supposed to have asked Subardjo to dictate to him from memory the relevant phrases which he wrote down on a piece of paper. The resultant sentence: 'We, the Indonesian people, declare herewith our Independence' was, according to Hatta, too abstract and after some deliberation the clause: 'Matters regarding the transfer of power and other affairs will be arranged in an accurate manner and within the shortest time possible was added.' The text was then typed out by Sajuti Melik and was presented by Sukarno to the meeting.

Sukarni, who spoke for most of the students present, vehemently objected to the wording of the Proclamation, because it was not explicitly directed against the Japanese. The general feeling of the meeting, however, was against the students. Sukarno's suggestion that the Declaration should be signed 'by the representatives of the Indonesian people' was also rejected by Sukarni, who apparently felt that he and the other student leaders, Chairul Saleh, Adam Malik, Djawoto, and Maruto Nitimihardjo, should be the signatories, rather than the members of the Japanese-sponsored Preparation Committee. Another suggestion from someone in the crowd that everybody present should sign was also opposed by the Sukarni group. It was Sajuti Melik who apparently caused a breakthrough in this impasse with a suggestion that nobody would mind if Sukarno and Hatta were the sole signatories. This was accepted with great applause by the majority.[13]

Sukarno also squashed Sukarni's idea that independence should be proclaimed at a mass meeting which he had arranged for the next morning on Ikada Square. Instead Sukarno suggested that a less conspicuous place was needed in order to avoid an open clash with the Japanese Army and suggested that the Proclamation should be made on the front lawn of his house at Pegangsaan Timur 56, at ten o'clock that morning.

On the morning of 17 August at 10.00 a.m. Sukarno, with Hatta at his side, read the Proclamation to a small crowd of people gathered in front of his home. At the same time a homemade red and white flag was raised and the national anthem was sung. This rather simple though moving ceremony must have been somewhat of an anti-climax to those who had for decades dreamt about this great moment. Everything was done in a makeshift fashion; there was no fanfare, and there were no great festivities.

Adam Malik who at the time was an employee of the Japanese news-agency *Domei* used the Djakarta radio station to transmit the news about the Proclamation to Indonesia and the rest of the world.

The following day the Committee for the Preparation of Indonesian Independence met in session, and Hatta read out to the members the Constitution of Indonesia. For the most part this Constitution followed the earlier draft of the Supomo sub-committee, with the important exception that the earlier compromise with the Muslims was not incorporated and that Article 29 no longer contained the clause concerning the duty of Muslims to live in accordance with the precepts of the Islamic law. Also the requirement that the President of Indonesia had to be a Muslim was deleted.

Unfortunately, most of the documents concerning the meetings of the Committee were destroyed during the Dutch attack on

Jogjakarta in 1948, and it is therefore almost impossible to pinpoint exactly why and how these changes were made.

The deletions were apparently insisted upon by Hatta, and the fact that they were accepted shows that the Islamic leadership had lost a great deal of their earlier political power and were now forced to play a role subordinate to the nationalists.[14]

On the other hand, the Five Principles, which were contained in the preamble to the Constitution, now featured as their first pillar the belief in God, which in the initial Sukarno version had been the fifth and last principle. While this might be taken as a victory for the Muslims, the substitution of the word Allah by the much vaguer word *Tuhan*, which means the Almighty One, would rather suggest otherwise. And it is clear that the Constitution envisaged that in addition to Allah there would be a place in the Indonesian republic for other concepts of the divine.

Hatta, who also seemed to have been responsible for this change in emphasis in the state ideology, explained in 1956 in a speech in Jogjakarta:

The leaders of all groups hoped that in an Independent Indonesia everybody would not only have religious freedom, but also that there would be religious peace. Therefore on the instigation of Bung Karno, who had formulated the *Panta-Sila*, the principle of the Almighty God was accepted as the fifth pillar and in this way the state ideology came to consist of two layers, namely a political foundation and a moral foundation. After the formulation of the *Piagem Djakarta* of 22 June 1945, which was to be included in the text of the Proclamation of Indonesian Independence . . . a change was made in the order of these principles . . . the result of this change . . . is that without changing the state ideology itself, the state had been given a strong moral basis. The expression 'Almighty God' does not only lead to mutual respect between the various religions as was at first argued by Bung Karno, but it became the basis which leads to truth, justice, goodness, honesty, and fraternity.[15]

It was also during the meeting of the Preparation Committee of 18 August that Sukarno and Hatta were elected as President and Vice-President of Indonesia. However, the Preparation Committee, in view of the considerable time lag involved in setting up the various representative bodies provided for in the Constitution, decided that for the next six months all state powers should be exercised by the President who would be assisted by a national committee. This decision gave Sukarno virtually dictatorial powers.

On 19 August the Independence Committee (the word Preparation was now deleted in line with the changed circumstances) divided Indonesia into eight provinces, each of which was to have a governor, a national committee, a resident with a national residential committee, and a village head with a village council. A sub-committee was set up to prepare for the establishment of the various central government departments. During the discussions the Muslims received a further setback when their demand for a department of religion was rejected by a majority of members.

On 29 August Sukarno abolished the Independence Committee and installed the *Komitee Nasional Indonesia Pusat* (Central Indonesian National Committee) or K.N.I.P. which counted 135 members selected by Sukarno and Hatta from all regions and from various political groups and racial minorities.

During the same meeting it was also decided to adopt a one party system and, rather significantly, this one government party was to be named after Sukarno's old P.N.I. According to Sukarno the K.N.I.P. was only a temporary institution, but the P.N.I. was to be a permanent organization, which was to be joined by all Indonesians in a spirit of mutual cooperation and help.

Immediately after the Proclamation the republic of Indonesia only existed in name. The government apparatus as well as most of the armed power were still in the hands of the Japanese, who were bound by the surrender agreement to maintain the *status quo*. Sukarno put the problem clearly in a radio broadcast to the nation on 23 August:

> To proclaim Independence is easy. To make a Constitution is not difficult. To elect a President and a Vice-President is easier still. But to establish the organs and offices of authority for the administration of a state, as well as to seek international recognition, especially under conditions such as the present, in which the Japanese government is still obliged by the international *status quo* to remain in this country to run the administration and maintain public order—these tasks are not easy.[16]

Contrary to the views of Sukarno and the older leaders, the students didn't think there was a problem at all, and in their usual hot-headed manner, they argued that the Japanese should be overthrown by force. But the views of the diplomatic party were to prevail for some time, and by diplomacy and negotiation the Sukarno-Hatta government was able to reach a type of 'gentleman's agreement' with the Japanese, which allowed Indonesians gradually to take over the civil service and public utilities. Most of the first cabinet ministers and Indonesian high public officials were drawn from the existing Japanese-controlled agencies and for some time they held the dual function of Japanese and Indonesian republican official. As one American scholar succinctly put it:

> By this neat device both the Indonesian leadership and the Japanese were satisfied. The former now had a cabinet, both an important symbol of the state they were constructing and a means by which they could expect to increase their control over the rank and file of the civil service. The Japanese authorities, for their part, continued to consider the ministers as officials subordinate to them and could use this fact both to hinder the drift of the Indonesian civil servants towards the republic and to justify themselves to the Allies who wanted the *status quo* preserved.[17]

Undoubtedly even more galling to the students and other strongly revolutionary groups in Indonesian society was the comparative unconcern with which the Sukarno-Hatta government allowed the Japanese on 18 and 19 August 1945 to disarm the PETA force of sixty-six battalions, numbering in total about thirty-five thousand trained men. The republican government was apparently not sure that it could control PETA, and considered that any premature armed uprisings would completely sabotage its attempts at a peaceful takeover from the Japanese. The Sukarno government, although clearly realizing the need for a strong national army, was apparently first concerned to maintain peace and order. And on 22 August *Badan Kemanan Rakjat* (the People's Security Agency) or B.K.R. was set up which for all practical purposes was a type of police force rather than an army.[18]

Ostensibly Sukarno's personal power and authority seemed very great at the beginning of the revolution. He was the one who proclaimed independence. And the state ideology, the Constitution with its emphasis on unanimous agreement, full deliberation, strong presidential leadership, and the one party system, bore the distinct imprint of the political philosophy which Sukarno had preached since the mid-1920s.

To the Indonesian masses Sukarno was the great national hero.

In comparison to Sukarno the popularity of other leaders such as Sjahrir, Hatta, Subardjo and the Communists, Tan Malakka and Musso, was minimal.

Sukarno had made good use of the opportunities provided by the Japanese occupation to extend and consolidate his pre-war popular image. He had taken the initiative from most of the other leaders and had fastened on every chance that came about to put himself into the limelight. He had almost totally monopolized the mass media and millions of Indonesians had regularly heard his voice on the radio. Any criticisms or doubts that might have arisen in the people's mind about Sukarno's intentions and motives during the Japanese occupation, seemed to have quickly disappeared when most of the other leaders insisted that he should make the Proclamation and be the first President of the republic.

Sukarno's greatest asset was his mesmerizing power over the people, of which he gave another example on 19 September, when a vast crowd—estimated at 200,000—led on by Tan Malakka and his followers, gathered on Ikada Square vigorously protesting against the Japanese. The Japanese military government expecting trouble had cordoned off the area with strong detachments of heavily armed troops. Considering the ugly mood displayed by the crowd, bloodshed seemed unavoidable. But to the great astonishment and admiration of the Japanese and the equally great chagrin of Tan Malakka and his associates who for weeks had been carefully planning this move, it took Sukarno less than five minutes to defuse this extremely explosive situation and to send the people home quietly and peacefully.[19]

However, the initial victory of the 'diplomatic party' and the general quiet and peaceful atmosphere which was prevalent during August and most of September, cannot solely be ascribed to the power and prestige of Sukarno and his associates. The lack of violence and the absence of other outward signs of a physical revolution were in part a backlash of the fear and terror inculcated in the people by the Japanese. Many Indonesians, although happy about the Declaration, were confused and uncertain about what would happen next, and remained inactive. For some time, then, Indonesia, or at least Java, lived in a type of political vacuum. The people were dazed and generally adopted a wait-and-see attitude:

Even after people began to take action of one sort or another, however, this feeling of waiting persisted. Shock and inertia kept the shell of social order substantially intact while the forces

1. Sukarno as a high school student in 1916.

2. *Sukarno with his second wife.*

3. *Sukarno: the charismatic speaker.*

4. *Under the protection of Japan (Sukarno is second from the right, Dr Mohammed Hatta, the leader of the oppostion and former Vice-President, is on the extreme right).*

5. *At an inaugural ceremony at Bandung, western Java, in July 1958. This was the last time the two former*

6. *Sukarno with his mother in March 1958.*

7. *President Eisenhower talking to President Sukarno's son in Washington in May 1956. Richard Nixon, t Vice-President, is on the left, and Foster Dulles, the American Secretary of State, is third from the left.*

Sukarno is presented with the Czechoslovakian Order of the White Lion by President Zapotocky, at Prague Castle on 26 September 1956.

In Cairo for talks with Islamic and Arab leaders in May 1956. The then Prime Minister of Egypt, Colonel Nasser, is on Sukarno's right.

10. Lunching as a guest of the Stockholm City Council in May 1959.

11. With Emperor Hirohito, Empress Nagako and Prince Mikasa in Tokyo.

12. *Sukarno, during a tour of Afro-Asian states, being met in Delhi by Mr Nehru, the Indian Prime Minister, and Dr Radhkrishnan, the President, in January 1958.*

13. *With the families of government troops soon after the putting down of Sumatran rebels in March 1958.*

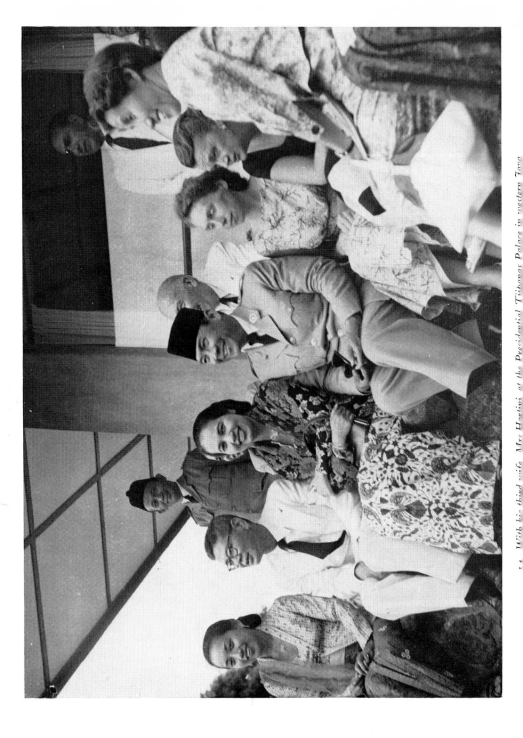

14. With his third wife, Mrs. Hartini, at the Presidential Tjitarua Palace in western Java.

15. *On a state visit to Iraq in April 1960. Praying at the tomb of the Moslem saint, Abdul Qaàir al-Qaylani.*

16. In August 1961.

which were to destroy it, anarchy from below and intervention from outside, were clearly visible. During most of August and September an air of unreality prevailed; for the time all sorts of people—nationalist leaders, militant students, *Kempeitai* troops, looters, Dutch from the internment camps—pursued their own courses in Bandung without seriously impinging on each other. It was only at the end of the period, in the latter part of September, that these antithetic forces which had been gathering converged in a sudden explosion that marked the real beginning of the revolution.[20]

But below this surface quiet, a strong revolutionary mood was gradually developing, often stimulated by the activities of the Dutch and Eurasians, who usually behaved in a pre-war, lordly manner and acted as if nothing had changed.

In 1945 Sukarno's ideal of a free Indonesia in which he would be the king-pin around which the life of the nation would revolve, was still far from being realized. It still took four years of intense struggle both on the diplomatic and military fronts before Indonesia finally gained its independence from the Dutch.

In August and September 1945 the young republic had successfully weathered its first storm and had been able to avert annihilation by the Japanese; then a new, and a more formidable threat to its existence arose when the first Allied occupation forces arrived in Java in late September.

Dutch radio reports from Australia had made it abundantly clear that Sukarno and other Indonesian collaborators with the Japanese were considered traitors and war criminals, who would be punished accordingly by the Netherlands Indies authorities on their return.

Feeling that the Allies would help to restore the Dutch to power, Sukarno was deeply disturbed about the future of the republic and his own personal fate, fearing that he might lose his life. He is reported to have expected immediate imprisonment on the arrival of the Allied forces, and soon after the Declaration of Independence he ordered his valuables, including his now famous collection of paintings, to be stored in a safe place.[21]

Lack of shipping and military personnel, and also the fact that because of defective intelligence reports Allied headquarters were not sufficiently aware of the urgency of the situation in Java, caused a considerable delay in the arrival of the Allied forces in Indonesia. In the meantime, the Indonesian revolution, which might have been smothered at its inception, was allowed to get off the ground and was beginning to gain momentum when the first British troops landed in Djakarta towards the end of September 1945.

The arrival of the first Allied forces, consisting mainly of British troops with a sprinkling of Dutchmen, appears to have caused an explosion of revolutionary activity, which had been simmering for months, all over the country and was spearheaded by the students. Indonesians took over complete control of the governmental administrative apparatus and public utilities; and even more important, Indonesians, often after protracted and bloody battles, obtained vast quantities of arms from the Japanese.

By the beginning of October 1945 the physical revolution was fully under way and the controversial *Bersiap* (literally 'get ready') period had begun. And as in most revolutions the situation soon deteriorated in some areas in bloody excesses on both sides. Thousands of innocent Indonesians, Dutch and Chinese, including many women and children, were murdered. Daily reports about killings and widespread pillaging poured into Djakarta. The country had run amuck and there was little that either the Allies with the weak forces at their disposal or the Indonesian government, including the charismatic Sukarno, could do to stop the carnage.

In addition to the regular government armed forces, hundreds of separate bands of irregulars sprang up all over the country; some sporting a medley of Japanese, Dutch or Australian uniforms and weapons, while many others were only armed with pointed bamboo sticks and *goloks* (hatchets). Some groups were better organized and showed a certain amount of internal discipline and cohesion; others were merely bands of criminals who were out to loot, pillage and rape.

In the midst of this frenzied melee the voice of the Central Indonesian government was hardly audible and in many areas its authority seemed to have collapsed completely.

The intense popularity of the revolution and the hatred shown against the Dutch took the British High Command by surprise and made it tread very warily in dealing with the Indonesian situation.

The initial policies of the British occupation forces must have come as a surprise and certainly as a relief to Sukarno and many other Indonesian leaders. To the amazement of many Indonesians and the horror of thousands of prisoners of war—mainly Dutchmen —the British Commander-in-Chief, Lord Mountbatten, ordered the Japanese forces to help to maintain law and order. And the Dutch became even more disgusted when the British reached a working agreement with the Indonesian republican authorities sharing the responsibility for internal security in their respective areas, and cries of *Perfide Albion* were loudly heard in the Hague and Batavia.

To the majority of Dutchmen at the time, the matter was perfectly simple. All that needed to be done was to pour in troops, put down the rebellion, and arrest the ringleaders, most of whom were to be shot or imprisoned as traitors and war criminals. Holland, however, was almost powerless at the time. The Netherlands had suffered severe war damage; the Dutch Merchant Fleet had been decimated and whatever shipping there was left could not be released from the Allied pool. Moreover very few Dutch troops were available in the South-East Asian area. It took Holland almost two years to raise, train, equip, and transport the military forces considered necessary to reoccupy Indonesia.

In the meantime the brunt of the task of disarming the Japanese and maintaining law and order fell on the British who were themselves short of troops, and had to rely heavily on their Indian divisions. In view of Britain's precarious political situation in India at the time, and also because most Indian soldiers could hardly be expected to agree to suppress another colonial people fighting for its independence, the British commanders were severely hampered in their actions. Moreover, another important factor which militated against any direct British military intervention in the Indonesian-Dutch dispute was the changeover in Britain from the Churchill-led Conservatives to Labour. The Labour party, which advocated the dismantling of the British Empire, could hardly be expected to favour the shoring-up of the Dutch East Indies by British troops.

The British forces in Indonesia therefore were ordered to stick to their original instructions which were: to accept the surrender of the Japanese forces; to release Allied prisoners of war and civilian internees; to disarm and repatriate the Japanese; to establish peace and order in preparation for the transfer of power to the civilian government; and to capture and try war criminals.[22]

In order not to spark off a widespread anti-Allied offensive by the Indonesians, the British High Command decided to postpone any further disembarking of Dutch troops. And on 28 September Lieut.-Gen. Sir Philip Christison, the Allied Task Commander in the Indies, made it clear in a broadcast from Singapore that British troops came to Indonesia to take care of the Japanese surrender and the release and care of Allied civilian internees, but that the British had no intention of meddling in Indonesian internal affairs. The General further stated that he would attempt to bring the

Dutch and Indonesians to the conference table. The next day on his arrival in Djakarta Christison conceded *de facto* control to the republic in their territories. Arguing that the Allies did not have sufficient forces at their disposal to occupy the whole of Java, Christison appealed to the Republican authorities to help the British in maintaining peace and order.

General Christison's actions, while being viewed with considerable suspicion by many Indonesians, caused a furore in Dutch circles, which immediately accused Britain of selling out a trusted wartime ally. And the Dutch adamantly refused to meet such Indonesian leaders as Sukarno and Hatta, whom they dismissed as traitors.

In the meantime, the *Bersiap* spirit continued to run its course. Clashes between Allied troops and Indonesians became more frequent; law and order was fast collapsing in many parts of Java; thousands of people were being murdered; and the lives of thousands of internees in the camps were in constant danger. The British, much against their will, were gradually drawn ever more deeply into the Indonesian conflict. Anglo-Indonesian confrontation culminated in the battle of Surabaja towards the end of October 1945.

On 25 October the 49th Indian Infantry Brigade had landed at Surabaja without any difficulty. But Indonesian nationalists, fearing that the British were only paving the way for the landing of Dutch troops which were supposed to be waiting in the harbour, soon clashed with the British troops. On 28 October, one Infantry Brigade was attacked by about 20,000 armed Indonesians supported by tanks while a large uncontrolled mob of people armed with rifles, daggers and clubs was milling around in the city.

In order to prevent a general blood bath, Sukarno agreed to the British request to fly to Surabaja in an attempt to ease the situation and to effect a truce. Arriving in Surabaja Sukarno's life was in serious danger. On landing, his plane was met by a hail of bullets from Indonesian forces which were mounting a full-scale attack on the airfield.

Sukarno's prestige was strong enough to stop the fighting for a few hours and a cease-fire was agreed upon. Furthermore, the Indonesians agreed not to interfere with the repatriation of internees from the various camps in East Java. It was also agreed that the British troops should take control of the harbour area and that the city as a whole should be patrolled in equal strength by both Indonesian and British troops. Any further disputes were to be settled in Djakarta after discussion between the British military authorities and Sukarno.

Sukarno's power over the masses, however, seems to have worn off soon after his departure, and a few hours later Brigadier Malaby and a number of other British officers were killed in a fracas in the city. A British observer writes:

The influence that Sukarno had over the masses of the Indonesian people fluctuated considerably. When he showed the Sukarno flag on tours through the country he was greeted with almost delirious enthusiasm, but he appealed many times with every appearance of sincerity for the cessation of fighting and nobody took any notice of him at all. His most successful speeches are those in which he tells the people in simple but vivid language what they want to be told, and it is possible that his undoubtedly great popularity rests on that basis. When he tells them something they do not want to hear they do not listen.[23]

After an ultimatum by Maj.-Gen. Mansergh, the Allied Commander in East Java, ordering Indonesian irregulars to disarm, had been ignored, British troops, aided by Naval guns, artillery and aeroplanes attacked Surabaja. After two days of fierce fighting, in which Indonesian suicide squads armed only with daggers threw themselves at Allied tanks, and went into machine-gun fire in wave after wave, the city was finally occupied.

The battle of Surabaja proved to be an important turning-point in the Indonesian revolution. The willingness of thousands of Indonesians to sacrifice their lives in defence of their freedom opened the eyes of the world and caused many foreign observers to dismiss the Dutch 'brush fire' theory as wishful thinking.

In the meantime the Dutch had been forced by the British to abandon their earlier insistence that discussion with the Indonesians could only take place after Dutch control had been restored. Also Governor-General van Mook began to realize that the other directive of the Hague, which stipulated that no discussions could be held with leaders such as Sukarno and Hatta and other Japanese collaborators, had become extremely unrealistic under the circumstances. And on 23 October a meeting was arranged between van Mook and a number of Indonesian leaders including Sukarno. At this meeting Mr Maberly E. Dining, the political adviser to Mountbatten, informed the republicans that the Allied Command recognized the Netherlands as the legitimate power in Indonesia. This statement caused strong protest from the Indonesians who refused to continue any further discussions. A further meeting between van Mook and

Sukarno was held on 31 October but very little was achieved. Sukarno excused himself from attending a third meeting which was planned for the beginning of November. The excuse given was that he had to attend to urgent political business in Central Java. It seems, however, that Sukarno had become extremely worried about a possible loss of prestige and power within the republic because of the severe criticism of his willingness to negotiate with the Allies including the Dutch, by leftist groups as well as by many sections of the Indonesian armed forces.

From then on Sukarno, who was always worried about his popularity, left the business of negotiations to other Indonesian leaders.

By October 1945 Sukarno's political position in the republic had considerably weakened. He realized that his personal charisma alone was not sufficient to sustain his position of national prominence. He also needed the support of a sizeable section of the national leadership. Ideological division, as well as the existence of mutually opposed power-hungry cliques were a serious danger to Sukarno's position.

Immediately after the Proclamation then, Sukarno's political position was rather weak. He had no political party of his own to lean upon, and on 1 September the idea of having one political party, the *Partai Nasional Indonesia*, a mass movement suggested by Sukarno and accepted by the Preparation Committee on 22 August, was abandoned by the K.N.I.P. which felt that such an organization would cause unnecessary competition and disunity. This left Sukarno and his government open to attack by the other powerful contenders for power: the moderate socialists led by Sjahrir, the national Communists headed by Tan Malakka, the Moscow directed P.K.I., and a strong authoritarian rightist party which had been built up by Subardjo during the last months of the Japanese occupation, and which consisted mainly of Indonesian officials who had cooperated with the Japanese.

Initially support for Sukarno and Hatta had rested to an important extent on former servants of the Japanese administration, which included most of the members of the Preparation Committee and many *prijaji*. Additional support came from some of the stalwarts of Sukarno's pre-war political party, the P.N.I.; and largely in spite of themselves also from a sizeable number of Muslim leaders, who either for reasons of self-protection, because of their collaborationist past, or because of their ideological opposition to Marxism, or both, preferred the Sukarno-Hatta government as the lesser of two evils.

For some weeks, Sutan Sjahrir and other Social Democrats had kept themselves apart from the Proclamation, because in their view the republic was a Japanese-sponsored affair. But after a fact-finding tour of Java, Sjahrir having noticed the general enthusiasm of the people for the Declaration of Independence and the immense popularity of Sukarno realized that the revolution was a fact and that participation could no longer be withheld. Moreover Sjahrir and his party became increasingly disturbed about the rapidly growing strength of the rightist—and in Sjahrir's view fascist—organization of Subardjo, and the equally authoritarian national-Communist group headed by Tan Malakka and such younger leaders as Adam Malik and Chairul Saleh.

Overtures by Tan Malakka to Sjahrir and Hatta to join him in a 'putsch' to overthrow Sukarno were abruptly turned down by both leaders; and Sjahrir eventually decided to throw in his lot with the existing republican government.

Sjahrir's support for Sukarno was purely tactical. The political and philosophical antithesis between the two leaders remained as strong as ever; nor was there any improvement in their personal relations. Towards the end of October Sjahrir published a small booklet *Perdjuangan Kita* (Our Struggle) in which he explained, mainly for the consumption of the outside world, his views on the objectives and conduct of the revolution. He reiterated his earlier views that the new republic was in many ways the product of fascist Japan, and he demanded that all former cooperators with the Japanese should be removed from high office. He blamed the wanton murders of foreigners and Indonesians alike on the fascistic upbringing of many young Indonesians during the Japanese occupation:

Initially the outside world was sympathetic to our freedom struggle. . . . But the increasing frequency with which events occur that show the state of confusion our people are in and which can hardly be accepted as expressions of our love for freedom—such as murder and robbery—public opinion overseas—as has lately been shown—can change. . . . Capitalists are frightened about the possibility that their investments will not bring the expected returns when peace has been re-established in our country. The workers of the world are suspicious of anything that looks like the cruelty of fascism, which is already so notorious all over the world at this moment, while they can hardly accept the murdering of foreigners and even less the murdering and the cruelties committed against Indos, Ambonese and Menadonese, who after all belong to our own people.

To Sjahrir the revolution was not a national struggle in the first place. It was primarily a fight for democracy. And Indonesians, he urged, should realize the important social changes that were occurring in their society. If they failed to do this then:

> There is a great danger that we would not recognize one of our enemies, namely feudalism, which is still present in our society. . . . Our nationalism then would look like a sort of solidarism, either of a feudal or hierarchical character, or in other words fascism, the greatest enemy of the progress of all peoples in the world.[24]

Sjahrir realized that the added strength of his group was sorely needed by Sukarno to even out the balance between the pro- and anti-government forces. He rightly speculated that he could sell his support to the President for an extremely high price, namely Sukarno's agreement to the introduction of a system of parliamentary democracy. On the other hand, Sjahrir had no illusions about going it alone and he clearly realized that in order to legitimize his political objectives in the eyes of the masses he needed the charisma of Sukarno.

Prodded on by Vice-President Hatta, whose own views were closer to Sjahrir's, and also perceiving that the Social Democrats were a lesser danger to his own political future than the Tan Malakka group, the President agreed to the demands of Sjahrir and his followers. Sukarno stood quietly by when during October and early November he was completely divested of the extraordinary, autocratic, powers granted to him in August and was reduced to a nominal President.

In addition to the Sjahrir group, there were also a number of democratic supporters within the Committee, who from the beginning had been opposed to the presidential system of government. On 7 October a petition was handed to Sukarno signed by a third of the 150-member K.N.I.P. demanding that the emergency powers of the President should be curtailed and that the K.N.I.P. should be changed into a legislative body.

On 16 October, Hatta with the approval of Sukarno issued a decree vesting legislative power in the K.N.I.P. conjointly with the President. Furthermore, a working committee of the K.N.I.P. was established which was to meet at least every ten days, while the whole of the K.N.I.P. was required to meet at least once a year. Sjahrir and Amir Sjarifuddin accepted the Presidency and Vice-Presidency of this committee on the condition that they were given a free hand in co-opting the other thirteen members. The working committee was empowered to participate in the shaping of general policy but the day-to-day executive powers remained in the hands of the President.

Further steps towards democratization of government were taken on 3 November when the working committee denounced the one party system and officially allowed the setting up of separate political parties; and on 11 November when Sjahrir announced that ministers of state were to be responsible to the K.N.I.P.

Sukarno offered the post of Prime Minister to Sjahrir, who accepted on the condition that he would be allowed to select his own ministers. The new cabinet, announced by Sjahrir on 14 November, consisted of leaders who had a clear anti-Japanese record. Many of the new ministers were also recognized expert administrators.

The most important political parties which were set up were: the P.N.I., the Masjumi, the Socialist party, the P.K.I., and the Catholic and Protestant parties.

The P.N.I. attracted a large mass following because many people saw a connection with the pre-war party of the same name set up by Sukarno. But in many ways, the new P.N.I. was a far cry from its radical and revolutionary predecessor of the 1920s and 1930s. The majority of the membership was drawn from the basically conservative *prijaji* class. The leadership of the P.N.I., however, was gradually monopolized by the smaller, more radical left-wing, led by such prominent pre-war nationalists as Sartono, Sastroamidjojo, and Wilopo. The P.N.I.'s immediate objective was independence and it advocated that matters of social, political and economic reorganization should be left until after freedom had been obtained. This was clearly the language of Sukarno.

The most explicit exposition of Sukarno's views on the Indonesian revolution are to be found in a booklet *Sarinah* written in 1947 primarily to espouse the cause of women's emancipation in Indonesia. Unlike some of the socialists and the Communists—either of the Tan Malakka or the Moscow variety—who considered the revolution foremost as a movement for social and economic change, Sukarno argued that the revolution was solely nationalistic and that a social-economic revolution should not be attempted until after complete national freedom and consolidation had been achieved.

Indonesia, according to Sukarno, had only reached the national revolutionary phase in the world-wide struggle against capitalism and imperialism; and all efforts therefore should be directed at establishing an Indonesian national state, which was a prerequisite for any true socio-economic development. National unity was of the utmost importance and a class struggle should be avoided. Not only were all groups in the Indonesian society opposed to foreign suppression and wanting to destroy colonialism, but it was also possible for all groups—the nobility, the common people, the intellectuals, the proletarians, the middle classes, the religious teachers, the officials—to work together and build up the national state:

> It is because of this that I always urge: unity, unity, and again unity. And we must understand that our revolution can only exert its maximum power when it is truly a national revolution, national and aligned. The revolution of a *people*. And *not* the revolution of one or another class. How often is the word 'people' misused. It is used as a mask to camouflage the interests of a particular class. . . . All social and religious sections of our people are without exception revolutionary, because the purpose of the struggle is to annihilate imperialism and the old order, and to accelerate the advent of a new order in the form of national freedom.

Sukarno strongly warned against those who in their misguided enthusiasm wanted to jump the nationalist stage and start a social revolution. These so-called Marxists, according to Sukarno, did not really understand socialism and did not realize that the conditions necessary for a complete social-economic renewal were as yet not sufficiently present in Indonesia. Sukarno argued that the evolution towards socialism should not be compared to the pre-ordained growth process of a plant or animal. People themselves had to do something about it, to suffer, to make sacrifices, to build, to renew. Foreshadowing his later concept of the *continuous revolution*, Sukarno wrote:

> The duty or historical task of our national revolution is the construction of a National Indonesian State. This historical task must be first accomplished and precede the social revolution. And how much time is needed to fulfil our historical task? Nobody knows how many years or how many decennia are needed—but it is certain that it is not a question of a few months. Much sweat and tears will have to be shed before this task is completed. The

Indian Ocean will still for years assault the shores of the Indonesian islands with its waves, before all the islands are finally united into one National Indonesian State. Yes, it will take years! We are already engaged for more than two years in a national revolutionary struggle, and the end is not in sight as yet. Yes, how numerous, how difficult, and how colossal are all the problems of a national revolution we must solve—both in the destructive and constructive sense! We must tear away power from the hands of foreigners, and build up our national armed forces to completely destroy colonialism. We must occupy all (government) positions with our own people, regulate the Indonesian finances, unify all the islands of Indonesia within one, independent state, make Indonesia strong in modern technical know-how. We have to devise a diplomacy designed to obtain *de jure* international recognition, we have to supress regionalism and coordinate all these millions of Indonesians into a state and a national consciousness, with a consciousness of belonging to a state, an army, a society. The creation of a 'stable government' both for internal and external purposes, etc., all these problems must be tackled and solved before the national revolution can be considered to have run its course. These huge problems cannot be solved in an offhand fashion and within a few days. This is a gigantic task, which needs our total energy, persistent willpower, and an enormous amount of calculation and planning. All this work must be completed before we can prepare ourselves in earnest for the destruction of the forces of capitalism and organize and unite Indonesia into a socially prosperous society.[25]

Sukarno, however, hastened to add that the Indonesian revolution was different from the French and American revolutions, and did not intend to set up a bourgeois state. Pointing to Article 33 of the Indonesian Constitution, which stressed that the economy should be run on the family principle, and that important industries were to be nationalized, Sukarno concluded that socialism was the final aim of the Indonesian revolution. He stressed that he was all for socialism and that all he wanted to say was that at this point in time, Indonesia was not yet ripe for a full-scale social revolution. This, of course, did not mean that Indonesians should not be allowed to spread socialist ideas and be strongly anti-capitalist:

It is just because I have socialist ideas that I am writing this book. It is just that because we long for a socialist society, we must know the way and the right way in which we can achieve such a socialist community. It is socialist theory which makes us understand that the present state of our revolution can be nothing else than a national stage. . . . The Indonesian nationalist who thinks and acts in a social-national way, is a socialist in the true sense of the word. Conversely, an Indonesian 'socialist' who already wants to 'organize' a social revolution, is a 'socialist' who harms the revolution![26]

To Sukarno then, the national revolution was a 'golden bridge' opening the way to the final realization of socialism in Indonesia.

The socialism Sukarno had in mind, however, was very different from that of Marx, Lenin, or Mao. Sukarno's socialism had a strong nationalistic imprint and although he defined it as a system of collective production and distribution based on the existence of a minimum of private property, he seems to have been far more interested in the result, a prosperous and economically strong Indonesia, rather than in the system itself. Moreover, Sukarno's insistence that the changeover to socialism should and could be gradual and without a class struggle shows how far removed he was from accepted Communist doctrine.

Sukarno argued that socialism was not the monopoly of one particular party and that, if they wanted to, people could use another word as long as it conveyed the same meaning, namely:

A society in which social prosperity and justice is prevalent. In which one human being does not exploit another, where there is no capitalism, poverty and slavery. Where women are not broken by misery because they have to carry a double load. . . . I value activity and the content of that activity; I don't care about names or formulas! I am a nationalist and I will, with God's help, in this revolution keep nationalism in the foreground. But I am also attracted to socialism because my brains tell me that in the final analysis only in a socialist society can humanity and the world find salvation. . . . And . . . no matter if people understand it or not . . . I love socialism because I believe in God and I adore Him. I love socialism because I love Islam. It is even as a religious duty to Allah that I love socialism and struggle for it. In my political ideas I am a nationalist, in my social ideas I am a socialist, in my spiritual life I am completely a theist; I believe in God with my entire being, and I desire to obey God in everything.[27]

While Sukarno's political and ideological syncretism was perfectly acceptable to many of the Javanese members of the P.N.I., it exasperated the majority of orthodox Muslims who had combined their strength in the new Masjumi party, which was founded on 7 November 1945. In addition to the primarily social-religious organizations, such as the Mohammadijah and the Nahadatul Ulama, the Masjumi also included a number of Muslim political parties, of which the most important was the Islamic Association. The Masjumi soon became the largest political organization in the country because it was supported by the majority of the village religious teachers and their pious followers all over Indonesia.

The main objective of the Masjumi was national independence. In addition members of the party also advocated, with varying degrees of intensity, the establishment of a *Negara Islam*, that is a state based on the principles of the Islamic law.

The party's leadership was divided into three sections: a conservative group consisting mainly of traditionalist, orthodox religious teachers; a modernist-fundamentalist group led by Mohammad Natsir; and a left-wing group of religious socialists led by Jusuf Wibosono and Abu Hanifah. The Natsir group, and even more so the religious socialists who held most of the posts in the party central committee, thought along similar lines to the secular social democrats led by Sjahrir.

The socialist party contained many of the Dutch-educated and Western-orientated intellectuals and also drew much of its support from the younger students, in particular those who had been connected with the anti-Japanese underground movement led by Sjahrir and Amir Sjarifuddin.

The Christian parties, although comparatively small in number, contained many Indonesian intellectuals. Many of their members were religious socialists and supported Sjahrir's policies.

The radical socialists and Communists were divided into the Moscow-directed P.K.I. and the national Communist group of Tan Malakka. Initially many of the Moscow Communists joined a number of smaller organizations in which they soon came to play a leading role, such as the Socialist party and its armed auxiliary organization Pesindo and the Labour party. The P.K.I., however, did not become a closely-knit and powerful organization until 1948 when it attempted to overthrow the Sukarno-Hatta government.

Tan Malakka's supporters had founded in November 1945 a Common People's party (*Partai Rakjat Djelata*). It was the Tan Malakka-Subardjo group which since the beginning of the revolution had attempted to oust Sukarno and Hatta from power. However, the political aspirations of Subardjo in particular received a severe setback when Sjahrir was appointed to the premiership and instituted a parliamentary democratic system of government. Sjahrir's strongly anti-fascist stand and his opposition to former collaborators with the Japanese caused the sudden dismissal of Subardjo from the cabinet; at the same time the mushrooming of new political parties ruined the ideologically heterogeneous organization set up by Subardjo and tore his political power to shreds.

Both Subardjo and Tan Malakka frantically kept trying to take control of the Indonesian republic. At the beginning of October Tan Malakka was able to convince Sukarno and Hatta of the urgent need for a political testament, which would name their successors in case they were killed. The danger of political assassination was very real at the time, and attempts had already been made on the lives of various Indonesian leaders by trigger-happy Dutch and Ambonese soldiers. Moreover, in the existing revolutionary frenzy the possibility that Sukarno and Hatta might be murdered by some fanatical Indonesian could not be completely ruled out. The killing by anti-Japanese groups of such prominent nationalists as Oto Iskander Dinata who had held top positions during the Japanese time clearly pointed that way.

Sukarno and Hatta agreed to draw up a document in which after their death the following four leaders would conjointly take over the government: Tan Malakka of the Marxist faction; Sjahrir representing the Social Democrats; Iwa Kusuma Sumantri representing the Islamic organizations; and Wongsonegoro representing the *prijaji* group.

Sukarno told his cabinet about the existence of the political testament, but Subardjo who had been party to it, and who had been given the task of informing those named in the document, did not do so until months later. In the meantime, Tan Malakka forged a testament of his own, in which he was named as the sole successor. Travelling widely through Java during November and December 1945, Tan Malakka flashed this political 'testament' around and many leading personalities who knew about the existence of such a document began to believe the Communist leader. Tan Malakka tried to reinforce his position by claiming that Sukarno and Hatta were *de facto* prisoners of the Allies in Djakarta, and were therefore no longer capable of carrying out their functions. Tan Malakka argued that under those circumstances he should become the leader of the state in line with the provisions of the testament.

In order to deflate Tan Malakka's claims, Sukarno was forced to make a lightning tour of Java in early December and fearing assassination either by Tan Malakka or Dutch agents in Djakarta, it was decided at the beginning of January 1946 to move the Indonesian government to the Central Javanese city of Jogjakarta, where Sukarno would be among his own people and where the risk of being murdered would be considerably less.

Far more dangerous to the republican government was the campaign mounted by Tan Malakka ostensibly against Sjahrir, although as many Indonesians soon realized, the real aim was to move Sukarno and Hatta from office.

Early in January 1946, Tan Malakka established the *Persatuan Perdjuangan* (United Fighting Front) or P.P.—which shows a distinct similarity in its conception to Ho Chi Minh's Viet-Minh. The programme of the P.P. stressed the need for a unification of all Indonesians into one strong organization to support the government in its anti-colonialist struggle. The P.P. wanted to abolish all political parties, demanded the confiscation of foreign properties, and strongly condemned the negotiations which had been started with the Dutch.

The Front was spectacularly successful and in February 1946 it had been joined by most of the major political parties and large sections of the armed forces. The motive for joining Tan Malakka varied from political group to political group and often from person to person. However, the majority of Indonesians agreed with Tan Malakka on one major point: his condemnation of negotiations with the Dutch. Nationalist feeling was running high and in this hyper-sensitive situation the calmer and calculated reasoning of Sjahrir and some other Indonesian politicians was entirely misplaced. In particular, large sections of the military and many of the armed irregulars demanded that the Dutch should be driven out by force and that only then should negotiations take place.

The Indonesian armed forces constituted a major political problem from their inception. For the first few years of the revolution the Central government had little or no control over large sections of the military, in particular many of the guerilla bands. The vast majority of Indonesians who took up arms during the revolution considered themselves as freedom fighters rather than as professional soldiers.

Serious divisions existed within the Indonesian officers' corps. Differences in military training and experience, and different cultural, religious and ethnic backgrounds, which often spilled over into the political arena, prevented the Army from putting up a united front against internal and external enemies.

A sprinkling of Indonesian Army officers had been trained by the Dutch in pre-war days. Most officers, however, originated from Japanese-sponsored military and semi-military organizations such as PETA. Another large group of officers owed their rank to the revolution. Most of the officers in this last group had been students or administrative officials without any previous military training who had assumed command of local sections of the official army or guerilla bands because of their educational status and leadership qualities.

This difference in military background also meant differing approaches in military tactics as well as in the opinion as to the role the Army was to play in the republic. Experience in tactical skill and organization was almost totally confined to the few Indonesians who in pre-war days had been trained either at the Military Officers' School in Bandung or at the Royal Military Academy at Breda in Holland. It was from this small group of Dutch-trained officers that most of the top-ranking republican military leaders originated, men such as Simatupang, Nasution, Urip, Hidajat, and Suharto. The rapid promotion of the Dutch-trained officers to the top posts in the Indonesian Army as well as their insistence on organizing the Indonesian Army along Western military lines caused a great deal of resentment from the ex-PETA officers and those who had been thrown up by the revolution into positions of military command.

The Japanese had concentrated on training lower-ranking officers and the most an Indonesian PETA officer could hope for was to be put into command of a battalion. Moreover, Japanese military training was concerned to create fighters rather than tacticians. Those who had volunteered to join PETA and other auxiliary Army units during the Japanese occupation had become imbued with the traditional Japanese fighting spirit. Many Javanese did not need much indoctrination by their Japanese officers because of the many similarities between the Japanese warriors' code and the traditional *ksatrya* philosophy of the Javanese nobleman.

Many of the guerillas who had joined the revolution to fight the Dutch were even more deeply imbued by the fighting spirit than the ex-PETA officers and were appalled at the willingness of the Sukarno-Hatta government to come to an agreement with the enemy.

The majority of the Army officers, in line with the ethnic population distribution, came from Java. As a result much of the traditional Javanese ethos was introduced into Army thinking and philosophy, and this was very much resented by officers who originated from other parts of Indonesia.

Moreover, the ethnic, religious, cultural and social divisions in Indonesia, which in politics had produced a multi-party system, were also carried into the armed forces, causing further serious cleavages in particular within the officers' corps. These differences were further accentuated by the fact that some of the major political parties had their own private armies, and that politicians in general tried to interfere in Army affairs. The Army of Allah was an armed force consisting of about 30,000 fanatical young Muslims, which was closely affiliated with the Masjumi. The various Socialist factions were supported in the field by the armed youth organization Pesindo. A number of Pesindo units joined the Communist uprising at Madiun in 1948. Another important armed youth organization was the *Barisan Pelopor*, which had already been set up under the Japanese, and which had now changed its name to *Barisan Banteng* (Buffalo Legion). The Buffalo Legion was originally closely supporting the P.N.I. but later almost exclusively supported Tan Malakka.

In addition to the widespread disapproval and opposition of the government's attempts to come to terms with the Dutch, many politicians and Army officers supported the Tan Malakka Front because of Sjahrir's anti-Japanese collaborationist policy. Many politicians who had collaborated with the Japanese during the occupation had been demoted or had lost their national prominence because of Sjahrir's rise to power. Many of these politicians and leaders joined Tan Malakka in the hope of regaining their earlier positions. Also many of the Indonesian officers who had been trained by the Japanese felt insecure in their positions because of Sjahrir's *razzia* against former collaborators, and they therefore supported the National Front of Tan Malakka.

During January and February 1946 the P.P. mounted its attack by pressing for the dismissal of Sjahrir and demanding that the membership of the K.N.I.P. should be changed to reflect more truly the actual political power structure of the country.

Sjahrir took up the challenge, and in a masterly tactical move he resigned from the premiership on 28 February 1946. Sjahrir's sudden resignation was accepted by the President who then asked the leaders of the P.P., but not Tan Malakka on his own, to form a new cabinet. And as Sjahrir had rightly foreseen, the internal cohesion of the P.P. proved to be rather weak. A struggle for cabinet positions ensured in which Tan Malakka was unable to gain the support of Sukarno and Hatta as well as the anti-Communist Muslims and the on the whole conservative leaders of the P.N.I. By this time it also began to dawn on many of the other nationalist leaders and many Army officers, including General Sudirman, the Commander-in-Chief of the Indonesian Army, who initially had strongly supported the National Front, that Tan Malakka was interested solely in gaining power for himself.

After some time the P.P. leaders had to admit defeat and were forced to hand their mandate back to Sukarno who then felt free again to offer Sjahrir the premiership for the second time. Then in a desperate move, Tan Malakka called a general meeting of P.P. leaders in the East Javanese town of Madiun, at which the Sjahrir government and its policies were condemned and it was resolved that the P.P. should now take matters into its own hands and set up a rival government. Sjahrir, who must have known what was in the wind, had the meeting surrounded by pro-government troops, and the main leaders, Tan Malakka, Sukarni, Mohammad Yamin, Chairul Saleh, and the Communist Soeprato and the Masjumi leaders, Abikusuno and Wondoamiseno, were arrested and jailed.

In June 1946, the P.P. leaders were released from gaol by the pro Tan Malakka Third Division of the Army. And during that same week Sjahrir, while on a tour of Central Java, was kidnapped in Surakarta by a unit of the Third Division, whose commander, General Sudarsono, together with Mohammad Yamin and other P.P. leaders, travelled to Jogjakarta to confront Sukarno with an ultimatum. The P.P. demanded that Sukarno dismiss the Sjahrir cabinet and replace it by a supreme political council headed by Tan Malakka. Sukarno refused point blank, and had the delegation arrested.

Sjahrir's kidnapping caused a serious national crisis. And as on earlier occasions of great danger to the state, Sukarno was charged to act as a national saviour. On the instigation of the Minister of Defence, Amir Sjarifuddin, the cabinet proposed that all powers should be transferred to Sukarno and that the ministers should be made responsible to the President. The Working Committee of the K.N.I.P. agreed, and Sukarno went on the air and proclaimed a state of emergency in Indonesia.

Large detachments of pro-Sjahrir Pesindo troops as well as units of the crack Siliwangi Division moved into Central Java. These pro-government forces completely outclassed the Third Division and the Buffalo Legion troops, which had thrown in their lot with Tan Malakka.

The chance of victory for Tan Malakka and his followers was

further weakened when General Sudirman, the Indonesian Army commander, on whose support they had pinned their hopes, remained on the fence. The end of the rebellion came when Sudirman finally made up his mind and agreed to Sukarno's plea to support the Sjahrir government and to put the P.P. leaders under arrest.

Sukarno had safely ridden out another storm. Undoubtedly, his own personal prestige and the fact that he was widely considered as the symbol of the free Indonesia helped to save his political skin. On the other hand the timely measure taken by the Sjahrir cabinet a few months earlier in setting up the Siliwangi Division and the Mobile Police Brigade, which were the nucleus of a modern disciplined Indonesian Army, was also an important factor in winning the day. Both these units were well trained, equipped with armour and artillery, and most of the higher-ranking officers were Dutch-trained. The arrival of Siliwangi units in Central Java and their apparent determination to crush the rebellion put General Sudirman in an impasse. As a true nationalist he was opposed to civil war which would seriously weaken the Indonesian defence position against the Dutch. Moreover, in the case of victory by the government troops—which was most likely—Sudirman's own position would be considerably weakened. He decided therefore on a compromise; except for the commanding general and some other officers, the rebellious Third Division and the Buffalo Legion were not to be punished, and the Pesindo troops who had freed Sjahrir from prison were to leave the Surakarta area as soon as possible.

After the collapse of the Tan Malakka rebellion, the K.N.I.P. in the middle of August 1946 assumed full powers again and demanded that a more widely representative cabinet should be formed. But strong opposition to the government's insistence on negotiations with the Dutch, caused the powerful Masjumi and the P.N.I. to refuse to have official representation in the new cabinet, although six Masjumi members and four P.N.I. members were allowed to take up ministerial posts as individuals without having any responsibility to their respective parties. Sjahrir again accepted the post of Prime Minister because he felt that he should continue to act as the major Indonesian spokesman in negotiations with the Dutch which he expected would soon be brought to a satisfactory conclusion.

On 15 November 1946 the so-called Linggadjati Agreement was signed in which the Netherlands agreed to recognize the *de facto* authority of the Indonesian republic in the islands of Java and Sumatra. It was also envisaged that a United States of Indonesia would be set up consisting of the republic of Indonesia, and the two states of Borneo and Greater Eastern Indonesia. The United States of Indonesia would form an integral part of a Netherlands-Indonesian Union which was to be headed by the Dutch Queen. The ultimate date for a federal Indonesia was to be 1 January 1949, and in the meantime there was to be a mutual reduction in the armed forces and a gradual withdrawal of Dutch forces from the republic. In another important clause the republic of Indonesia agreed to protect and uphold the rights—including property rights—of foreigners.[28]

The Masjumi, the P.N.I., and the followers of Tan Malakka were strongly opposed to the Linggadjati Agreement, and set up a powerful anti-government coalition: the *Benteng Republik* (Republican forces). Supporting the government was a leftist coalition (*Sajap Kiri*), which included the Socialist party, the P.K.I., and smaller leftist groups. The Christian parties also were in favour of the Linggadjati Agreement.

Sukarno tried to turn the intense political turmoil and division caused by the Linggadjati Agreement to his own advantage. Sukarno's emergency powers had been rescinded by parliament in August 1946, but in order to ensure ratification of the Linggadjati Agreement as well as to test the extent of his personal power, he issued a presidential decree on 26 December 1946 to raise the membership of the K.N.I.P. from 200 to 514, an increase of 250 per cent. Of the 314 additional members only ninety-three were to be representatives of political parties, while the others were to be divided over functional, regional, and racial minority groups.

To a certain extent, Sukarno's decree reflected the prevailing feeling in the country that the existing K.N.I.P. was far from being representative of the total complexity of political opinion in the country. On the other hand Sukarno's insistence on functional representation was obviously aimed at getting a step closer to his favourite system of *musjawarah* and *mufakat*. It was especially this last factor which was vigorously opposed by most political parties, in particular the P.N.I. and the Masjumi, who both felt badly under-represented.

The Working Committee of the K.N.I.P. although not denying that the President had the right to initiate legislation, insisted that its prior approval was needed for a presidential decree to become law. The question was finally settled after days of fierce debate at the general session of the K.N.I.P. at Malang from 25 February to the beginning of March 1946, when Vice-President Hatta in an unusually emotional speech confronted the assembly with an ultimatum, threatening that he and Sukarno would have to resign from office if the decree in question was not accepted. Fear of an intense power struggle for the Presidency and the Vice-Presidency, which might even result in civil war, caused the majority of the members of the assembly to pledge their support to Sukarno and Hatta. The Working Committee withdrew its objections and on 2 March 1947 the new members appointed by Sukarno took office.

On 5 March the K.N.I.P. passed a motion of confidence in the Sjahrir cabinet and ratified the Linggadjati Agreement, with the P.N.I. and the Masjumi abstaining.

As many Indonesians had suspected, the Linggadjati Agreement soon proved to be no more than a farce. Infringements in the military sphere occurred at an increasing rate on both sides. In the political sphere a serious dispute arose as to the meaning of the term 'federation'. Holland maintained that it had the right to create unilaterally member states in the area outside republican control. Like the French in Vietnam at that time, the Dutch attempted to curtail the power of the republic by surrounding it by a large number of Dutch-controlled puppet states. The Dutch also insisted that until 1 January 1949 the Dutch held *de jure* sovereignty over the whole of Indonesia, and that foreign affairs and all overseas trade dealings were to be under full Dutch control.

Sjahrir, realizing that the Dutch, who by this time had built up their military strength considerably, wanted to make war to crush the republic, was forced to make important concessions. This caused so much turmoil and political opposition to the government that Sjahrir was forced to hand in his resignation on 27 June. Sukarno, fearing the outbreak of civil war, immediately issued a decree in which he again assumed emergency powers. This was approved by the Working Committee on 28 June.

In 1947 then the outlook for the republic was bleak. The Dutch case, which was strongly reinforced by United States support, looked reasonable to most Western powers. As a result the new Indonesian cabinet headed by Amir Sjarifuddin was forced to go even further than Sjahrir in trying to appease the Dutch. When the Indonesians, however, refused to agree to the Dutch demand that joint control should be established over the Indonesian police force, the Dutch army launched a full-scale attack on the republic on 20 July. The reason given by the Netherlands was that the republic had no control over extremist elements in many of its areas.

Aided by modern tanks, artillery and aeroplanes, the Dutch forces quickly sliced through large parts of republican territory, occupying most of the important towns. Realizing that their ill-equipped forces had no chance against the Dutch in a pitched battle, the Indonesians resorted to hit-and-run tactics and most of the republican forces melted away intact before the advancing Dutch columns, disappearing into the forests and remote and inaccessible areas from where they planned to conduct guerilla operations. The scorched earth policy planned by the Indonesian government was less successful because of the rapidity of the Dutch army's advance, and large stocks of export produce fell into Dutch hands.

The Dutch attack was severely condemned by the United Nations, in particular by the Asian states and the Communist bloc. The United States protest was rather weak, as Washington was at that time still impressed by Dutch reports that the republic could go Communist at any time. Proposals by Russia, India, and Australia, which strongly condemned Holland and demanded withdrawal of Dutch troops could not get acceptance at the United Nations. Finally an American proposal was accepted which called for the immediate cessation of hostilities and a settlement of the dispute by arbitration or other peaceful means. The Netherlands government agreed and ordered its troops to halt their advance on 5 August.

Following the acceptance of the American proposal in the United Nations Assembly the Security Council sent a Commission of Good Offices to Indonesia, which consisted of one American, one Belgian, and one Australian.

The Dutch, however, took little notice of the recommendations of the Commission, and went their own way. A military demarcation line 'the van Mook line' was established unilaterally by the Netherlands, which brought the richest food-producing areas into Dutch hands. Moreover, the Dutch Navy and Air Force put an effective blockade around the republic cutting off much-needed supplies of arms, food, clothing and drugs and medical equipment.

Urged on by the United Nations Commission of Good Offices, and with its stocks of food and ammunition running very low, the Indonesian republic, which feared another Dutch military attack, was finally forced to accept the so-called Renville Agreement on 19 January 1948.

The signing of the Renville Agreement caused a serious cabinet crisis when both the P.N.I. and the Masjumi withdrew their support from the government. Amir Sjarifuddin was forced to resign and Sukarno appointed Hatta to form a presidential cabinet in which all the major parties were to cooperate. This proved impossible owing to the unwillingness of the P.N.I. and the Masjumi to collaborate with the leftist group. The Hatta cabinet when finally established drew most of its ministers from the P.N.I., Masjumi, and Christian parties.

The left-wing Sajap Kiri group suffered a serious split on the issue of the Renville Agreement. The smaller Sjahrir faction, which had become increasingly concerned about the radicalization of the Marxist faction led by Sjarifuddin and its orientation towards Moscow, finally separated from the Socialist party and on 13 February 1948 founded its own *Partai Socialis Indonesia*. The Socialist party and the remainder of the Sajap Kiri, which on 26 February 1948 changed its name into *Front Demokrasi Rakjat* (People's Democratic Front) or F.D.R., called for the repudiation of the Renville Agreement, the cessation of all negotiations, and the nationalization of all foreign properties. Attempts by Hatta to include the F.D.R. in his cabinet failed. The F.D.R. obtained a great deal of its support from labour and also from various sections of the armed forces. Amir Sjarifuddin had held the post of Minister of Defence, and by means of promotion and handouts he had been able to make a large number of Army officers beholden to him. In any case many of the officers in the regular Army, as well as the irregulars, were violently opposed to the Renville Agreement and to the government which in their view had betrayed the ideals of the revolution. Sjarifuddin also had the trusted support of a vast number of local militia which he had set up during his term of office as well as of the 200,000 members of the labour organization SOBSI.

The Hatta government which was acutely aware of the danger posed by the F.D.R. tried to cut the ground from under Sjarifuddin by proposing a rationalization programme in the armed forces. It was planned to demobilize 160,000 men and on Colonel Nasution's suggestion, to establish a well-equipped, trained, and organized striking force of about 57,000 men, which would be able to fight a well-planned guerilla war campaign against the Dutch if they attacked again. A beginning was made with this rationalization programme in mid-1948 and in order to weaken the F.D.R. support in the Army even more, a number of high-ranking officers and well-known Sjarifuddin supporters were transferred to innocuous positions.

The Renville Agreement was a clear victory for the Dutch cause. The Indonesian republic was forced to accept the van Mook military demarcation line and agreed to become a member of the United States of Indonesia, which in turn was to constitute an integral part of a Netherlands-Indonesian Union. Netherlands sovereignty was recognized until such time as the federation of Indonesia was established and for all practical purposes the Netherlands were given the right to create in the territories under their control new member states of the future federation. The only clause which could be considered as favourable to the Indonesian republic was the stipulation that a plebiscite was to be held to determine whether the population in specified areas desired to join either the Indonesian republic or another member state.

In spite of the favourable conditions of the Renville Agreement, the Dutch were still bent on destroying the republic once and for all. And van Mook, after having created in quick succession thirteen new states, called a meeting of representatives of the states on 17 July 1948 and, ignoring the provisions of the Renville Agreement, proceeded to set up a Federated States of Indonesia without the republic.

The intransigence of the Dutch was intensified by a change of government in Holland in August 1948 in which the majority of cabinet posts went to hard-line members of the Catholic party. This caused great anxiety in government circles where it was expected that a second Dutch attack could occur at any moment.

In this rather bleak situation, and with the enemy massing its troops on the Indonesian border, the republic was suddenly called upon to defend its life against an internal enemy when the P.K.I. staged a rebellion in Central and East Java and set up a rival government in the East Javanese town of Madiun.

During the first few years of the revolution the P.K.I. had followed the Moscow directive laid down in 1943 of joining a united front against fascist aggression. During the German occupation a number of Indonesian students with P.K.I. affiliations had fought courageously in the Dutch underground against the German Nazis and had become Dutch national heroes.

When the Indonesian revolution broke out Indonesian Communists in Holland and other overseas countries followed the Dutch Communist party's lead and condemned Sukarno and Hatta as 'fascist collaborationists'. The Dutch government attempted to make use of this situation and sent a number of Indonesian Communists back to Indonesia, where it was hoped that they would continue their anti-republican activities. Soon after their return, however, these young Indonesian Communists realized that the revolution was a widespread and popular movement; they therefore decided to continue the previous united front policy and they attempted to infiltrate the Socialist party and various other smaller leftist organizations. In this way Communists had been able to obtain positions of leadership in the Sajap Kiri (left-wing group) which had been set up in 1947.

The adoption of the Zhadov line in Moscow in September 1947 which divided the world into an aggressive capitalistic bloc led by the U.S.A. and a Communist bloc led by the U.S.S.R., between whom no compromise was possible, seems also to have had an impact on South and South-East Asian member parties. After the Calcutta conference of Asian Communist parties in February 1948 at which the new Moscow line was explained: Communist-led strikes occurred in India; Communist uprisings occurred in Burma in March; the Malayan Emergency began in June; and the Indonesian Communists revolted in September.

In Indonesia gradually more people began to look to Russia and consequently the P.K.I. for support, when it became clear that the U.S.A. favoured the Dutch.

In August 1948 Musso, a prominent P.K.I. leader of the 1920s who had lived in exile abroad, suddenly returned from Moscow. He immediately took over command of the P.K.I. and attempted to prepare the party for a revolutionary takeover with the help of the F.D.R.

Speculating on the widespread discontent with the Renville Agreement and the dissatisfaction in the armed forces with the Hatta-Nasution rationalization programme, and the economic distress, the P.K.I. staged a widespread propaganda campaign attacking the government on its policies. Dismissing the Sukarno-Hatta government as lackeys of capitalist imperialism, Musso pointed out that they had to make a choice between Russia, which had consistently supported the Indonesian cause of freedom, and the United States which obviously supported the Dutch.

The republican government tried to meet the growing threat of the P.K.I. by pressing its demobilization programme and by transferring or pensioning outright known P.K.I. or F.D.R. sympathizers in the Army. In another counter-move Sukarno tried to sow division in the leftist camp by releasing from gaol in the middle of August Tan Malakka and other leaders of the *Gerakan Revolusi Rakjat* (G.R.R.) who immediately began an anti-Musso-P.K.I. campaign.

After attempts by Musso to join the P.N.I. and the Masjumi in an anti-government nationalist front had failed, and he and other top leaders of the P.K.I. had gone on a speaking tour of various provincial centres, the initiative in P.K.I. affairs was taken out of their hands by a number of deputy leaders and various pro-P.K.I.

army units and irregulars. In the Surakarta area in particular there were many leftist-inclined Army units and irregulars who refused to carry out government orders to demobilize. Also in and around Madiun pro-Communist units took matters into their own hands, and when Musso and other high-ranking Communist leaders arrived in Madiun on 18 September a Communist anti-government rebellion was in full swing.

Sukarno, who on 16 September had already placed Surakarta and the surrounding countryside under martial law, made a radio broadcast on the evening of 19 September in which he accused the Communists of high treason:

> Brothers, consider carefully the meaning of this: Musso's Communist party is attempting to seize our beloved republic of Indonesia. My beloved people, in the name of the struggle for independent Indonesia I call on you at this extremely critical moment when you and I are experiencing the greatest test to make a choice between following Musso and his Communist party, who will obstruct the attainment of an independent Indonesia, or following Sukarno-Hatta, who, with the Almighty's help, will lead our republic of Indonesia to become an independent Indonesia which is not subjected to any country whatsoever. . . . Support the government; exert yourself to the utmost in supporting the organs of government in combating the insurgents; and restore the lawful administration in the region concerned. Madiun must be returned to our hands as soon as possible.[29]

On that same evening Musso went on the air exhorting Indonesians to overthrow the Sukarno and Hatta government which he dismissed as corrupt and bourgeois-nationalist:

> Actually those in the government have used our revolution for enriching themselves. During the Japanese occupation these persons acted as quislings, *romusha* dealers and *Heiho* (work corps) propagandists. More than 2,000,000 became widows, because their husbands were *romushas*. And now, the same persons are going to sell Indonesia and her people once more to the American imperialists. . . . It is clear that during the past three years Sukarno-Hatta, the *ex-romusha* dealers, the sworn quislings, have executed a capitulation policy to the Dutch and the British, and at this very moment they are going to sell out Indonesia and her people to the American imperialists. Can people of this kind claim that they

have the just right to govern our republic? The people of Indonesia are not blind! They understand that these *romusha* dealers are not fit to rule the country. The citizens of Madiun and some other places are breaking off connections with these imperialist satellites.[30]

Caught between the two fires of an imminent Dutch attack and the Communists, the republican government had to act quickly. The Communists whose armed strength amounted to about 25,000 men were engaged in battle by a force of equal numbers consisting of such crack republican troops as the Siliwangi Division and the Mobile Police Brigade, aided by units of the Sungkono Division.

In the absence of a general uprising these pro-government forces were able to eliminate the Communist forces fairly quickly and by the end of October the rebellion was broken. Musso was killed in battle on 31 October and soon after some of the other top P.K.I. leaders, such as Amir Sjarifuddin and Suripno, were captured and executed.

The Madiun affair cost thousands of people—most of them innocent bystanders—their lives. Many Indonesians, in particular orthodox Muslims, who were known opponents of Communism, were liquidated, and the Communists became even more savage when it was clear that they were losing. During the last few days before the occupation of Madiun by government troops, hundreds of people, many of them Muslim teachers, were butchered and their bodies mutilated. This murderous rampage by the Communists was never forgotten and after the abortive coup of September 1965 the Muslims took more than full advantage in getting their own back.

Sukarno's reaction to the Communist coup and in particular its bloodshed, was one of genuine horror. In a small booklet called *Kepada Bangsku* (*To My People*) which was published towards the end of 1948, Sukarno wrote:

Our duty at present is to build up national independence through a struggle of national unity and to give substance to national independence with spiritual requirements and material requirements in order that this national independence may become a sound stepping stone to a social independence of the future. A sound stepping stone! Not a stepping stone inflicted by ferocity, savagery and bestiality. Not a stepping stone used as a foundation for the butchering of men who are God's creatures. How horrifying and how far from unitarianism was the 'social revolution' provoked by irresponsible persons in Madiun and in other regions. There was no nobility of character whatsoever about it. The reason is that the 'Madiun social revolution' was a social revolution, it was provoked, a social revolution that was forced years and perhaps decades before its time. The 'Madiun social revolution' was cruel and savage because our society in general is indeed not yet ready for a social revolution—in general is not yet willing to have a social revolution—so that those disrupters who, because of the superficiality of their knowledge felt themselves 'obliged to lead a social revolution right away', then felt themselves 'obliged' to push aside those people who don't want it yet, by means of torturing them, murdering them, cutting them up as a butcher does with animals. . . . The results they have achieved are just devastation and condemnation. . . . There were no millions of the people or masses who answered their call. There were no mothers who greeted them with shouts and cries of joy and gladness. Ninety-nine per cent of our people did not approve of their revolution, a very large part indeed even actively opposed their revolution. . . . Plain signs and proof that a revolution certainly cannot be 'made' at someone's will. Plain signs and proof that revolutions indeed await their respective periods. . . . In reality, the 'Madiun revolution' was not a revolution at all. The term revolution is too noble, gives too much respect to what people did there. The 'Madiun revolution' was an act of revolutionaryism gone astray. In its deeds it was a revolt in a sense that it was a *putsch*. For people who really know revolutionary literature and revolutionary terms, that is, those who are learned in the theory of socialism, the term 'putsch' contains the sense of blame and judgment well enough . . . thus, the social revolution to which I refer—the social revolution that proceeds from a 'sound stepping stone'—the social revolution after the national phase is finished—the social revolution to which I refer will not have the character of a murdering and butchering revolution. Because the social revolution to which I refer comes about . . . after we have 'given content to national independence of the whole of Indonesia, its spiritual requirements and material requirements, in order that national independence can be a sound stepping to social independence in the future'.[31]

It is significant to note that Sukarno did not put the blame for the Madiun affair on Communism as such, but he put the blame squarely on the perpetrators of the coup, whom he considered criminals and not really Communists, because they apparently did not understand the Marxist theory of revolution. It should also be noted, however, that immediately after his condemnation of the P.K.I., Sukarno himself deviates again quite markedly from accepted Marxist doctrine, and again stresses that the Indonesian social revolution could be achieved without a bloody class struggle.

There is no doubt that if the Communists had been successful Sukarno would have lost his prominent position, and might even have lost his life. The Communists failed partly because they were ill-prepared and the coup was started prematurely by younger cadres without the consent of the top party leaders. There is also no doubt that the Communists had far overestimated the extent of their popular support; and that in trying to replace Sukarno and Hatta they attacked, in the view of many people, the concept of Indonesia itself. Again it was the personal stature of Sukarno, the fact that he stood for independent Indonesia, which played an important role in defeating the Communist threat. However, Sukarno's charisma alone would not have been enough to defeat the Communists. It was the speedy and determined action of the pro-government armed forces, particularly of the Siliwangi Division and the Mobile Police Brigade, which saved the government and Sukarno from extermination. The fact that they were repeatedly called upon to save the state gave the military an important stake in the revolution, and caused them gradually to interfere more and more in Indonesian political affairs.

In addition to the danger posed to the Indonesian state from the extreme left, the Sukarno government was also assailed from the extreme right by certain groups of fanatical Muslims. Some of the more fanatical *santri* were bent on doing away with the *kafir* (unbeliever) secular republic, and creating an Indonesian state which was based on the tenets of the Islamic law. The first successful attempt in establishing an Islamic state occurred in Atjeh (North Sumatra) which between December 1945 and February 1946 was the scene of a bloody civil war between the Muslim teachers under the leadership of Daud Beureuh and the *adat* chiefs and their followers. Many *uleebalang* families were murdered down to the last male members, and Daud Beureuh proceeded to realize his theocratic ideals. In order to keep Atjeh within the republican fold the central government appointed Daud Beureuh as its provincial governor.

To ameliorate the growing dissatisfaction of many orthodox Muslims, the republican government felt obliged, on 3 January 1946, to reverse its earlier position and create a Department of Religious

Affairs. This gesture, however, was taken as an insult by those Muslims who were striving for an Islamic state. In their view a Department of Religious Affairs accentuated the fact that Indonesia was basically a secular state.

At a conference of West Javanese Muslim leaders called by Kartosuwirjo in March 1948, it was decided to fuse the Army of Allah with the whole of the Islamic community in West Java to form one united Islamic country (Darul Islam) in the struggle against the Dutch. At a second conference towards the end of March 1948 the final step was taken towards the realization of the Muslim theocratic ideals and the Sudanese region (West Java) was proclaimed as an independent Islamic state, headed by a cabinet of ten ministers with Kartosuwirjo as the president. The Darul Islam openly turned against the Indonesian republic during the course of 1948; and it informed Sukarno that if the Indonesian republic desired to join the Darul Islam it would be welcomed and all that had happened in the past would be readily forgiven. The Darul Islam meant business and killed many Indonesians in various parts of West Java who took part in the celebrations of Proclamation Day on 17 September 1948. Darul Islam troops also attacked republican forces and began to terrorize the West Javanese countryside. It was not until 1963, after the capture and execution of Kartosuwirju, that the Darul Islam problem was finally settled.

With the Communist rebellion hardly out of the way, and the Darul Islam problem gaining momentum in West Java, the Indonesian republic was attacked again in full force by the Dutch on 19 December 1948. The main target was the republican capital of Jogjakarta, which fell quickly into Dutch hands. On the morning of the 19th planes bombed and strafed Jogjakarta airport which was then quickly taken in a surprise attack by Dutch paratroops. By the afternoon the airborne troops, reinforced by units of the Royal Netherlands Indies Army brought in by road from Semarang, had occupied most of the city, and the Indonesian cabinet including Sukarno, Hatta, Sjahrir, and many other high officials were taken prisoner. All other major cities in Java were taken by the Dutch and the republican government was moved to Sumatra where a caretaker cabinet was set up under the leadership of the Minister of Finance, Sjaffrudin Prawiranegara.

But the Dutch had by no means won the battle. The Indonesian Army remained almost intact, and withdrew according to plan into the more rugged parts of the countryside from where they attacked the often tenuously held communication lines between the Dutch-held cities. Admittedly, the blockade of the Dutch Navy around the Javanese and Sumatran coasts was tight and supplies were running very low in the republican areas, but resistance by guerillas, living off the land and aided by the people, could have continued for years.

Sukarno's behaviour during the battle of Jogjakarta has been questioned by many Indonesians, in particular by the Army. Not long before the Dutch attack, Sukarno in a fierce speech told the people of Jogjakarta that he would go into the mountains and become a guerilla leader if Holland again made open war on the republic. The crowd became wildly enthusiastic, but some of the president's colleagues, including Sjahrir, were rather doubtful whether Sukarno would really join the physical struggle. As it turned out these critics were proved right. When the Dutch forces were nearing the city General Sudirman went to the Palace to keep Sukarno to his promise of leading the guerilla struggle. To the great amazement and disgust of Sudirman and his fellow officers, Sukarno and most of his cabinet refused to leave the Palace. Some cabinet members, however, such as the Minister of the Interior, Dr Sukiman, and the Minister of Justice, Mr Soesanto, joined the republican forces and took an active part in the fighting. When the enemy was nearing the Palace Sukarno instructed his bodyguards to put up a large white flag on the front porch and he asked his guards to surrender when the Dutch opened up with mortars.

Some Indonesians have accused Sukarno of cowardice. Another explanation given is that he was strongly advised by his *dukuns* against joining the guerillas because he would lose his life. In fact, Sukarno had strong reasons for not going into the remoter country areas where, in addition to thousands of pro-government soldiers and irregulars, there were also thousands of Communists, who had been released from prison when the Dutch attacked and who were roaming around and would have needed no compulsion to kill Sukarno.

After his capture Sukarno was first brought before Major-General Meyer, the Dutch Army Commander in Central Java, who demanded that he order the republican troops to surrender. The importance attached by the Dutch General to Sukarno's power over the Indon- esian forces at that time was certainly somewhat unrealistic and flattering. His prestige was low in the Army, and it is highly doubtful whether very many Indonesian commanders would have obeyed an order to surrender.

The next day Sukarno together with Sjahrir and Hadji Agus Salim were flown to Brastagi in North Sumatra and a few days later to Prapat on Lake Toba in Central North Sumatra. Sukarno was apparently in great fear of his life there after a Dutch officer with a lugubrious sense of humour had spread the story that he would be shot the morning after his arrival. Certainly it was strongly felt in many Dutch colonial and military circles at the time that Sukarno should be condemned as a traitor and war criminal and executed. There is a story that a summary execution was planned soon after the arrival of the Dutch army in Jogjakarta and that it was only after strong representations by Monseigneur Sugiopranoto, the Roman Catholic bishop of Semarang, to the Dutch authorities that Sukarno's life was spared. This is said to have been one of the major reasons for the close friendship between the Bishop and Sukarno and the favoured view in which he always held Indonesian Catholics.

Sjahrir, apparently disgusted with Sukarno's behaviour, is reported to have often clashed sharply with him during their stay in Prapat:

> No, Sukarno and Sjahrir didn't live harmoniously together. Sukarno complained to Hadji Agus Salim many times that he must do something about Sjahrir's attitude towards him. Agus Salim happened to be Sjahrir's uncle. Hadji Agus Salim tried to convince Sjahrir that, after all, Sukarno was still Indonesia's President, and he should stop calling Sukarno 'stupid, idiot, coward' and other ugly names. Sjahrir was not willing to stop so the harmony was never restored between the two leaders during the rest of the revolution; even after we had been freed and had become independent and Sukarno was President, the ill-feeling continued.[32]

Somewhat later Sukarno, Sjahrir, and Hadji Agus Salim were transferred to the island of Bangka where they joined Hatta and other members of the Indonesian cabinet who were held there. In Bangka relations between Sukarno and Sjahrir went from bad to worse, and Sjahrir is credited with the following remark about their exile: 'We were not really badly off. Hadji Agus Salim had a large double bed, Hatta had a large case full of books at his disposal, I had a large tennis court to amuse myself on, and Sukarno had a room with seven mirrors.'[33]

The second Dutch 'police action' against the Indonesian republic caused world-wide condemnation. On 20 December 1949 the Security Council of the United Nations called on the Netherlands to cease hostilities immediately, and to release Sukarno and other members of the Indonesian cabinet. When the Dutch took no notice a similar Resolution was passed on 28 December, which again was ignored by the Netherlands.

Continued Indonesian guerilla resistance and the flouting by the Netherlands of successive United Nations Resolutions, also caused strong criticism within the U.S.A. which hitherto had been rather lukewarm in its support of Indonesian freedom. Particularly after the Indonesian republican government had shown that it could deal effectively with the Communist threat, opinion in Washington became more favourable to the Indonesians and the American government began to put stronger pressure on the Dutch. The Dutch Foreign Minister Stikker, when visiting Washington in March 1949, was told by the State Department that the United States might consider economic sanctions in the form of a reduction in Marshall Aid, if the Netherlands continued refusing to comply with the directives of the Security Council. This threat by the United States caused the Dutch position to erode rapidly. On 14 April the Dutch resumed negotiations with the republic. This resulted on 7 May 1949 in the Roem Van Royen Agreement in which the republic agreed to stop its guerilla warfare and to attend a Round Table conference at The Hague, to discuss the speedy and unconditional transfer of sovereignty to the United States of Indonesia. For its part the Netherlands agreed to restore the Jogjakarta republic and to release all political prisoners arrested since 17 December 1948.

On 6 July Sukarno and other members of the cabinet were able to return in triumph to Jogjakarta. Sukarno was on top of the world. When the commander of the Indonesian Army, General Sudirman, who was suffering from an advanced stage of tuberculosis, was carried into Jogjakarta on a stretcher at the head of some of his troops accompanied also by other ministers of the Indonesian cabinet who had shared the dangers of the guerilla war, he and his group received an even greater ovation than that given to Sukarno. As an eye-witness describes it:

Sukarno had the grace to run into the arms of the tragic but still spirited fighter of the republic. The people who witnessed this were touched and forgave, for the moment, most of the mistakes and failures of Sukarno. General Sudirman was a real hero in the eyes of the soldiers, officers, and also in the estimation of the Indonesian people. He was the perfect example of the man who killed his own body to fight the enemy of his beloved fatherland and people. He was already very ill when he arrived in Jogja, lying on a primitive kind of stretcher carried on the shoulders of his faithful and loyal men. In fact, that day during the meeting of Sukarno and General Sudirman, the love and sympathy of the people were more on the side of General Sudirman, but Sukarno nearly stole the show by his seeming gesture of affection and the touching emotion he displayed. At that moment, he identified himself with the heroic figure of the General. I saw all this with my own eyes; this return of all the Indonesian leaders to Jogja which they had left nearly a year ago, under the explosions and thunder of the Dutch guns and bombs. I must admit that Sukarno was indeed a man who could adjust himself to all kinds of situations, and come out as a winner.[34]

The Round Table Conference in The Hague lasted from 23 August to 2 November 1949. Hatta headed the representatives of the Indonesian republic, while Sultan Hamid II of West Borneo led the delegation of the other member states.

The Netherlands finally agreed to transfer its sovereignty over the Netherlands East Indies unconditionally and completely to the United States of Indonesia. The area of West New Guinea was to be excluded from this agreement, and further discussions on the political future of this region were to be held within one year from the date of the actual transfer of sovereignty. There was to be no interim Dutch caretaker government and full independence was to be granted not later than 30 December 1949. Holland and Indonesia were to form a loosely constructed union, of which the Queen of the Netherlands was the nominal head.

Indonesia granted the Netherlands privileged trade terms, and agreed to take over existing international trade agreements made by the Netherlands Indies government. Furthermore, Indonesia was forced to take over most of the existing debts incurred by the Netherlands Indies government totalling about 400,300 million guilders (100,130 million dollars).

On 27 December 1949 Hatta, as head of the Indonesian delegation, accepted, in a moving ceremony on the Dam Square in Amsterdam, the freedom of his country.

On the same day in Batavia the Dutch red, white and blue flag was lowered for the last time on the Governor-General's Palace. Three hundred and fifty years of Dutch power had finally come to an end.

The following day Sukarno arrived from Jogjakarta in a plane which had hastily been painted in glaring red and white, the Indonesian national colours. He took up residence in the Palace, which was now re-baptized Freedom Palace. Batavia reverted to the old Sundanese name Djakarta and other Dutch names of public buildings, streets and parks were rapidly changed into Indonesian ones.

Sukarno received a rousing welcome on his return to Djakarta, hundreds of thousands of people crowded the streets, shouting with joy. Undoubtedly this must have been one of the most moving days of Sukarno's life. He writes:

At 11.40 a.m. the presidential vanguard, the sole plane of the day-old Garuda Indonesian Airways, taxied into Kemajoran airport. With beating heart I stepped down into the sea of people. We could not get through the crowd. Millions upon millions flooded the sidewalks, the roads. They were crying, cheering, screaming . . . 'Long live Bung Karno'. Soldiers beat a path for me to the topmost step of the big white palace. There I raised both hands high. A stillness swept over the millions. There wasn't a sound except for the silent tears; nothing moved. *Alhamdullillah*—thank God I cried, we are free.[35]

CHAPTER V

Constitutional President

O**N 27 December 1949 the red and white national flag was waving triumphantly all over Indonesia; banners on walls and buildings were covered with the word *merdeka* (freedom); politicians made rousing speeches; the armed forces proudly marched past; thousands of people thronged the streets and squares, in an excited, festive mood, highly charged with expectations about a golden future.

Indonesia was indeed free from Dutch colonial rule. But it was still tightly shackled to the emotions of the colonial past, and the complex divisiveness of traditional ingrained cultural and socio-religious patterns. Personal, ethnic, and inter-group competition for power and prestige caused great political instability for many years. In 1949 a united Indonesia with a strong sense of national purpose was hardly more than an aspiration; there was no national consensus of opinion about the direction the new Indonesia was to take ideologically, economically, and socially. The fierce pre-war inter-necine struggles within the nationalist movement had only been temporarily quietened down during the all-out drive against the Dutch during the revolution. But now, with the common enemy— the Dutch—gone, the country was soon torn apart again by internal strife, caused in the main by the unwillingness of the competing political and ideological factions to play the rules of the game; and the general refusal of politicians and leaders to compromise; to put aside personal, sectional, regional, and ideological interests for the sake of the general good of the state.

Independent Indonesia came into the world in 1949 as a federation consisting of fifteen states, including the Indonesian republic. The Constitution provided for a democratic system of government on the European model, featuring proportional representation, a multi-party system, and ministerial responsibility to parliament. The powers of the President were largely nominal.

Federation which was widely felt to be a Dutch imposed, neo-colonialist system hardly outlasted the removal of the statutes of the Dutch empire builders from the various parks of Djakarta, and by August 1950 the republic of Indonesia was able to impose a unitary state on the whole of the country without running into any serious and protracted opposition from the other federal member states.

The provisional Constitution of 1950, which was largely a copy of its 1949 predecessor, stipulated that Sukarno and Hatta would continue in their positions as President and Vice-President until such time that the Constituent Assembly had decided on a permanent Constitution.[1]

Sukarno as constitutional President felt in a strait-jacket. His vitality, vanity, and ambition demanded a position of real power. This he was eventually able to obtain by gradually stepping into the power vacuum created by the inability of the Western-style parliamentary system to achieve political stability and a degree of social and economic development and prosperity which was satisfactory to the majority of the Indonesian people.

The basic causes of the failure of Western parliamentary democracy in Indonesia were twofold: the absence of grass-root support for such a system of government; and the lack of a sufficient number of politicians who were principally committed to parliamentary democracy.

The revolution had changed the power structure in favour of the comparatively small Dutch-educated indigenous élite, who in the pre-war colonial period had only been allowed to play a minor role in the political and administrative decision-making process. It was from this new Western-trained élite that most of the prominent nationalist leaders had emerged. However, it was only a minority group within this Dutch-educated nationalist leadership which was Western-orientated in its political thinking. The vast majority, including Sukarno, were strongly nativistically inclined and condemned the complete Westernization of Indonesia, claiming that modernization need not necessarily occur at the cost of losing Indonesian national-cultural identity. During and after the revolution the traditionalist and neo-traditionalist sector of the political élite was often supported by the Dutch-trained corps of indigenous— mainly Javanese—local and regional administrators. These *Prijaji* or *Pamong Pradja*, despite a considerable loss of prestige because of their colonial collaborationist past, have remained until the present day one of the few stable and relatively efficient elements in the governmental administrative apparatus.

In addition, the Japanese occupation and the revolution had spawned large numbers of younger Indonesian semi-intellectuals who held strongly anti-Western views. Large sections of the Army officers corps—the most powerful extra-parliamentary force—was composed of these individuals.

In terms of the total population the number of Indonesians who showed a degree of political awareness at a national level was small. The general average literacy rate in 1949 was probably no more than 10 per cent, although a rapid improvement occurred during the 1950s and the 1960s with the present average literacy rate standing probably around 60 per cent. Perhaps a more accurate indicator of the size of the politically conscious public is the number of regular newspaper readers, which Feith estimated at $1\frac{1}{2}$ million Indonesians at the end of 1950. Using the same methods of calculation the newspaper-reading public had by the end of 1956 increased to approximately 3 million people, or roughly $2\frac{1}{2}$ per cent of the total population.[2]

National politics, the prerogative of this small élite which was almost totally concentrated in the national capital of Djakarta, mostly passed over the heads of the vast majority of Indonesians, who continued to live in their segmented ethnic-religious units in accordance with long-established socio-cultural patterns of behaviour.

Perhaps even more important in the final collapse of parliamentary democracy in Indonesia was the fact that most parties failed to carry out their democratic functions properly, because there was a general unwillingness to compromise and the golden rule that party interests end where the national interest begins was seldom adhered to.

The fundamental cleavage underlying Indonesian politics was still the age-old division between Javanese traditionalism and neo-traditionalism on the one side and the *santri* philosophy of life of the orthodox Muslims on the other.

As we saw in an earlier chapter, traditional Javanese civilization sees human life and the socio-political order as a reflection of the cosmic order. As a result order and harmony are the main objectives in Javanese life. These goals can only be reached by striving to reach a state of *rasa* (inner harmony) by means of perfecting such qualities as self-control, asceticism, and etiquette. Order means hierarchy and the traditional Javanese state was centred hierarchically around the autocratic, divine king in his *kraton* from which the life blood of the state emanated, permeating all ranks of society. These traditional views of the state still influence much political thinking

of many Javanese today. And, as the eminent Indonesian scholar
Sudjatmoko points out, this explains the existence in modern Java
of 'the tendency towards paternalistic authoritarianism, the inclina-
tion to seek employment in the civil service, the preoccupation with
prestige and status rather than function and performance, the un-
questioning obedience to authority, the almost exclusive concentration of politics in the capital and the emphasis on strengthening the
national will through indoctrination and revolutionary fervour
rather than the solving of practical problems'.[3]

In this divinely ordained status-seeking society radical change
from within was not possible. And over the centuries Javanese people
who had their share of oppressive and unjust rulers developed the
messianic expectations about the coming of the *Ratu Adil* (Just King),
who would bring a golden age of prosperity and justice. The Just
King myth introduced a revolutionary element in the Javanese
situation which exploded at various times during the island's history
both in the pre-colonial, colonial, and independent eras.

A large section of the Indonesian Nationalist Party (P.N.I.) and
some other smaller Java-based nationalist organizations were deeply
imbued with neo-Javanistic thinking. It was these parties who were
most closely in alignment with the *Pantja-Sila* and mufakat doctrines
of Sukarno. The P.N.I. attracted most of its support from the
abangan masses, from many *prijaji*, and also from many younger
urbanized intellectuals in Java.

The Communist party (P.K.I.) also drew most of its support from
abangan Java as well as from many of the workers in the plantations and
mines in the outer islands, in particular in Sumatra. Reinvigorated
by a new leadership which had gradually been able to erase the
national shame of the 1948 Madiun affair, the P.K.I., by coating its
doctrines with a Javanistic veneer, was soon able to attract large
numbers of followers in Central—and East—Java, and by the mid-
1950s was close to surpassing the P.N.I. in terms of membership.
But while many P.N.I. leaders and followers were genuinely
Javanistic in their outlook, the P.K.I. only paid lipservice to Javanese
tradition and because of its Marxist-Leninist programme the party
was essentially Western in character.

Orthodox Islam in Indonesia, which was strongly opposed to the
kafir (unbeliever) mentality of Javanese traditionalism as well as
Western secularism, was organized mainly in the Masjumi party.
Most orthodox Muslims advocated the establishment of an Islamic
state, which is usually rather vaguely defined as a state based on the
principles of the Islamic law. Views as to the role which Islam should

play in government and politics appear to vary largely in relation to the degree in which particular Islamic leaders have been subjected to Westernization. To many Western-orientated Muslim reformist leaders the concept of the Islamic state seems to mean little more than a religious-socialist structure based on the European Christian Democrat model, while at the other end of the spectrum there were the Darul Islam leaders who attempted to impose by fire and sword a theocracy reminiscent of Calvin's Geneva and the Spanish Inquisition.

Orthodox Islam then was by no means a monolithic force and suffered from severe internal divisions which tended to make the Muslims politically ineffective. The pre-war division in the orthodox Muslim camp between modernists and traditionalists came to the fore again soon after independence was achieved. Objecting to the strong hold which modernist religious socialists such as Mohammed Natsir held on the Masjumi leadership, the traditionalist-orthodox organization Nahdatul Ulama separated from the Masjumi in 1952 and constituted itself into a separate political party.

In addition to the basically Western-orientated P.K.I. there was the Murba party, the successor of Tan Malakka's nationalist-communist organization which envisaged a Titoist type of Indonesian state.

Supporters of Western social-democracy were small in number. They were almost solely concentrated in the Socialist party (P.S.I.) of Sjahrir and the Christian parties, while also most of the modernist leadership of the Masjumi was committed to a Western-type parliamentary democracy.

Ideological divisions were often accentuated by regional and ethnic differences. The P.N.I. and P.K.I. were based mainly in Central and East Java, which contained about 45 per cent of the total Indonesian population. The Nahdatul Ulama, although in principle opposed to the P.N.I. and the P.K.I., drew most of its support from *santri* pockets in East Java and was sufficiently imbued by the eclectic Javanese ethos to object to the 'Western-liberal' doctrines of the modernist Masjumi, which had its strongholds in the ethnically different regions of West Java (Sunda), parts of Sumatra, and the other outer Islands. The Christian parties also gained most of their strength from the islands outside Java; such as Ambon, Minahassa, the Batak regions (Protestant) and Flores (Catholic). The P.S.I. and the Murba party were mainly urban-based.

With the exception of the P.S.I., the P.K.I. and also perhaps the

Christian parties, political parties in Indonesia were on the whole rather amorphous institutions, lacking cohesion and discipline. Parties were usually controlled by a strong leader backed by a powerful clique. These leaders had to defend their position almost constantly against rival groups and this caused serious strife within the parties and weakened their effectiveness at the national level. Party leadership was a highly coveted post conferring high social prestige, always a consideration of extreme importance particularly in the strongly status-conscious Javanese milieu. The reverence, obedience, loyalty and respect, in which the traditional feudal rulers had been held, was now also extended to party leaders, who in turn were expected to take care of the spiritual, economic and social interests of their devoted followers. The relationship between leader and follower is often one of deep personal attachment similar in the Indonesian mind to the feeling of trust and respect between a father and his children. As a result many parties, in addition to pushing their particular ideological interests to the hilt, also became patronage-dispensing institutions, rather than instruments of democratic government.

The greater the pressure a party could exert on the government, then the more lucrative positions in the civil service, the more overseas trips and government contracts and other tit-bits of public revenue it was able to divert to its members. Some of the many smaller parties that mushroomed during the 1950s were solely mutual provident societies set up to obtain a share of the spoils. In the larger parties, however, the quest for the greatest possible slice of public funds tended to aggravate the already fierce ideological, and often ethnic-regional divisions, which further minimized the chances of achieving compromise solutions on matters of general national interest.

Political parties because of their power of patronage also had their tentacles deeply entwined in the government service, and most civil servants were party members and party appointees. Constant meddling in Army affairs by politicians was strongly resented by the officers' corps and was an important contributory factor to the demise of the political parties at the end of the 1950s.

Partly cutting across and partly flowing from this intense rivalry between the political parties, the national leadership was also seriously divided on the question of national priorities. In the view of the small group of Western-orientated leaders the revolution had been completed in 1949 with the transfer of sovereignty by the Dutch to the Indonesian state. The major tasks ahead, according to this group, were economic and social rehabilitation and development. These 'administrators'—to use Feith's terminology—including such important leaders as Hatta, Sjahrir and his followers, most Christian leaders, many Masjumi leaders, and a number of leaders of the P.N.I., had to fight a tremendous uphill battle against the 'consolidarity makers' who pointed to the divisive tendencies in the state and argued that national unity should be given first priority. Moreover, most 'consolidarity makers' strongly opposed the complete Westernization of the country and advocated neo-traditionalist solutions to Indonesia's economic and social problems.

The insistence by the 'administrators' on such qualities as technical ability, sound educational background, competence, and devotion was strongly resented by the hundreds of thousands of *nouveaux riches* who had obtained positions of importance on account of their participation in the revolution rather than on the basis of their skills and education. Any attempts by the government to rationalize the civil service and the armed services, which had been greatly inflated by the influx of thousands of revolutionary veterans who considered such jobs their just reward for risking their lives in the freedom struggle, was strongly resisted. Considerable weight was added to this opposition by President Sukarno, who as a nominal President often over-stepped his constitutional prerogatives by actively interfering in politics.

To the Indonesian masses the revolution was a chiliastic key which was expected to immediately bring about an era of happiness and prosperity for all.

In addition to the uneducated and politically unsophisticated masses, this Just King mentality also seems to have retained its hold on a sizeable section of the new political élite, in particular those who with little education and practical background, had been catapulted by the Japanese occupation and the revolution into positions of responsibility and leadership. Suffering from a 'fountain pen, attache case, motor car' fixation, many of these semi-intellectuals seem to have considered that the possession of these élitist symbols was in itself sufficient to automatically ensure the appropriate economic gains which could normally only be expected after considerable effort and hard work. As a result the mentality of 'administrators' such as Hatta and Sjahrir was often incomprehensible to the vast majority of Indonesians.

The single-minded concern of the majority of politicians and parties with their own particular interests resulted in a great deal of political bickering and manoeuvring for position and power, while the major tasks of economic and social rehabilitation were largely neglected.

Another important contributory factor to the popular discredit and the final collapse of constitutional democracy in Indonesia was President Sukarno. Speculating on his tremendous national prestige and popularity, Sukarno was repeatedly able to transgress with impunity the constitutional limitations to his power and he took an active part in national politics throwing the full weight of his great authority as the 'father of the nation' against the existing political system.

As early as August 1951 Sukarno, in his Independence Day oration, ridiculed the fact that Indonesia had so far already seen twelve cabinets and 121 ministers come and go and he exhorted the Indonesian people to solve their problems on the basis of his *Pantja-Sila* and *mufakat* doctrines.[4]

In 1952 Sukarno directly interfered in a serious crisis which had developed in the armed forces. The rift which had originated during the revolution in the Indonesian military between the small group of Western-orientated officers and the much larger group of Japanese trained *semangat* (fighting spirit) officers, was severely exacerbated during the 1950s owing to the continuous interference by the government and the political parties in army affairs.

The first major clash between the *semangat* section of the officers' corps and the Indonesian government occurred in 1952 when Sultan Hamengku Buwono, Minister of Defence in the 'administrator' Wilopo cabinet, submitted a plan to parliament for a considerable retrenchment of the armed forces. This plan was part of the new budget policy forced on the government by the serious financial impasse it had to face in the post-Korean war slump. In 1952 Indonesia suffered from a severe balance of payments problem caused by a steep decline in the world prices of primary exports, in particular rubber. Government revenues were falling sharply and gold reserves were being rapidly depleted. Attempts to stimulate exports and local production by such means as import restrictions were insufficient to solve the problem and a considerable reduction in government expenditure was also needed. As a result the 1953 budget envisaged a retrenchment of 60,000 civil servants, 60,000 soldiers, and 30,000 policemen.[5]

Rationalization was strongly supported by the Central Army Command, which was composed mainly of Dutch-trained and 'administrator' type officers such as Nasution. The High Command had since 1950 been able to exert firmer control over the rather amorphous mass of military and semi-military forces and had been able to exert its will in appointments at the regional and regimental level. It saw retrenchment, particularly of the often unruly, ill-trained, *semangat*-type officers and soldiers, as a further important step to the creation of a modern, well-trained, and disciplined standing army, an ideal which had been strongly advocated by Nasution as far back as the early days of the revolution.

The planned reorganization, however, was obviously highly unpopular among those most affected by it, in particular many of the ex-PETA officers and those who had risen through the ranks during the revolution.

Sukarno, as well as the political parties, lost no time in trying to gain the greatest possible political benefit out of this growing dissension within the Army. The *semangat* officers faction was on the whole culturally and ideologically on the Javanistic side of the Indonesian political spectrum, and was closely supported by the 'solidarity makers' faction of the P.N.I., the smaller Java-based parties, the Nahdatul Ulama, and the greatest 'consolidarity maker' of them all, President Sukarno.

Sukarno's influence within the Army had rested mainly on its close personal rapport with many of the *Bapakist* regional commanders, particularly in Central and East Java, who because of the family-like loyalty of their troops could exert a certain degree of independent pressure on the Djakarta High Command. Nasution's move in 1952 of transferring many of these regional commanders to other units, considerably curtailed the power of these officers to act independently and as a result Sukarno also suffered. Perturbed by the increasing power of the Western-orientated High Command, Sukarno strongly opposed the rationalization programme and was actively involved in a move by some Army officers, led by one of his distant relatives, Colonel Bambang Supeno, to have Nasution removed from his post as Chief-of-Staff of the Army. When Nasution sacked Colonel Bambang Supeno there was a furore in parliament where the 'solidarity making' elements, including the P.K.I., strongly attacked the Western-inspired army modernization pro-gramme, claiming that the High Command had been used by the Dutch Military Mission for its own devious purposes and that the Army was rapidly being fashioned into the strong-armed instrument of the P.S.I., Sjahrir's Socialist party. The Army was accused of corruptive practices, and Army files were openly read in parliament. A P.N.I. motion—supported by Sukarno—censuring the Army leadership and asking for a committee of investigation consisting of government and party representatives was finally passed by 91 to 54 votes.[6]

The humiliation suffered by the Army on account of these accusations heightened the intense dislike for 'scheming and wrangling' politicians, which had existed since revolutionary days, and stung the Army leadership into action. On 17 October 1952 a crowd of about 5,000 people, instigated by the Army, suddenly appeared in the streets of Djakarta demonstrating against the political parties and demanding the dissolution of parliament and immediate general elections. By the time the demonstrators had reached the Presidential Palace the crowd had swelled to about 30,000. This was the right setting for Sukarno to demonstrate again his tremendous hold over the people. As Feith describes it:

After some time the President came out and walked, among general cheering, to the fence where the demonstrators were standing. Then, in a masterly speech made from the Presidency steps, he both rebuked and soothed them. There would be elections as soon as possible, he said. But meanwhile he could not simply dissolve parliament. To ask him to act thus was to ask him to become a dictator, to bring to nought what the people had fought so long and hard to win. In this way Soekarno sent the demonstrators home. They cheered him and went. Even if one admits that this was a hastily assembled group of people, it was an extraordinary demonstration of the President's authority.[7]

The fact that the Army during the Presidential speech had surrounded the Palace with armour and artillery does not appear to have worried Sukarno unduly. A delegation of Army officers who demanded that the President should dissolve parliament forthwith and that interference by politicians in Army affairs should be stopped came back empty-handed, the leaders obviously having been mesmerized again by the dazzling personality of Sukarno.

This sudden concern of Sukarno for the continuation of a system of government, which he had constantly reviled and dismissed as unsuitable to Indonesian conditions, needs some further explanation.

There is strong evidence that for months prior to the '17 October Affair' Nasution had been planning a coup to establish a more efficient government in which Sukarno backed by the Army, would be given considerable power. The President, as well as Hatta and Prime Minister Wilopo, had been sounded out about this plan by Nasution. And Sukarno appears to have supported the idea of a coup. But a few days before the 17 October he fell out with Nasution over the question of which politicians and officers were to be put out of circulation. Nasution wanted to arrest a number of important 'consolidarity maker' politicians and officers, and naturally this was strongly resented by Sukarno, who was partly dependent on these men for his political support.

The main reason, however, for the failure of the 17 October coup was disunity of action and purpose within the officers' corps itself. The Chief-of-Staff, General Simatupang, as well as the Minister of Defence, were opposed to Nasution's plan on the grounds that the Army was not equipped to play a major political role. Nasution was strongly supported by a number of mainly younger staff officers including Lieut.-Col. Sutoko, who led the delegation to the President on 17 October. The majority of Army leaders, however, appear to have been confused and to have taken a wait-and-see attitude.

In this situation, everything came to depend almost solely on Sukarno who in deciding not to cooperate with the demonstrators administered the death blow to the coup. The reasons for Sukarno's opposition to the coup were personal as well as tactical. Sukarno was not a man to be bullied into anything, and the threatening stand taken by the plotters in surrounding his Palace with guns was a major psychological error. Moreover, Sukarno obviously did not fancy becoming the tool of a military junta. He wanted power handed to him on a platter by popular acclamation. Sukarno, who often has been acclaimed as the great unifying force in Indonesia, was at this stage of his career more interested in accentuating disunity. In 1952 the Western parliamentary system still had a considerable degree of support in the country, although definite signs of its unworkability were already apparent. Sukarno decided to bide his time until the system had completely run aground.

In the meantime Sukarno tried to strengthen his support in the 'consolidarity maker' sectors of the party system and the armed forces. He actively encouraged anti High Command coups in East Java, South Sumatra, and South Celebes, in which regional commanders appointed by Nasution were ousted and replaced by *semangat*-type officers.

By accentuating disunity within the armed forces in this way, Sukarno increased his independent political power. Moves which were contemplated by a number of officers in the Nasution camp to force the issue in the 'rebellious' military regions floundered on the realization that a disunited army was bound to come off second best in a political battle with President Sukarno and his supporters. Also the 'modernizing' faction in the Army felt powerless when on 27 November 1952 the Chief-of-Staff, Colonel Nasution, and his close associates, Colonel Sutoko, Deputy Chief-of-Staff, and the Commander of the Military Police, Colonel Parman, were suspended from their duties.[8]

With the threat of an Army takeover temporarily averted, and with his national prestige considerably boosted, Sukarno now proceeded to take an increasingly active interest in politics, particularly in the serious ideological disputes which severely hampered the normal business of government during 1953 and 1954 when the campaign for the 1955 general elections began to gain momentum.

The debate between the proponents of an Islamic state and a *Pantja-Sila* state, which in 1945, owing to the threat of the common enemy, the Dutch, had been temporarily suspended in favour of the latter, was now taken up again in earnest by orthodox Muslims.

In 1953, during a tour of the outer-islands, Sukarno took issue with the Muslims and beseeched his listeners to continue to support the *Pantja-Sila* ideal. A speech made by Sukarno on 27 January 1953 in the strictly orthodox town of Amuntai in South Kalimantan (Borneo) in which he rejected the concept of an Islamic state, caused a furore in the Indonesian Muslim world. Sukarno argued that in addition to Islam there were many other religions in Indonesia and that the *Pantja-Sila* protected the interests of all denominations:

The *Pantja-Sila* is not opposed to Islam, because the Divine Omnipotence which is such an important tenet of Islam, is contained in the first pillar of the *Pantja-Sila*. The unity of the Indonesian people is also in accordance with Islam and the *Pantja-Sila*, because Islam would not condone that we are split into many groups. The sovereignty of the people is also not opposed to Islam and neither is the principle of social justice.[9]

The Masjumi paper *Abadi* commented that it was not up to the President to decide on what foundation the Indonesian state was to be based, but that this was the right of the Constituent Assembly which was to be set up after the general elections. The paper further accused Sukarno of having given the impression that there would be no freedom of religion in an Islamic state and that other denominations would be persecuted. This was a complete misrepresentation of the Muslim position because in an Islamic state all religious minorities were guaranteed freedom of religion and freedom to sustain and develop their own culture.[10]

The reassuring effect that this statement might have had on other religious groups in the country was almost immediately destroyed by an article in the same paper by a certain Hadji Mohammed Saleh Suaidy, who retorted that only a national state which was based on Islam and the tenets of Islamic Law was in accordance with Islam. The Hadji further argued that the rights of men as specified in the United Nations Charter had already long been vested in the Qur'an and the Hadits (Islamic tradition) and therefore non-Muslims should also be subjected to the precepts of the Islamic Law with the exception of the theological and ceremonial aspects.[11]

In the fanatically Muslim region of Atjeh (North Sumatra) Sukarno's oration about the virtues of the Pantja-Sila made little impression; and an anti-Sukarno sermon was given in the main mosque of Kotaradja, the Achinese provincial capital.

Sukarno had far more success in the Christian areas of the Batak lands (Sumatra), where the people asked for his continuous protection and demanded the abolition of the Department of Religious Affairs. Also in Ambon (Moluccas) Sukarno made a tremendous impression when he asked the Christians to forgive the misdeeds committed against them by Muslim fanatics and presented the Christian community with a large new Church.

The Masjumi leader, Kasman Singodimedjo, followed Sukarno step by step on his national tour trying to counteract the impact the President might have made on the people. On occasions some Muslim leaders went to ridiculous lengths to get nominal support for their cause, as when the Minister of Religious Affairs, Fakih Usman, declared that for a religion to be recognized by the state it would have to satisfy the following conditions: it would have to possess a holy script, a founder, unity of doctrine, and international recognition. Furthermore, the minister argued that the Pantja-Sila envisaged only monotheism and therefore polytheism and atheism were forbidden.

When a number of Muslim officials of the Department of Religious Affairs armed with his dictum tried to enforce this regulation in the predominantly Hindu island of Bali, telling the Balinese to register themselves as nominal Muslims, they almost caused a rebellion. The local press and parliamentarians protested strongly and Balinese priests travelled to Djakarta to have this ministerial pronouncement revoked. A number of Balinese even threatened: 'If they want to

Islamize us, then it would be better for Eastern-Indonesia to separate itself and to call for the protection of Australia.'[12]

The question was finally settled by a government statement to the effect that the Minister for Religious Affairs had only acted in his capacity as a private person. Moreover, the Balinese Hindu-Dharma religion was officially recognized and a separate section for Balinese religious affairs was established within the Department of Religion under the leadership of Balinese. These bungling efforts by some Muslims lost them whatever support they might have gained politically in Bali, and many Balinese joined the P.N.I. which had strongly supported the Balinese religious case in Djakarta.

In the meantime, the *Pantja-Sila* versus Islamic State question raged in parliament and in the cabinet.

By the middle of 1953 the Wilopo cabinet, the last major 'administrator'-dominated government, was replaced by a new cabinet led by the P.N.I. stalwart Ali Sastroamidjojo. The new cabinet appealed to radical-nationalistic sentiments, and the major coalition partners, the P.N.I. and the N.U., attempted to strengthen their position in the forthcoming elections by increasing their hold on the civil service and the armed forces. Many top public servants were replaced by P.N.I. adherents, while the Nahdatul Ulama gained major control of the Department of Religious Affairs. In addition the unpopular financial and trading policy of the previous 'administrator' cabinets was abolished. The result was a rapid increase in inflation and malpractices became rife.

The Ali Sastroamidjojo government also attempted to keep the Army divided by playing out the pro and anti '17 October Affair' factions in the officers' corps. In November 1953 the post of Chief-of-Staff of the armed forces was abolished, thus removing Major-General Simatupang—the last major figure of the anti-government group in the '17 October Affair'—from a position of power. In addition, a number of anti-Nasution officers were appointed to general-staff posts.

Conflicts between individual Army commanders and the cabinet increased during 1954, and many officers gradually began to realize that if the armed forces were ever to defend their interests effectively, a greater degree of consolidarity was needed in the officers' corps and existing rifts would have to be healed as far as possible. It was with this in mind that a number of top Army officers, representing both of the warring sides, started travelling up and down the country in an attempt to unify the armed forces. A preliminary meeting was held in Djakarta in October 1954. This was followed by a larger conference of Army officers in Jogjakarta in February 1955, at which a general rapprochement was achieved. The general staff as well as the majority of commanders and officers were united in their opposition to the ever-increasing interference by government in Army affairs. The longstanding antithesis between the armed forces and politicians was further sharpened by the attempts of the Sastroamidjojo government to counterbalance the power of the military by trying to arm outside groups such as the pro-Communist veteran organization *Perbepsi* and the Front for the Liberation of West Irian (West New Guinea). This was considered by the officers' corps to be a direct attack on what they saw as the prime function of the armed forces, which was to defend the state and the ideals of the revolution from external as well as internal enemies.

Another grievance which tended to bridge the division within the Army was the apparent unwillingness of the government to allocate sufficient funds for defence purposes. The Army leaders claimed that lack of finance not only impaired the technical efficiency of the forces but also lowered the social status—always an extremely important consideration in Indonesia—of the officers' corps. Whereas during the revolution and the early years of independence local commanders had enjoyed a very high status, second only to the top civilian administrators, they now could no longer keep up with politicians and even middle-ranking public servants who had been able to secure for themselves the largest share of the spoils of the revolution.

Many officers were also insulted by a government decree forbidding Army personnel to take part in the national elections. But perhaps most important of all, many Army officers, who in 1948 had saved the state from a communist takeover, were incensed about the willingness of the Ali Sastroamidjojo government and the P.N.I. to accommodate the P.K.I. within the government structure. All these factors tended to unite the officers' corps in opposition to the government and in many cases also against the system of constitutional democracy as well.

The conference in Jokjakarta was attended by all the leading figures in the armed forces and although by no means all the differences were settled, a sufficient agreement was reached to condemn the government for continuously meddling in Army affairs and a resolution was passed stressing that the sole criterion for military appointments should be proven ability—and not political patronage. The conference also declared that the '17 October Affair' should from now on be forgotten and demanded that the government should endorse this view.

The government helped to dig its own grave when it completely underestimated the spirit of unity underlying the Jogjakarta officers' conference, and continued its policy of divide-and-rule in the Army. Matters were brought to a head by the appointment of a government supporter to the vacant post of Chief-of-Staff. Vehement opposition by the military finally forced the government to resign.

The apparent power of the reunited Army in toppling the Sastroamidjojo government bode ill for the future of parliamentary democracy and the party system. However, the Army refrained as yet from establishing a military dictatorship, a move advocated by a number of junior officers. The majority of Army leaders, in line with the thinking of the general public, were still apparently hopeful that the general elections scheduled for September would bring a much needed solution by giving one of the major parties a clear mandate to govern.

On the other hand the Army exerted pressure in various political quarters on the question of the new cabinet. The hostility of the officers' corps to the Sastroamidjojo government, which it had helped to overthrow, strengthened the position of the 'administrators' of the Masjumi and the P.S.I., which were given the major posts in the next government led by Burhanuddin Harahap. As a compromise the Ministry of Religion remained in the hands of the N.U., while the other remaining cabinet posts were divided between a number of smaller parties to the exclusion of the P.N.I.

The new cabinet tried to initiate an 'administrator' type of government and hopefully attempted to stave off the bankruptcy of the parliamentary system and increase public confidence by such means as a widespread anti-corruption campaign. Whatever gains the Burhanuddin government was able to make in the few months before September 1955 were lost when the country was again thrown into political disarray by the outcome of the general elections of that month.

In the national elections the pro-democratic parties, the Masjumi and in particular the P.S.I., polled rather poorly, while the P.K.I. (the Communist party) and the N.U. received much greater support than had been expected. The election results not only impaired the viability of the Burhanuddin government but also showed a sizeable swing against 'administrator'-type governments, a situation which could only be favourable to Sukarno's plans. By the end of 1955 the Burhanuddin government was succeeded by the second Ali Sastroamidjojo government, which although ostensibly committed to an 'administrator'-type policy, was in fact largely ineffective in achieving any of its major goals. The second Ali Sastroamidjojo government also suffered from the chronic inability of all the previous governments to instil a reasonable degree of political stability, to root out corruption and to solve the economic problem (the Djakarta price index rose by 84.4 per cent between June 1955 and March 1956).

The credibility gap between the government and the general public became so wide during 1956 and 1957 that the extra-parliamentary forces of the Army and President Sukarno were gradually able to usurp supreme power in the country demolishing the system of constitutional democracy in the process.

An important milestone in the final disintegration of liberal democracy in Indonesia was the growing rapprochement in 1955 and 1956 between Sukarno and Nasution. This resulted in the re-appointment of Nasution to the post of Chief-of-Staff of the Army with the rank of Major-General. Nasution, during his years of inactivity since 1952, had begun to realize that: 'He had made serious mistakes in his earlier period as Chief-of-Staff. He had attempted to move too rapidly against the officers without professional training. ... He had gone too far in ignoring civilian politics, underrating the political importance for the Army of maintaining good relations with the politicians. Above all he had not appreciated the power and central importance of President Sukarno.'[43]

In his Independence Day oration on 17 August 1955, Sukarno launched a seething attack on the parliamentary system of government. He argued that contrary to the hopes of many people the general elections could not completely solve the problem of political disunity in the country and he beseeched the people to set aside their ideological difficulties, which endangered the life of the nation, and preserve Indonesian unity. Dissociating himself completely from any responsibility for the country's political turmoil, Sukarno squarely blamed Hatta who on 3 November 1945 had signed a decree allowing a multi-party system. Sukarno charged the parties with having neglected the real interests of the nation in favour of their own, and he went so far as to call the parties traitors to the holy rights of the Indonesian people, the *Pantja-Sila*, the republic, and the Proclamation.[14]

In the last quarter of 1955 Sukarno travelled widely throughout the country in an obvious effort to influence the elections for the Constituent Assembly which were to take place in December. In his speeches he warned the people that a few groups were out to destroy the *Pantja-Sila*, and he repeatedly stressed that it was he who had founded the P.N.I. in 1927 hoping in this way to draw away votes from the Masjumi and other Western-orientated parties.[15]

On 19 November 1955 the President told a meeting of police officials at Bogor:

The old established Indonesian democratic principles must be implemented. The parliamentary democracy of Indonesia does not have to be the same as in Western countries. In the Western countries there is no economic democracy. We use the concept of guided economy and why then should we not use the term guided democracy? Guided democracy—or in other words democracy with leadership fits our situation. . . . We must adhere to the Proclamation of 1945 and we may not change it. The *Pantja-Sila* is not something temporary in character but it must together with the proclamation of 1945 be the basis of the Constituent Assembly.[16]

Officially opening the newly elected parliament on 26 March 1956 Sukarno beseeched the members to work on the basis of real Indonesian democracy and to abandon the Western system of 50 per cent of votes plus one. This might suit the individualistic Western societies he argued, but in Indonesia with its strongly communalistic tendencies the principles of 'mutual help', as it was practised in the villages, were also suitable at the national level.[17]

Then, showing complete unconcern for the tottering government and washing his hands of the serious economic difficulties and the growing trend of rebellion in the non-Javanese regions, Sukarno went on a grand tour of the major capitals of the world.

On this first extended overseas trip as head of state, Sukarno was feted and honoured and headline news. In the United States and West Germany he was presented with honorary doctorates of law. China and the Soviet Union tried to outdo the glittering reception of the Western countries, playing on the impressionable and vain Sukarno. Characteristically he seemingly had no difficulty in praising Lincoln in Washington, and lauding Lenin in Moscow, Sun Yat Sen in Peking, and Tito in Belgrade.

Sukarno felt on top of the world and his tour could only strengthen the admiration of the Indonesian people for their President who was honoured and wooed by the leaders of the great nations of the world.

There are also many stories about Sukarno's sexual exploits during his tour. It is alleged by various Indonesians that the

Communist governments were able to gather sufficient compromising evidence on film and tape to blackmail Sukarno and to force him closer to the Marxist block.

More impressive and typical of the ease and fatherly affection with which Sukarno was able to bind his people to him is the following story reported about the presidential visit to France. While in Paris a young official in the presidential entourage was in a tremendous quandary when he passionately desired to phone his sick mother in the Netherlands. In view of Dutch-Indonesian relations, which were at a very low ebb at the time owing to the West Irian dispute, the young Indonesian was frightened that he might become the victim of the President's anger, if it leaked out that he was in secret contact with Holland. Sukarno, after having been told about the young man's dilemma, burst out spontaneously: 'I hear you want to telephone your mother in Holland. Now, listen carefully. A mother is always more important than all political differences and has preference above everything. You phone her and give her my best wishes. You can ring her every day and I'll pay the bill.'[18]

It was at the University of Heidelberg that Sukarno made perhaps his most significant speech of the year. In this speech entitled 'The spiritual movement in Asia as a world moral force', Sukarno argued that industrial, economic, and military power and efficiency on which the Western nations set such great store were far less important than moral principles. He then went on to explain the Indonesian state philosophy of the *Pantja-Sila*, arguing that Indonesian nationalism was different in kind from its nineteenth-century European counterpart. Indonesian nationalism was not chauvinistic or arrogant and did not want to isolate itself from the rest of the world. 'Our nationalism', he said, 'flows from what is truly indigenous in our people. It is a Renaissance of fundamental principles which for centuries have been embedded in the Indonesian people.' And then, giving a preview of the policy priorities he was soon to stress during the period of Guided Democracy, he lashed out against the Western preoccupation of judging Indonesia and its people solely in terms of economic achievement:

It is true indeed that our economy is underdeveloped and that our economic potential is not fully used. But a nation does not only live on her economic performances. A state or nation lives basically on its moral values and its spiritual being. . . . Special spiritual and moral forces have enabled the Indonesian people to develop a new type of foreign policy. This policy is determined partly by geopolitical and geographical factors and partly by the character of the Indonesian people. . . . We strive for a united world which is composed of different countries with their own national character. We strive for unity in diversity for the whole world. All nations and their different social and economic systems must learn to live together and in that way we follow in fact the teachings of the founders of the great religions. Because all religions are founded on love for God and love for humanity. Jesus, Buddha, Mohammed, Confucius, all have taught this. When we forget our duty towards God and humanity, we end up in a state of hate and barbarous wars. . . . The strongest power in this world is the idea. Our philosophy rests on ethical principles and our state is founded on this ethical basis. And ethical principles determine the whole of our life. The power of the idea is superior to all other forces and all nations have at all times recognized this and have established a spiritual and moral order. But you have often misused this order and have given it a materialistic imprint with the result that there is a conflict between principle and practice. We in Indonesia hold firm to our *Pantja-Sila* principles. We can be consistent in our policies even if we do not take sides, because our ideals are always valued higher than realistic objectives. We strive for the absolute truth, the absolute good in the words. We recognize the fundamental rights and duties of man, the right of the full development of one's own national life, and the right of self-determination of all peoples. What we are propagating is not a theoretical idea, but a confession of faith. . . .[19]

This 'Heidelberg Catechism', as the Dutch scholar Muskens has aptly termed it, constitutes one of the most explicit keys to Sukarnoist thinking. The emphasis on idealism and the search for the absolute good flowing from a Javanistic craving for harmony between the microcosms and the macrocosm; the condemnation of Western materialism; the right and duty of Indonesians to retain their own national and cultural identity; and the disdain with which economics is relegated to an inferior place on the value scale; all these were soon to become the major features of Indonesian life during Sukarno's reign as supreme Guide and Great Leader of the Revolution.

On his return to Indonesia, Sukarno, whose visions about guided democracy had been reinforced by what he had seen in the Communist countries, began to criticize constitutional democracy even more vehemently. He asked for a 'burying of the parties' and in his opening speech to the Constituent Assembly in Bandung he told the delegates that they should keep constantly in mind that the new Constitution was meant for Indonesians and that it should reflect the Indonesian identity:

> Indonesian problems can only be solved by means of Indonesian formulas. And only when we are intelligent enough to create our own formulas for our own national problems, will we be able to act decisively and without hesitation. . . . Our Constitution may not be a mere copy, because the Indonesian people has its own needs, its own identity, its own characteristics.[20]

Many Western-orientated Indonesian politicians viewed with great misgiving the growing power of the anti-democratic forces in the country, which they were powerless to stop. Vice-President Mohammad Hatta, who since the 1920s had been the antithesis of Sukarno and Sukarnoism and who had become deeply disappointed with the political and economic chaos in Indonesia, resigned from the Vice-Presidency on 1 December 1956 and officially retired from politics altogether.

The disappearance of Hatta from the national political scene symbolizes the end of parliamentary democracy in Indonesia. Hatta, the rationalist and pragmatic counsellor, who by Sukarno's own admission had often held him back from committing romantic follies, was not replaced by a man of similar calibre. Instead Sukarno surrounded himself by a group of younger men from the so-called 1945 revolutionary generation, such as Chairul Saleh and later also Subandrio. These were ambitious 'yes men', who encouraged Sukarno in his schemes, hoping eventually to benefit from the resulting chaos.

So far, Sukarno had only spoken in vague terms about guided democracy, but on 21 February 1957 the President presented Indonesians with a more detailed outline—*Konsepsi Presiden*—of his plans for political and economic innovation. There was to be a *gotong-rojong* (mutual help) cabinet in which all parties would have to be represented and which was to conduct its affairs on the principles of *musjawarah-mufakat*. Furthermore, Sukarno proposed the establishment of a National Council which in addition to political parties would also be composed of such functional groups as the armed forces, religious leaders, farmers, students, and racial minorities.

Only the Masjumi, the P.S.I., and the Catholic party strongly opposed the *Konsepsi Presiden*. The Nahdatul Ulama and the

Protestant party agreed to the proposal on the condition that the P.K.I. would be excluded. The P.N.I., and the P.K.I., were in full support. But even if all parties had opposed the presidential blueprint for guided democracy, the power of decision had already largely passed from their hands. The opinion of the political parties came to matter even less when, after the outbreak of open rebellion in Sumatra and Sulewesi, Sukarno, in March 1957, proclaimed martial law, which gave the armed forces almost complete authority in the country.

The power of the Army was further increased when in December 1957 it took control of Dutch business and plantation interests that had been seized by Indonesian workers largely on the instigation of the P.K.I. The reason for this takeover was the persistent refusal of the Dutch to hand over West New Guinea to Indonesia. The Round Table Conference in 1949 had excluded West New Guinea, and provided that the political status of the territory was to be decided within a year from the transfer of Dutch sovereignty to Indonesia. Holland, however, proved unwilling to transfer New Guinea and attempts in 1954, 1956, and 1957 by Indonesia to ensure support within the United Nations for her claim failed to obtain the necessary two-thirds majority in the General Assembly. When on 29 November 1957 Indonesia's claim was again rejected in the United Nations, most of the remaining 40,000 Dutchmen in Indonesia were expelled and more than 500 Dutch-owned enterprises representing an estimated capital investment of 2 billion dollars were nationalized.

With their power being constantly eroded by the Army and the President, the political parties could do little to prevent their final downfall. Weakened by internal rivalries, the various governments were unable to tackle the fundamental economic and regional problems. Instead they were forced to buy off various discontented groups by patronage, ignore the major problems, and try to divert people's attention to such nationalistically charged issues as the New Guinea dispute with the Netherlands. By 1957 the patience with which most Indonesians had for so long endured the wrangling and bungling of the politicians had worn thin. And the promises of the President and the Army that guided democracy would solve the nation's problems drastically, efficiently, and speedily had given many people great hopes. Liberal democracy in Indonesia had slowly strangled itself to death with Sukarno and the Army applying the rope ever more tightly in the last agonizing stages.

CHAPTER VI

Great Leader of the Revolution

BY March 1957 the second Ali Sastroamidjojo government had collapsed. The President ignoring the constitutional limits to his power, took it upon himself as 'private citizen Sukarno' to form a new government, which was headed by the 'administrator' Djuanda, an engineer by profession who had previous ministerial experience and who was party-less. Sukarno's new protege, the enigmatic and highly ambitious Dr Subandrio, was appointed to the important Foreign Affairs post.

One of the specified tasks of this 'extra-parliamentary emergency cabinet' was the creation of a National Council, as suggested by Sukarno in his *Konsepsi*.

At the inauguration of the National Council on 12 July 1957, Sukarno announced with obvious self-satisfaction that the Council was fully in line with the ideals of the 1945 Proclamation. The National Council was headed by Sukarno and the Vice-President was Ruslan Abdulgani, a P.N.I. leader and former classmate of the President in the Surabaja High School. Ruslan Abdulgani was to play a very important role during the hey-day of guided democracy in the early 1960s when he was Minister for Information and master-minded and directed the vast Sukarnoist indoctrination programme. The major task of the National Council was to advise the government when requested, although the Council could also make proposals on its own initiative.

The first major activity of the National Council was to call a vast *Musjawarah Nasional* (national deliberation) between all the leading national personalities in order to achieve the normalization of the political and economic situation in the country. Even the retired Vice-President, Mohammed Hatta, was persuaded to take part in these discussions. But apart from some vague general resolutions, no really tangible results were achieved.

The National Council was strongly opposed by the democrats,

in particular by the Masjumi and the P.S.I., who considered that they could further their interests much better in parliament and the Constituent Assembly, institutions which were now in serious danger of being eliminated by the political manoeuvring of Sukarno and the Army.

Then the unexpected happened. On 30 November 1957 the first open attempt was made on Sukarno's life. On that morning Sukarno attended a prizegiving ceremony at a private school in the Djakarta suburb of Tjikini, where his eldest son and daughter were studying. As he was leaving the building around 9.00 a.m. surrounded by throngs of people, mainly children, three hand grenades were thrown in quick succession. Sukarno, although splattered with blood and dust and in a state of shock, was not hurt, but eleven people, mostly children, were killed and a number of others were badly wounded.

The assassination attempt was considered to be the work of Darul Islam fanatics. The Indonesian nation was shocked and outraged at this wanton murder of children. Moreover, the miraculous escape of the 'father of the nation' from death caused the charismatic prestige of Sukarno to rise even higher. Many of the common people began to believe that the President was not only politically indestructible but also especially protected by destiny to perform even greater deeds of glory.

In the meantime the rift between the regionalists and the Djakarta government had widened very seriously, and by the end of 1957 full-scale rebellions had broken out in parts of Sumatra and Sulawesi. In February 1958 the rebels were joined by a number of prominent Masjumi and P.S.I. leaders, who, unwilling to acquiesce to the Sukarno-Army takeover, set up a rival government, the *Pemerintah Revolusioner Republik Indonesia* (P.R.R.I.) in West Sumatra.

In spite of the active support of the United States, Malaya, and Singapore, for the strongly anti-Communist P.P.R.I., the central government forces under the leadership of Nasution were able to break the back of the rebellion by mid-1958, although guerilla warfare in Sulawesi still continued for a few years.

The failure of the rebellion meant that the power of many of the anti-Sukarno officers was eliminated. In addition the position of Nasution vis-à-vis the central government was greatly strengthened and he was now able—with the support of other politically conscious officers—to press for a more dominant role for the armed forces in government and for the elimination of the power of the political parties.

To achieve these ends the Army decided to continue the alliance with President Sukarno. Although having the power to establish a militarist government there and then, the Army—in common with all previous regimes in Indonesia—still needed the charismatic Sukarno to instil a greater degree of unity in the country and to legitimize the increased military control of political affairs. Moreover, the armed forces were still far from being a united, purposeful, political force, and Nasution still had an extremely difficult task to forge an *esprit de corps* which was strong enough to withstand the overtures of President Sukarno and the other major contender for autocratic power, the P.K.I.

With the Masjumi and P.S.I. generally discredited because of their involvement in the P.R.R.I. rebellion, Sukarno, backed by the Army, continued to crusade for the introduction of his system of guided democracy during 1958 and 1959. The last remnant of democratic opposition which still stood in the way of the realization of his cherished plans was the Constituent Assembly which had been debating in Bandung since 1956 on the vital Islamic versus *Pantja-Sila* state controversy without being able to reach a final solution. By 1959 the odds on Indonesia becoming an Islamic state had become very remote, and the resistance of the Islamic as well as the other political parties in the Constituent Assembly to the demotion in status they would have to suffer in a system of guided democracy soon collapsed like a pack of cards after the first major attack by Sukarno.

On 29 April 1959 Sukarno in a speech to the Constituent Assembly made it clear that nothing short of an agreement to his principles would be acceptable. Pointing to the Darul Islam and the regional movements, Sukarno argued:

These disturbances of security must be considered counter-revolutionary acts, and constitute a deviation of the soul and spirit of our National Revolution, which exploded on 17 August 1945 based on the Constitution of the Proclamation of 1945. And that is also true for deviations in the field of politics, in the military field, and in the field of social-economy. . . . And in order to restore—at least to enlarge—our national potential, efforts must be made to create the greatest possible unity between all groups within Indonesian society, including the Muslims, who compromise the largest group in our society. This can be achieved, if God is willing, by returning to the 1945 Constitution. I believe that this will be approved by the Muslim community, considering that full acknowledgment will be accorded to the Djakarta charter of the 22 June 1945.[1]

The President's stand was strongly supported by the P.N.I. and the P.K.I., but various Masjumi spokesmen, although not rejecting a return to the 1945 Constitution altogether, argued that such a move should be postponed until Indonesia could produce leaders who would be able to revive the spirit of 1945. Hamka, an important Muslim leader, openly declared that Sukarno wanted to impose a dictatorship. Voting on the government's proposal to reintroduce the 1945 Constitution and the Djakarta Charter did not reach the required two-thirds majority; and on 2 June 1959, when both the P.N.I. and P.K.I. declared that they would no longer attend the meetings of the Assembly, the resultant lack of a quorum caused the legal death of the Constituent Assembly.

Sukarno, who had put his proposals to the Constituent Assembly on a take-it or leave-it basis, had left the next day, apparently unconcerned, on another overseas tour, visiting Scandinavia, Italy, South America, Turkey, Russia, and Japan. While in Tokyo Sukarno was informed about the outcome of the voting in the Constituent Assembly and he received a telegram from the P.N.I. urging him to reintroduce the 1945 Constitution by decree. So again Sukarno was asked to save the situation and as if to get the full benefit of his final thrust against constitutional democracy, he kept the country in suspense for a few days and happily paid a visit to North Vietnam, returning to Djakarta on 28 June.

Sukarno was received with great fanfare after his sixty-seven-day overseas visit and on 5 July he issued a decree abolishing the Constituent Assembly and reinstituting the Constitution of 1945. The last vestiges of parliamentary democracy in Indonesia had now been eliminated and in rapid succession the various instruments of guided democracy were constructed.

On 22 July 1959 Sukarno announced the composition of the *Madjelis Permusjawaratan Rakjat Semantara* (M.P.R.S.) or Provisional People's Congress for National Deliberation. In accordance with the 1945 Constitution the M.P.R.S. was the embodiment of the people's sovereignty and was thus the highest-ranking institution of authority in the state. Its membership was comprehensive and covered a cross-section of national groups including representatives of political parties and groups of farmers, officials, students, teachers, academics, religious leaders, journalists and the military. The main task of the congress was to define broad policy outlines, and to elect the President and the Vice-President. The M.P.R.S. was not meant to be an instrument of day-to-day government. It was required by law to meet at least once every five years, and the business of the government was left to the President and the instruments of guided democracy, such as the *Dewan Pertimpangan Agung* (D.P.A.) or Supreme Advisory Council, which was set up on 26 August 1959 replacing the earlier National Council of 1957. The D.P.A. was headed by the President and consisted of twelve representatives of the political parties, eight from the regions, and twenty-four from the functional groups. The main function of the D.P.A. was to advise the President, although it could also initiate proposals itself which were not, however, binding on the President.

Legislation severely curtailing the sphere of action of political parties was brought into force on 12 January 1960. Parties were only allowed to exist if they were willing to uphold the 1945 Constitution. The President was given wide powers to eliminate political organizations.

In March 1960 the Indonesian parliament, which had been elected in 1955, was summarily dismissed by Sukarno after it had rejected the government's budget. The elected parliament was succeeded in June 1960 by the *Dewan Perwakilan Rakjat* (D.P.R.) or People's Representative Council. The members of the D.P.R. were selected by Sukarno from the parties and the functional groups. Although the President could ignore decisions of the D.P.R., he was required by the 1945 Constitution to obtain the D.P.R.'s approval for all legislation. Similarly Presidential approval was needed for D.P.R.-initiated legislation. In case of conflict between the President and parliament the former could issue government regulations, which could be revoked again at the next session of the D.P.R.

Sukarno's refusal to include representatives of the Masjumi, P.S.I., and the Army-sponsored League of Supporters of Indonesian Independence (I.P.K.I.) in the new parliament, caused the Sukarno opposition to make a final frantic attempt to turn the clock back. Some leaders of the Masjumi, the P.S.I., the I.P.K.I., and the Christian parties formed the Democratic League which declared its opposition to Sukarnoism and stressed the need to combat the growing influence of the Communists. The League, which seems to have momentarily heightened the hopes of democratic supporters as well as regional interest groups, grew rapidly. It also attracted the support of some P.N.I. and N.U. leaders and a considerable number of Army officers, some of whom demanded that Sukarno, who was overseas at the time, should be dismissed from the presidency. The Army, however, was not sufficiently united and when the President returned and the clash came, the military leadership stood aside. In August 1960 Sukarno banned the Masjumi and the P.S.I. on the grounds of their connection with the P.R.R.I. rebellion and five months later he had most of the top leaders of these parties, including Sutan Sjahrir, arrested.

Of a host of other guided-democracy institutions, perhaps the most typically Sukarnoist of all was the National Front which was inaugurated on 28 March 1960 and was the realization of Sukarno's ideal of 1927 of an ideologically unified national body, which would have the task to guide the country on the road to Indonesian socialism.

By 1960 the structure of guided democracy was completed and Sukarno after a long and tortuous journey which began in the 1920s had finally achieved his ambition and, as he strongly believed, his destiny, of becoming the great leader of the people: the pivot around which the whole of Indonesian life revolved.

The vast majority of Indonesians had welcomed the debacle of liberal democracy and believed that Sukarno possessed the magic key which would finally open the door to the long promised and fervently expected era of prosperity and happiness. But neither Sukarno nor his system of guided democracy was able to solve the basic problems of political and ideological segmentation and economic deterioration. Sukarno was able to impose a pseudo-political stability on the country by forcing the political factions to kowtow to his ideas and by eliminating those who did not comply.

Guided democracy, however, did not eradicate the inherent political and ideological divisiveness in the country; all the new system of government did was to streamline the problem by reducing it basically to a power contest between the Army and the Communists. Sukarno had by no means become a complete dictator and his power depended on his success in manipulating this power struggle.

The power personally vested in Sukarno flowed from his charisma; from his long and distinguished record as a fighter against colonialism; and as the first and sole President of the republic. He was without doubt the most popular man in Indonesia, highly esteemed and revered as 'the father of the nation'. To the vast majority of his countrymen he was the symbol of independent Indonesia and its legitimate ruler.

After independence Sukarno, who in the 1920s had headed the

P.N.I., had no mass organization at his disposal to support him in his quest for power. Just before the 1955 national elections both the P.N.I. and the Masjumi are reported to have offered Sukarno the chairmanship of their respective organizations, being sure that whichever party he elected to lead would win a landslide victory at the polls. To the P.N.I. proposal Sukarno is said to have replied that this party lacked revolutionary spirit and was no longer dynamic enough for his taste.[2] Soon afterwards he took up a closer relationship with the P.K.I., a party which he was wont to hold up to the Indonesian people as an example of the true spirit of revolution and progress.

On the other hand Sukarno was not the type to allow himself to become too dependent on one particular source of support. He was a loner, driven by a very powerful and explosive mixture of vanity, conceit, and belief that he was destined by the gods—not men—to become the great ruler of Indonesia. This point is well illustrated in the following conversation which took place in the early 1950s between the Masjumi leader Abu Hanifah and Sukarno:

> I said to Soekarno . . . that he should have a party of his own. We had a short debate on the question of Marxism which I believed was incongruous with the religious Indonesian people. His only answer, which I still clearly remember, was that he knew that whatever he believed in, the people would believe in too. His vanity had already taken on such proportions, even then! He said: 'Bung Abu, do you believe me that in an election where I will put my ideas at stake, that I will win the majority of the people to my side. I don't need a party at all. The people, whatever party they belong to, will follow me, because I am Soekarno, their real leader.'[3]

Ostensibly Sukarno was by 1960 the most powerful man in Indonesia. In reality he held his authority to a large extent by the grace of the Army, which because of its own internal problems, its unpopularity, and its quest for legitimacy, was not yet in a position to exert its full power and take over the government on its own account.

The relationship between the President and the Army leader Nasution was in many ways as incongruous as the earlier partnership between Sukarno and Hatta. Nasution was born in Sumatra. He was a devout Muslim, honest, incorruptible, hardworking, a brilliant tactician, and had a genuine interest in the advancement of the

Army as well as the country as a whole. Modern, basically Western-orientated, an 'administrator' type, and as pragmatic and realistic as Hatta, he was in many ways the complete antithesis of Sukarno, the flamboyant, romantic dreamer, but also the wily politician, and the ruthless goal-getter.

The Nasution-Sukarno alliance was an uneasy one, based solely on political necessity, with each partner constantly trying to improve his position to the point where the power stalemate would be broken and the other contender discarded.

Sukarno was able to extend the limits of his independent action by the skilful exploitation of internal division within the Army and the inter-services rivalry.

The basically anti-Sukarnoist forces within the Army were mainly concentrated around Nasution and the Djakarta High Command, which had the committed support of the highly professional crack units in West Java, such as the Siliwangi Division, the Rangers, and the R.P.K.A.D. (Army Para-Commandos) which controlled the strategically important Bandung-Djakarta artery. The support for the Nasution group was also strong in the predominantly orthodox Muslim and Christian areas of the outer-Islands, where many military commanders as well as the people strongly objected to Sukarno's flirtation with the Communists. Moreover, the conciliatory attitude of the High Command to the P.R.R.I. rebels, which had been deeply resented by Sukarno, had resulted in a rapprochement with Nasution.

More strongly committed to Sukarno and ideologically less opposed to Communism were many of the officers and ranks of the ethnic-Javanese Diponegoro Division (Central Java), and the Brawidjaja Division (East Java), as well as the K.K.O., Marine Commandos (Surabaja), who were on the whole more imbued with the *semangat* spirit, and being Javanese their thinking was more closely attuned to Sukarnoist doctrine. Many of these *semangat* officers accused the 'administrators'—modern, largely Dutch-speaking and often high-living Djakarta staff officers—of having betrayed the ideals of the revolution. This cleavage was further exacerbated by the jealousy of these officers over the quick promotions of 'administrators' to lucrative positions near the seat of power and by the lack of modern armour and artillery, which put the Javanese divisions at a distinct tactical disadvantage compared to the modern, well-equipped armoured units in West Java.

The Navy and the Air Force were comparatively small and resented the preponderance of Army officers in the national councils.

Many of the officers in these services also hailed from Java; the Navy drew most of its strength from the traditionally 'red' areas of Surakarta and Surabaja, while many top Air Force officers originated from the Jogjakarta area, which in some ways was a reflection of the centuries-old rivalry between these two Central Javanese principalities.

In addition to his attempts to keep the armed forces divided, Sukarno also tried to widen his scope for independent political action by ensuring the support of the remaining political parties: the P.N.I., the N.U., and in particular the P.K.I. which was the largest and best organized party in the country with its roots deeply embedded in the rural areas as well as in the poorer sections of the cities, and to a lesser extent in the civil service and the armed forces. However, the Army had never forgiven the Communists for having stabbed the republic in the back in 1948, and Sukarno's protective attitude towards the P.K.I., while it gave him an extra lever against the military, also tended to accentuate the divisions within the armed forces between anti- and pro-Sukarnoist officers; a situation which could only benefit Sukarno's cause even more.

Furthermore, Sukarno was also able to strengthen or in some cases gain the allegiance of a vast section of the politically conscious population by creating employment for them in the highly prestigious government service. Completely reversing the policies of the earlier 'administrator' governments, the proliferation of new guided-democracy institutions and organizations provided Sukarno and the clique around him with a great opportunity for dispensing patronage. The already inflated bureaucracy and armed forces increased to unmanageable proportions. A type of 'bureaucratic involution' took place, creating a situation in which officials were forced to work less and share the same cake with an ever-increasing stream of newcomers. Salaries were often hardly more than nominal, and became even less with the steep and continuous rise in inflation. As a result inefficiency and corruption became widespread in the public service. Many of the top and middle-ranking posts in the government service were filled by political appointees or army officers who more often than not held their positions as a result of patronage rather than on account of their skills and education. It was this large group in particular which stood to lose a good deal by any change of the *status quo*.

Indonesia then became a vast *Beambtenstaat* during the period of guided democracy, strongly reminiscent of the old Javanese kingdoms, in which the court and a vast bureaucracy staffed by the privileged orders were supported from below by the labour and services of the toiling peasantry.

Sukarno was not simply a dictator, but together with the Army formed a duumvirate, although in many ways an incongruous one. Cooperation was possible because each partner was allowed a near monopoly in certain fields of action.

Sukarno was needed by the Army for his charisma and legitimizing power. And the President was therefore able to deploy to the fullest his 'consolidarity maker' talents, devising and constantly revising the ideological slogans and symbols of guided democracy. Sukarno was also the dominant force in Indonesian foreign policy. It was in this field of international politics that Sukarno really let his imagination run wild, when he tried to create a new world order which would fit the situation he had, or rather hoped to create, in Indonesia.

The Army stayed very much in the background, leaving Sukarno to steal the limelight and fashion and perfect his own pet ideas. The officers' corps steadily consolidated its power in the regions, and the civil service and export companies. Moreover, the armed forces now received the lions' share of the budget and were able to equip themselves with modern weapons, ships, and aircraft.

While Sukarno's ideological acrobatics and symbolmongering was hardly taken seriously by many of the more Western-orientated and hard-boiled officers or by civilian intellectuals, there was a fundamental aspect of Sukarnoism on which practically the whole of the officers' corps was agreed: first, the need to return to the spirit of the revolution and, secondly, that the right to govern should be invested only in those who had actively been involved in the struggle for freedom. The advent of guided democracy was in many ways the victory of the 'consolidarity makers' within the Army as well as within the civilian sector over the 'administrators':

> More important, symbols and ritual made it possible to act out the central doctrine of the regime, the doctrine that the revolution was still being fought. . . . The importance of this doctrine can scarcely be exaggerated. It is partly that a sense of crisis serves to make material deprivation more acceptable: if the struggle against imperialism is still all-important, guns must come before butter. There is, however, more to the doctrine of the unfinished revolution that that. For if indeed this was a period of revolution, if its tasks were essentially the same ones which were faced in the days of the guerilla struggle against the Dutch, then it follows that the

national leaders needed were men who could rally and inspire the people to fight against the enemy and men who could organize the actual shooting; Indonesia therefore needed the leadership of specialists in symbols and military activity, not of specialists in economics and administration.[4]

The basic ideas underlying guided democracy were by no means new and had been continuously propounded by Sukarno since the mid-1920s. What was new was perhaps the presentation in magically charged symbolic forms.

The Sukarnoist Political Manifesto which is contained in the Presidential Independence Day Address of 17 August 1959 presented a more systematic exposition of the major principles of the new state ideology. Sukarno pointed out that the nationalist stage of the new revolutionary process was almost over and that Indonesia should continue the great struggle to enter the socio-economic stage. Sukarno stressed that during the period of Constitutional democracy people had become self-satisfied and had lost the revolutionary spirit. In order to progress, to reach the goal of a just and prosperous society, Indonesia should return to the spirit of the 1945 revolution and adopt the system of guided democracy and guided economy which was based on the true Indonesian spirit of unity and mutual cooperation. Only in this way could the stable government be achieved which was necessary to satisfy people's immediate economic needs, to rid the country of rebellions and restore internal security, and to continue the anti-colonialist struggle and return West Irian (West New Guinea) to the mother country.

The new creed was officially formulated as MANIPOL-USDEK, actually standing for *Manifesto Politik* (Political Manifesto) which was further elaborated into the following components: the Constitution of 1945; Indonesian Socialism; guided democracy; guided economy, and national identity.

Sukarno further argued that if such basic concepts of guided democracy as *musjawarah-mufakat* and mutual cooperation were to have any real meaning at all then the Communists should be included in the system. To facilitate this Sukarno fashioned a new symbol, NASAKOM, an abbreviation for *Na*sionalisme (Nationalism); *A*gama (Religion); *K*ommunisme (Communism). NASAKOM was in fact a reformulation of Sukarno's doctrine of 1927 when he had argued that nationalism, Marxism, and Islam were quite compatible if they were looked at in the right spirit, that is in terms of the Javanistic view of the world which tends to blur fundamentally antagonistic principles, stressing that 'many are the ways' to achieve final unity.

As he had done in 1927, Sukarno argued that these three forces in Indonesian society were basically striving for the same goals:

> Thus all three want freedom and socialism. Thus all three contain progressiveness. For that reason NASAKOM is a progressive necessity of the Indonesian revolution. Whoever is opposed to NASAKOM is not progressive! Whoever is against NASAKOM in reality cripples the revolution, disbalances the revolution. Whoever is anti-NASAKOM is not fully revolutionary, nay, is historically even contra-revolutionary.[5]

The other important theme which is repeated over and over again in the Presidential speeches is the need for strong and united leadership, which brought about another important slogan, RESOPIM— *Revolusi* (Revolution), *Socialisme* (Socialism), *Pimpinan Nasional* (National Leadership). As Sukarno put it:

> This trinity is a law for all nations. It is a universal law. . . . No single nation can carry out a great struggle radically altering a rotten situation into a new situation without fulfilling these three requirements. . . . Should some nation have a revolution and possess a national concept or ideology, but have no national leadership—its revolution is like an army without a general and it becomes like a banked fire that cannot flame but merely emits puffs of smoke here and there.[6]

The final objective of the revolution was the achievement of justice and prosperity. To carry out the Mandate of the People's Suffering is a constant theme in Sukarno's exhortations:

> Guided democracy . . . means that there is democracy and there is guidance, there is guidance and there is democracy, because it is a democracy to carry out the Mandate of the People's Suffering. If not, it will no longer have any basis, it will no longer have any objective. For this reason, guided democracy must also be directed towards protecting and increasing the rights of the People—the common people, *si-Marhaen* [the peasants], *si-Murba* [the proletariat]. In addition to that, it must also be directed towards reducing or abolishing the excessive privileges of the imperialist

agents and the contra-revolutionaries, the anti-progressives and the exploiters of the People. . . . If it is turned upside down, the A.P.R. (Amanat Penderitan Rakjat) would mean not Mandate of the People's Suffering, but Mandate of the Suppression of the people.[7]

In the same way as liberal democracy was not the answer to Indonesia's political problems, Sukarno argued that also social justice could not be obtained under a liberal-capitalist system and therefore a guided economy was to be established, which was to be seen as a necessary stage to Socialism. Sukarno declared in his MANIPOL speech in 1959: 'It is obvious here that no room may be given to liberal economy wherein every individual is given the opportunity to scoop up wealth at the public expense. . . . The Indonesian revolution does not permit Indonesia to become a field for scooping up wealth for anyone . . . foreign or non-foreign.'[8]

Capitalism and imperialism were to be destroyed not only in Indonesia but also throughout the world. A new world order had to be established on the pattern of the Indonesian new order, because the newly independent countries, the New Emerging Forces, were still threatened in their freedom, in particular in their independent economic existence, by the old imperialist powers, the Old Established Forces. At the Afro-Asian Conference in Bandung in 1955 Sukarno told the delegates:

. . . we may not deceive ourselves into thinking that the history of the world will end when the last nation has won political independence! The elimination of the physical occupation by the colonialists is just the first stage of national independence in this age. Willy-nilly, however, we must go further and eliminate all kinds of exploitation, direct or indirect, mental and material. . . . To release ourselves from the spiritual and mental bondage of the colonial past, and then to explore and exploit our personality, our potential and those of our nation—these are the essentials of nationhood in the modern age. It is the search for these things as the basis for new nationhood that is the cause of this upheaval in our continents, and upheaval which constitutes a confrontation between the New Emerging Forces and that Old Established Order which throve upon the explanation of its fellow men. . . . Sisters and brothers, I am well aware that these words of mine are not the product of conventional thinking. They have nothing to do with the conventional idea that we wait until we are 'mature', the colonial powers who bestow independence upon us as a gift. They do not conform to the conventional idea that all we need after independence is technical skills, capital and machinery with which to develop nationhood. . . . Far more essential, however, is the question of the basic concepts produced by the society as a foundation for its activities. It is these basic concepts that will ensure that these activities do gradually round out and perfect the independence already gained. No matter what errors of judgement, no matter what mistakes are made through lack of skill in the meantime, these basic concepts will ensure the correct direction, if only they are sound, if only they are in harmony with the Revolution of Mankind, if only they express the genius of the nation.[9]

The New Emerging Forces were defined by Sukarno as the newly liberated areas of Africa, Asia, South America, the Communist countries, and the progressive groups in the capitalist countries.

What is significant about Sukarno's concept of the New Emerging Forces us that he rejected the generally accepted division of the world into a Capitalist, Non-Aligned, and Communist bloc and instead superimposed on the international world scene the bi-polar division between the Old Established and New Emerging Forces. To Sukarno the all important issues at stake were not the nuclear threat and the cold war, but the fight against colonialism and neo-colonialism. While Sukarno agreed that peaceful coexistence between the Communist and Capitalist countries was possible and necessary for the survival of the world, such coexistence was not possible between the imperialist and anti-imperialist forces.

At the Belgrade Conference of Non-Aligned Nations in 1961 Sukarno stressed that the old colonial powers refused to realize the historically inevitable march to power of the New Emerging Forces and were constantly attempting with every means available to obstruct progress in the newly developing countries:

It is common knowledge to us all that the old colonial powers, in having to leave their colonial territories, want to preserve as much as possible of their economic—and sometimes also their political and military—interests. This is carried out in various ways: by creating strife amongst all layers of the local people; by provoking the secession of one part of the old colonial territory from the rest under the pretext of self-determination; creating chaos through military provocation or—and this is also common—

by fortifying their economic interests, at the last moment, using even the most unscrupulous means.[10]

Therefore, according to Sukarno, the New Emerging Forces had to be constantly on the alert and fight the colonial forces:

Yes, STRUGGLE; STRUGGLE!—The struggle against imperialism is in this present period of nation building as imperative for us as is the struggle for liberation that led to our national independence. . . . We may never forget that we fight for all humanity. We may never forget the past sufferings of our people so that we lose sight of our original goals, and become deflected from our original course through the machinations of the forces of domination, which seek to destroy us in order to maintain themselves.[11]

As a result, Indonesian foreign policy during the Sukarno regime became far more radical and, shedding its earlier non-violent neutralist stance, swung towards the Communist bloc.

The first target in the anti-colonialist struggle was the Netherlands, which since 1950 had consistently refused to hand over its last stronghold in the area, West New Guinea (Irian Barat) to Indonesia. After the takeover of Dutch enterprises in 1957 and the exodus of the 40,000 or so Dutchmen, many of them Eurasians, relations between the two countries went from bad to worse. The former United States Ambassador to Indonesia, Howard Palfrey Jones, and a personal friend of Sukarno, aptly describes the feelings of the majority of Indonesians on the West Irian question:

To most Indonesians, West Irian was not a matter of money, or even of territory. It was a matter of principle, patriotism, and completing their revolution. Sukarno's golden voice and flashing eyes carried conviction. With *merdeka*, the people were for the first time free from foreign masters. They had endured the Dutch for centuries, and the Japanese for four cruel years. It was hard for the Indonesians to believe the Dutch would not return. If Sukarno said their economic hold must be broken, then it must. He was the Moses who had led them out of captivity.[12]

The West Irian dispute united the Indonesian people behind their government and there is also no doubt that Sukarno in this way attempted to divert people's minds—in particular the increasing masses of paupers among the landless peasants in rural Java and the unemployed and the underemployed in the urban centres—from the economic deterioration, inflation, corruption, and official malpractices. The people were told that the continuous revolution, the struggle against imperialism, meant suffering and hardship. The fight against colonialism had to take preference over economic development, increasing productivity, and rooting out inefficiency and corruption, because, according to Sukarno, true social justice and prosperity could only be achieved after the defeat of capitalist imperialism.

To the P.K.I., who supported the President to the hilt in his West Irian campaign, sometimes outdoing the Great Leader himself, the New Guinea issue proved to be a great boon. The apparent close relationship between Sukarno and the P.K.I., and the ferocity with which the Communists pressed the issue, made some nations in the Western bloc, such as the U.S.A., adopt a neutral stand, and others like Australia, which feared to have a common border with a country that could go Communist at any time, oppose the Indonesian claim outright.

With the Afro-Asian bloc and the Communist bloc strongly backing Indonesia, the West Irian dispute became a cold-war issue.

To the Army a more radical departure in dealing with the Dutch was also advantageous, because it would put the country on a war footing, which meant that the armed forces could legitimately continue to exert control in civilian affairs. It also meant that in order to provide for an actual armed confrontation with the Dutch, the generals had a legitimate claim to a larger share of the budget to pay for the necessary armaments. The proportion of the national budget spent on the armed forces rose from 32 per cent in 1960 to 50 per cent in 1961. As most Western nations were unwilling to supply the arms, ships, and aircraft demanded by Indonesia, the Russians were only too willing to comply.

General Nasution, after returning empty-handed from Washington in October 1960, was ordered by Sukarno to go to Moscow, where he was received with open arms and presented with armaments worth 360 million dollars, which Indonesia is still desperately trying to pay off.

By 1961 Indonesia had a large Soviet-built cruiser, modern motor-torpedo boats, and the most modern Russian aircraft, including the latest MIG fighters.

In July 1959 Foreign Affairs Minister, Subandrio, announced

that Indonesia would no longer refer the West Irian dispute to the
United Nations, but would take more radical measures.

In late 1959 and 1960 various attempts were made by small
armed Indonesian groups to infiltrate into New Guinea. On 19
December 1961 Sukarno gave his Trikora command (People's
Triple Command for the liberation of West Irian), calling for a total
mobilization. General Suharto, who later became President, was
given the command of the Trikora operation and began to assemble
troops, ships, and aircraft in Eastern Indonesia, apparently preparing
for a full-scale military onslaught on the Dutch.

Military pin-pricking tactics increased during 1961 and 1962,
when groups of paratroopers were dropped in various parts of West
New Guinea. On 15 January 1962 a naval engagement took place
off the coast of New Guinea in which a Dutch frigate sank two
Indonesian motor torpedo boats.

The international situation was considered extremely grave and
war was expected to break out at any time between Holland and
Indonesia.

The Indonesian High Command, although ostensibly strongly
supporting an armed clash with the Dutch, was in fact trying to
avoid an open war. General Nasution, reportedly with Sukarno's
backing, made informal contacts with important Dutch businessmen
and political figures to find a way out of the conflict. The General
Staff was seriously concerned about the over-enthusiastic attitude
of the P.K.I. War would have meant the commitment of Indonesia's
élite troops and its new and modern equipment. Apart from being at
a disadvantage as the attacker and having to sustain heavier losses
than the defender, Nasution realized that open war would also
lessen the Army's ability to control the Communists effectively.

The United States, worried about the outbreak of war in West
Irian which might extend into a global conflict, finally abandoned
its uncommitted attitude and attempted to get the Dutch and the
Indonesians to the conference table. In the case of the Dutch this
did not prove difficult, because Dutch public opinion was either
lukewarm or directly opposed to going to war to defend a territory
which yearly cost the Dutch taxpayers millions while they were
getting nothing in return.

Although the Dutch, in order to save face, caused the negotiations
to be protracted for a considerable period, Sukarno finally won out.
Agreement was reached on 15 August 1962 that West Irian would be
transferred to Indonesia on 1 May 1963. The views of the Papuans
were not ascertained before the event. As an afterthought, and as a

sop to the principle of self-determination, Indonesia was forced to agree to hold a plebiscite not later than 1969 on whether the Papuans wanted independence or elected to stay with Indonesia.

The Dutch, as a whole, were happy to leave West Irian, which had cost them a vast amount of money and a great deal of heartache. In particular, large Dutch business interests, which had played an important role in getting the negotiations started, were keen to get Dutch-Indonesian relations back to a friendlier level. Australia, which had strongly supported the Dutch on the West Irian issue, was left holding the baby after the United States had indicated that it would be unwilling to give military support to the Dutch in case of an armed clash with the Indonesians.

Sukarno's Independence Day address on 17 August 1962 was appropriately called 'A Year of Triumph'. The President told the people that it was the adoption of guided democracy, the return to the spirit of the revolution, which had brought about the recovery of West Irian:

It is well for me to affirm positively here that 1962 has brought us good results because we have the Political Manifesto. Yes, because we have the Political Manifesto! . . . Indeed, in past years Indonesia has been known as a country with many intentions but few achievements. A nation that is very clever at laying foundation stones but that rarely lays the final stone within a reasonable time. 'A nation with a large gap between idea and act . . .'

These sneers were a challenge for me. A challenge for me personally, as a son of Indonesia. A challenge for me as the President of the republic of Indonesia. A challenge for me as the formateur of the cabinet and the drafter of the Three-Point Programme. A challenge for me, even, as the Great Leader of the revolution. I know that the potential strength and capabilities of the Indonesian Nation are tremendous, and that the Indonesian People likes to struggle. . . . How can you unite all the funds and forces if you advocate liberal parliamentary democracy? This very liberal parliamentary democracy itself contains within it the principle of setting one group against another, one individual against another. And more than ever in this century of the decline of capitalism—this century of Kapitalismus in Niedergang— more than ever in this century, the principle of setting one against another in liberal parliamentary democracy is exploited by foreign subversion for its own interests. How can you rally the people to struggle for justice if you want to take them to a liberal economy that contains the element of exploitation *de l'homme par l'homme*? How can you rally the common people to defend the State, to liberate West Irian, if necessary with their blood and their lives, if that State does not undertake to provide the common people—*si Dadap, si Waru, si Suta, si Naja*—with a just and prosperous life, with a life of tranquillity and plenty?[13]

While the fanfare and celebrations about the West Irian victory were still in full swing. Sukarno was already planning another venture in diplomatic and military brinkmanship. This time the presidential rage was gradually gaining momentum against (what Sukarno termed) the neo-colonialist stooge Malaysia.

The creation of Malaysia, a federation consisting of Malaya, Singapore, and the North Borneo territories, had first been officially mooted by Tungku Abdul Rahman, the Malayan Prime Minister, in 1961.

Indonesia's first official reaction came in November 1961, when the Foreign Minister, Subandrio, approved of the proposal with apparent indifference. During 1962 Djakarta's attitude changed gradually to one of outright hostility. And when on 8 December 1962 Inche Azahari started an uprising in Brunei, Sukarno was provided with a plausible pretext to dismiss Malaysia as a NEKOLIM plot, which should be strongly opposed by the New Emerging Forces.

Indonesian opposition to Malaysia was motivated by a number of factors. The ready assistance given by Malaya and Singapore to the P.R.R.I. rebels in 1957 and 1958 had never been forgotten by Sukarno and the High Command. There was a genuine fear in Djkarta that a strong and prosperous Malaysia might cause dissident groups in Sumatra to seek admittance to the new federation. Also, the spectacular economic development of Malaya and Singapore was a thorn in the flesh of Sukarno, because its continuance might prove to his own people that guided economy was not all it was trumped up to be.

Sukarno was no doubt also moved by genuinely ideological reasons. Malaya in his view had not experienced a true revolution and was still ruled by the old feudal aristocracy under the protection of the colonial British. Malaysia therefore was a perfect target for an Indonesian revolutionary export drive. A further factor involved—although perhaps not as important as the others—was the craving of nativistically inclined nationalists, such as Sukarno, to recreate the ancient Indonesian empires of Sriwidjaja and

Modjopahit, which supposedly had exerted control over the Malayan peninsula and the coastal areas of Borneo.

Moreover, as in the case of West Irian, Sukarno no doubt also saw the Malaysia crisis as a device to draw the attention of the people away from their economic problems and as an extended opportunity to further indoctrinate his people with his views about the continuing revolution.

To the Communists confrontation with Malaysia provided another splendid opportunity to increase their hold on affairs. The P.K.I. with Peking's blessing pushed itself into the forefront of the 'Crush Malaysia Campaign', pressing for an all-out war against the NEKOLIM forces.

Compromises reached between Indonesia, Malaya, and the Philippines in May and August 1963 in Tokyo and Manilla were repudiated again by Sukarno in September on the grounds that Malaysia, egged on by the British colonialists, had declared itself into existence without having consulted its closest neighbours.

A few days later mobs—led by Communist cadres—burned down the British embassy in Djakarta, and British-owned firms and estates were confiscated.

Indonesia's confrontation with Malaysia was condemned by the United Nations, which accepted the new state as a member in November 1964. Angered by the NEKOLIM attitude of the United Nations Sukarno in a fit of rage withdrew Indonesia from the world body in January 1965. Sukarno received little support within the Afro-Asian bloc, with most members condemning Indonesia outright and with a minority giving only lukewarm support. It was only Communist China which fully backed Sukarno in his Malaysian venture; with the result that Indonesia became more and more diplomatically isolated and the Peking-Djakarta axis was strengthened.

With the President leaning ever more dangerously towards Peking and with the Communists at home intensifying their demands for a full-scale attack on Malaysia by the armed forces supported by a vast People's army of armed workers and peasants, the Army High Command refused to weaken its position on the home front vis-à-vis the P.K.I. Moreover, Nasution and many other staff officers realized that in view of serious logistics problems, and the lack of spare parts and landing craft, an open war with the British could turn out to be an extremely hazardous venture. As a result the High Command quietly toned down the military aspects of confrontation and allowed only a token commitment of troops and equipment to be used, keeping most of its crack troops in Java and indulging only in small-scale military operations, which had no more than a nuisance value.

While West Irian had been a complete victory, although at great cost to the economy, the anti-Malaysia campaign, because of the soft-pedalling of the High Command and the more vigorous opposition of Britain, Australia, and to some extent also the U.S.A., ran into a military-diplomatic stalemate which completed the final disintegration of the Indonesian economy and pushed the country into financial bankruptcy of gigantic proportions.

Sukarno, the Great Leader of the Revolution, the Paku Alam (the pivot of the world), the Great Dreamer, who wanted to perform great deeds, to reform the world so that the people could reflect in his glory, had little interest in economics. Questions of finance and economic planning bored him stiff and militated against his craving for the spectacular.

Sukarno hated the discussion of practical problems and on average no more than two cabinet meetings were held per month and even then he tried to subject his ministers for hours to expositions of his revolutionary theories. As soon as the cabinet was allowed to get on with the business of the day, Sukarno lost interest and often handed over the chairmanship to one of his favourite ministers, such as Subandrio.[14]

Sukarno's knowledge and understanding of economic problems was minimal and apparently much below the level expected of a moderately intelligent high school student. In his Independence Day speech in 1963 he frankly admitted:

> I am not an economist. I am a revolutionary, I am just revolutionary in economic matters. . . . My feelings and ideas about the economic question are simple, very simple indeed. . . . If nations who live in dry and barren deserts can solve the problem of their economy, why can't we? . . . If we are unable to provide clothing and food in this rich country of ours, then in fact it is we ourselves who are stupid, we ourselves who are completely stupid.[15]

Brilliant Indonesian economists such as Sumitro, who had been forced to leave the country after the collapse of the P.R.R.I. rebellion probably fully agreed with Sukarno's conclusion. But what did the President, the carrier of the Mandate of the People's Sufferings, actually do to alleviate, or solve the mounting economic problems, the growing poverty, the financial debacle? The answer is: nothing tangible. Perhaps Sukarno's aversion to economics also flowed from the Javanese concept that the Ruler, the divinely ordained, should not contaminate himself with such *kasar* matters as finance, production and trade, but leave these things to his underlings. And that is exactly what Sukarno did. The ministers were there to provide the President with the funds for his schemes both public and personal. Sukarno apparently could not care less where these funds came from. A special budget—nobody actually knows, or if so refuses to disclose the figures involved—was set aside for Sukarno's expenditure on his overseas trips, his mistresses, his wives, girl friends, and lavish entertainments. A minister could just be called and bluntly asked— as is reported to have happened on various occasions to Chairul Saleh—to produce a few million dollars for the President's pleasure. If the Great Leader of the revolution himself indulged in playing about with public money with such unconcerned abandon, it seems hardly surprising that similar practices became common at lower levels of the sycophantic presidential entourage.

Guided economy seems to have been somewhat of an afterthought in the MANIPOL-USDEK. And all the guidance Sukarno seems to have been prepared to give in the economic field was regularly to spout out new magic formulas in the hope of sustaining a little longer the messianic expectations of the people about the coming of the golden age.

The National Planning Council, founded in 1959, produced in 1960 a vast document containing an Eight-Year Plan of Indonesian Economic Development. The planners, however, seem to have been more concerned with the symbolic importance of the plan than with its implementation. The document contained 5,000 pages divided into 17 volumes, and 8 books, containing exactly 1,945 paragraphs. The implication, of course, was that the plan was based on the spirit of 7–8–1945. Admittedly this massive blueprint for economic development contained many sound suggestions, such as the concept of profit-sharing with foreign investors, and the emphasis on becoming self-sufficient in food and clothing before starting large-scale industrial development projects. But the political climate and the chaotic situation in the civil service, which was choked by excessive regulations, over-staffing, and corruption, made the execution of this promising plan impossible.

And then there was Sukarno's Economic Declaration—or *Dekon*— of 1963 which set out how the Eight-Year Plan was to be implemented. Even more vague than usual Sukarno decreed that the growth of the economy was to occur in two distinct stages: first a truly national and democratic economic structure had to be established; and then the second stage of Indonesian Socialism would be reached in which, 'each and every person would be ensured work, food and clothing, and housing, together with a proper cultural and spiritual life'.[16]

The Economic Declaration further promised that firm leadership would be given in economic development and that matters such as foreign investment would be taken in hand.

The Western powers, in particular the U.S.A., were sufficiently impressed by the Eight-Year Plan to increase their aid to Indonesia which, however, continued to be largely squandered on such unpracticable projects as the 'Crush-Malaysia' campaign. The liberal flow of American money was abruptly halted by Sukarno himself, when incensed by the United States condemnation of the anti-Malaysia stance by Indonesia, he told Ambassador Jones, on 25 March 1964, 'Go to hell with your aid', and in April 1964 coined a new magic catch-cry: *Banting Stir Untuk Berdiri Diatas Kaki Sendiri*— Throw around the wheel completely to stand on your own feet— or *Berdikari* in short. Sukarno exhorted his people to reject the idea of foreign assistance and the dependence on foreign imports. But the various government measures to instil new life into the economy by stimulating local production had very little effect. The economic situation towards the end of the Sukarno regime is described by an Australian economist as follows:

The country was in default on a foreign debt officially estimated at $2,400 million. Current foreign exchange earnings in 1966 were unlikely to cover much more than one-half of foreign exchange requirements for imports and (unrevised) debt service. Tax collection had been falling even further behind almost uncontrolled government expenditure. In consequence, inflation, as reflected both in rising money supply and rising prices, was continuing and indeed still accelerating. Shortage of imported raw materials and other factors had reduced industrial production to below 20 per cent of capacity. While rice production was seemingly well maintained, production of estate and other rural products, with few exceptions, continued to stagnate and decline. Shipping, rail and road transport and all other public services were suffering from years of running-down of equipment and were operating with difficulty and intermittently. The whole elaborate system of government controls of the economy was rendered practically inoperative by evasion and corruption. The relevant laws and regulations were neither respected nor enforced.[17]

The only people who benefited greatly from the system of guided democracy and guided economy was the vast number of higher-ranking public servants, including the bureaucratic army officers administering state enterprises, many of whom were able to enrich themselves at the cost of the general good.

The greatest beneficiary, however, in this situation of economic disintegration was undoubtedly the Communist party. Membership of the P.K.I. had risen from a moderate beginning in 1950 to a claimed three million in 1965. In addition the party had built up a series of auxiliary organizations such as SOBSI (Indonesian Federation of Trade Unions); the Veterans Organization (*Perbepsi*); LEKRA (an organization of leftist writers and artists); the GER-WANI (Women's League); and the vast youth organization, *Pemuda Rakjat*, which all in all are estimated to have added an extra 20 million supporters to the Communist cause in 1965.

In the 1955 national elections the P.K.I. received over 6 million votes or 16·4 per cent of the total, while at the 1957 elections for the regional assembly this percentage had doubled. Aidit, the Communist leader, boasted in 1964 that if general elections were held there and then the P.K.I. would gain 50 per cent of the votes.

The key to this phenomenal success of the Communists was partly the continuing deterioration in the people's economic condition, and partly—and perhaps more important—Sukarno's open patronage.

As in the early days of the P.K.I. many *abangan* people in Java were influenced by messianic expectations in their decision to join the Communists. Moreover, the Communists presented their doctrine in Javanistic form; in images and symbols which were familiar to the villagers.

With the Army waiting to pounce on them, the Communists found their protector in Sukarno and out of self-protection were forced to support Sukarno's doctrines to the utmost. In particular the NASAKOM concept was pushed to the hilt by the P.K.I., because it legitimized the party's entry into the councils of the nation. And although the belief in the one God, as specified by the *Pantja-Sila*, must have caused the convinced Marxists in the party leadership some qualms of conscience, to many of the Javanese peasantry the P.K.I. doctrine came simply to be known as *Agama Merah* (Red Religion). It is significant that *abangan* means red in Javanese, and that orthodox Muslims had for centuries designated the syncretic-animistic peasantry, on which Communism had the greatest impact, as *abangan*, the red ones, meaning pagans and unbelievers.

To Sukarno the rise of the P.K.I. proved advantageous in that he was able to strengthen his own power by playing out the Communists against the arch-enemy the Army, and vice versa.

During the period of martial law the Army could and did obstruct P.K.I. activities at will—and it was widely expected in Indonesia in 1961–62 that the military was planning to put the Communists out of action completely.

But unity within the Army proved to be rather brittle when in June 1962 Sukarno hit quickly and appointed General Nasution to the newly created and innocuous position of Chief-of-Staff of the armed forces, and had the post of Chief-of-Staff of the Army filled by General Yani, who was supposedly less antagonistic to the Communists.

The removal of Nasution from the Army leadership and the subsequent juggling of Army positions apparently opened up again many of the old wounds in the officers' corps which Nasution had steadily tried to heal since 1955.

The next serious blow to Army power was the abolition of martial law on 1 May 1963.

The Communists were not slow in taking advantage of this relative decline in the political power of the armed forces and the P.K.I. increased pressure on the President for inclusion in the NASAKOM cabinet and for more representation in other national policy-making bodies. Sukarno, who had so far kept the Communists out of important governmental positions, now changed his attitude and from 1963 onwards Communists were appointed in increasing numbers to important policy-making institutions, including the cabinet.

In an attempt to take the wind out of the sails of the P.K.I., Chairul Saleh and Adam Malik, leaders of the MURBA (National Communist Party), founded in August 1964 an organization called the Body for the Promotion of Sukarnoism (B.P.S.), which soon attracted the support of a number of Muslim politicians, members of the P.N.I. and the Catholic and Protestant parties, as well as Army officers, including General Nasution.

For some time Sukarno wavered in his attitude to the B.P.S. and he is reported to have sharply reprimanded Aidit, who demanded that the President should ban this obviously anti-Communist—and therefore anti-NASAKOM—organization. Sukarno is reported to have told Aidit: 'I do not like *demands* being made of me. If I ban the B.P.S. I should have to ban *all* political parties.'[18] A week later, however, on 17 December 1964, when it would be clear to the people that it was his own decision, Sukarno turned around suddenly and banned the B.P.S. on the grounds that it was counter-revolutionary in spirit. The President also forced the political parties to sign a statement in which they reaffirmed their right to work for the achievement of national unity on the basis of MANIPOL-USDEK, the *Pantja-Sila*, and NASAKOM.

To counteract the Communists again and to preserve the rather delicate balance of forces on which his power rested, Sukarno steadily refused to give in to P.K.I. demands to ban the strongly anti-Marxist Islamic Students Association (H.M.I.). Sukarno feared that forcing the H.M.I. out of existence would cause a tremendous upheaval in the Indonesian Muslim world, which might result in a rapprochement between the Nahdatul Ulama, an important partner in the NASAKOM structure and the openly anti-Sukarnoist Masjumi.

The P.K.I. then tried to get at the orthodox Muslims in another way and turned its attention to the land problem, in particular to the poorer areas of Central and East Java, where the number of landless labourers was greatest.

Land reform legislation had been passed in 1960 but so far had not been implemented. It was the P.K.I. which from the closing months of 1964 onwards took it upon itself to introduce these land reform regulations, while Sukarno stood by silently. More prosperous farmers, who owned a few hectares of rice land and who usually were affiliated to the Nahdatul Ulama or to a lesser extent to the P.N.I., were suddenly designated as landlords by the P.K.I. Led by cadres of the Communist-controlled Peasants Organization, landless peasants began to take over farmland, causing several bloody clashes in which a number of Muslim landowners were killed. It was this high-handed action by the P.K.I. which was an important factor in the final breakdown of the already tenuous coalition factor of the N.U. and the Communists within the NASAKOM framework.

The Communists also clashed with the Army on the land question in the large plantations areas such as in East Sumatra, which since 1957 had been under Army control. Orders to remove squatters who had been living on these former Dutch plantations for years presented the P.K.I. with another opportunity to create turmoil. Several clashes occurred and on one plantation an Army officer was beaten to death by Communist cadres.

Even more pointedly directed at the Army was the P.K.I.

demand for the creation of a Fifth Force of armed peasants and workers ostensibly to wage a total people's war against Malaysia. So far as it is known Sukarno never officially agreed to this request by the Communists. On the other hand, Sukarno no doubt knew about the agreement between Subandrio and the Chinese Foreign Minister, Chen Yi, made during August 1965 about the secret delivery of vast quantities of Chinese arms to equip the Fifth Force. Some of these arms began to arrive towards the end of August in Tandjung Priuk, the harbour of Djakarta, in cases which supposedly contained materials for the *Ganefo* (Games of the Newly Emerging Forces), which were to be held in 1966. A number of these cases are said to have been transported by Air Force trucks to Halim airbase, just outside Djakarta, where already for some months groups of anti-Malaysia volunteers, mainly drawn from Communist youth organizations, had been training under the supervision of Air Force personnel.

From the beginning of 1965 Subandrio and the P.K.I. began to spread rumours about plots by renegade Indonesian generals to overthrow the Sukarno regime. And in May 1965, on the occasion of the forty-fifth birthday of the P.K.I., Indonesia was rocked by the publication of the so-called 'Gilchrist letter', a document, probably faked by Subandrio, alleging subversive activities by an American, Bill Palmer, a film importer who was on friendly terms with Sukarno. When Palmer was on a business visit to Bangkok, a number of Communist youth cadres broke into his bungalow in the mountain resort of Tjipajung, west of Djakarta, where they supposedly found a letter implicating the C.I.A., Britain, and a number of Indonesian generals in a plot to overthrow Sukarno. Subandrio promptly named this document the 'Gilchrist letter' after a former British ambassador to Indonesia. According to Subandrio, he, Sukarno, and the Army Chief-of-Staff General Yani would be murdered by NEKOLIM agents. This was to be followed by an attack by British and American forces from Malaysia which would enable the pro-Western Indonesian generals to take over the country.

The publication of the 'Gilchrist letter' was followed by a spate of anti-British and anti-American demonstrations by Communist-led mobs.

Sukarno, who from the early 1960s onwards had distanced himself from his old comrades in arms—even Ali Sastroamidjojo complained that during 1964 and 1965 he found it difficult to gain access to the President—readily believed what he wanted to believe. He had complete trust in Subandrio who often deliberately fooled the

President by making false reports. For example, there is the story told by Ali Sastroamidjojo, who having attended the United Nations session in 1964 with Subandrio heard the latter blandly declaring to Sukarno that the whole of the Third World was behind Indonesia on the Malaysia issue. When Ali Sastroamidjojo pointed out that the Foreign Minister was far too enthusiastic in his report and that in fact most Afro-Asian nations disapproved of Indonesia's policy, Sukarno turned a deaf ear and agreed with Subandrio.[19]

Apparently during the last years of his reign Sukarno had become so cocksure of his divine mission, and of the perfection of his system, that he firmly believed he *must* be right. Moreover, even if his closest advisers had been more interested in the good of their country and had possessed the courage to tell the President the actual state of affairs, they would probably have been dismissed from office as NEKOLIMS and renegades smitten with the disease of Communist-phobia. There was apparently nobody in Sukarno's immediate entourage whose love of country and people was strong enough to overrule personal ambition. As a result the President was left to indulge in his dreams of grandeur.

Some Indonesian doctors believe that some of Sukarno's antics during the last years of his presidency—such as telling the U.S.A. to go to hell with its aid, and his enraged withdrawal of Indonesia from the United Nations in January 1965—were the result of momentary mental abberrations caused by nephritis, an advanced stage of kidney poisoning.

Whatever the reason, his vanity, his stubborn belief in his destiny, his mental condition or a combination of these factors, Sukarno took the 'Gilchrist letter' for granted. On 26 May 1965 the President called a conference of the leaders of the armed forces, which was attended by Nasution, Yani, Admiral Martadinata, Vice-Air-Marshal Herlambang, and police chief General Soetjipto Joedodihardjo. Sukarno told these officers that the most effective way to counteract the threat contained in the 'Gilchrist letter' was to 'NASAKOM-ize' the armed forces. This meant the implementation of the earlier demands of the P.K.I. for the introduction of Political Commissars in the armed forces and the creation of a Fifth Force of workers and peasants.

This presidential order went beyond the limits of what many officers considered as a reasonable basis for partnership with Sukarno, and they blandly refused to comply. During the next few months Sukarno kept insisting on the NASAKOM-ization of the armed forces and it is reported that in August a number of generals, including Nasution, Yani, Parman, Harjono, Pandjaitan, Suprapto, and Sutjojo, held a stormy meeting at the palace in which Sukarno was told to stop furthering the Communist cause or the generals would take matters in their own hands.

During 1965 it seems that most Indonesians began to believe that a Communist takeover was inevitable and some of the less scrupulous sections of the community were gradually adapting themselves to fit into the new situation. A case in point was the P.N.I. which in August 1965 fell apart into pro- and anti-Communist sections. Still more important, also the Communists were increasingly successful in attracting new recruits within the armed forces. The extent of P.K.I. infiltration is by no means clear, and estimates range from 10 per cent to 40 per cent depending on the region and the particular unit concerned.

Sukarno still persisted in believing that he could continue to balance the situation. He firmly believed that he had domesticated the P.K.I. and that leaders such as Aidit and Njoto were nationalists first and Communists second. Sukarno did not apparently see or perhaps did not want to see that his NASAKOM structure was already beginning to collapse around his ears even before it had been properly built. It is true that on various occasions the President warned against pseudo-NASAKOM followers, who were only interested in gaining as many benefits as possible for themselves. But he failed to see that most of the Palace clique only paid lip-service to his ideas. Undoubtedly NASAKOM meant something to the millions of primary school and high school students who had been indoctrinated. But the indoctrination programme had been less successful among university students and already in 1963 there was a great deal of grumbling behind the scenes. NASAKOM meant little or nothing to many members of the national leadership, who in private conversations often ridiculed Sukarnoism and secretly guffawed behind the President's back. To support NASAKOM meant to the majority of Indonesians a secure job, power, and prestige. To the P.K.I. it meant a necessary stage towards a final takeover; to many Army officers it meant a temporizing device which enabled them to marshal the strength they needed for the final struggle with the Communists.

The final showdown between the Army and the P.K.I. was hastened along during 1965 when Sukarno began to show sure signs of failing health and rumours circulated regularly in Djakarta about the President's imminent death.

On 4 August 1965 Sukarno fell seriously ill. Advised by Subandrio about the rapid deterioration in the President's health, the Communist leaders Aidit and Njoto hurriedly returned from a visit to Peking. Accompanying them was the Chinese medical specialist Dr Woe Ping Chie, who diagnosed a severe but not yet fatal attack of kidney stones, Sukarno's chronic ailment. However, stories about Sukarno's imminent death, supposed plots by rightist generals, and attacks by the American 7th Fleet were circulating wildly throughout rumour-prone Djakarta. Added to this, reports reached Djakarta about further clashes between Muslims and Communists in East Java.

Both the P.K.I. and the Army appear to have become extremely nervous, while Sukarno—at least on the surface—remained undisturbed, dismissing repeated warnings by loyal officers about an imminent Communist coup as examples of Communist-phobia. The President was still apparently convinced that whatever happened, whatever direction events might take, he would be asked, even beseeched to continue to lead the nation. In fact, however, Sukarno's magic spell had already lost a great deal of its potency and matters had moved beyond his control:

> Without any self-criticism he seated himself on an unsteady throne, in the belief that his services had made him indispensable. Showing off his popularity which he was in the course of losing he believed passionately in the ingenuity of his concept of unity, which in reality was on the point of bursting into smithereens. While Sukarno was believed to be sitting safely at the top, he was in fact in the field of fire. And when the first shots were fired the victim was Sukarno's vanity.[20]

The first shots were fired during the early hours of the morning of 30 September 1965 when a number of Army units, aided by groups of Communist volunteers who had been trained at Halim airbase, attempted a *putsch* against the Army High Command.

Nasution was able to escape, but the other five generals who in August had laid down the law to Sukarno about his Communist leanings, were either killed outright or slowly tortured to death by squads of frenzied girls and women of the *Gerwani* (the Communist Women's Organization). The bodies of the generals were severely mutilated, hacked into pieces, and thrown into a disused well (Crocodile Hole) at Halim airbase. In Djakarta rebel forces surrounded the Presidential Palace and occupied the radio station and the central telecommunications office. A little after 7.00 a.m. the

Djakarta radio informed the Indonesian people that in order to prevent a coup by a council of rightist generals the government had been taken over by a group of progressive-revolutionary officers and political leaders calling themselves the '30 September Movement' or *Gerakan Tiga-Puluh September* (GESTAPU).

The troops involved in the coup were the Tjakrabirawa regiment (the Presidential Body Guard), one battalion each from the Diponegoro and Brawidjaja Divisions, which were in Djakarta at the time to take part in the armed forces day celebrations to be held on 5 October, some troops under the command of Colonel Latief, the commander of the Djakarta garrison, a number of officers and men of the security battalion at Halim airbase led by Major Sujono, and about 2,000 Communist troops who had been trained at Halim in the previous six months.

In addition to Djakarta, coups were attempted in Jogjakarta, Surakarta, and Semarang by junior officers of the Diponegoro Division, while in Surabaja the K.K.O. (Marine Commandos) declared its support for the '30 September Movement'.

The major figures involved in the coup had set up their headquarters at Halim airbase and included Omar Dhani, the Air Force Commander, Brig.-Gen. Supardjo, the commander of the Indonesian forces at the Borneo front against Malaysia who the previous day had hurriedly returned to Djakarta, Colonel Untung, a battalion commander in the Tjakrabirawa regiment and a known protege of Sukarno, and the Communist leaders Aidit and Njoto.

Early in the morning this group was joined by no less a person than Sukarno himself. But the President refrained from publicly committing himself to either side until the situation became clearer towards the end of the day. By that time the *putsch* in Djakarta had fizzled out owing to the speedy and efficient counter-measures taken by General Suharto, the commander of the Strategic Reserve (KOSTRAD). By the evening of the 30 September most of the plotters had left Halim. Omar Dhani took a plane to Madiun from where he hoped to continue the struggle. Aidit flew to Central Java where he was eventually captured by an Army patrol in October 1965 and shot.

In and around the Central Javanese cities of Jogjakarta and Solo some hard fighting took place, but pro-Suharto troops quickly regained control and drove rebellious Diponegoro units and Communist youth cadres into the mountainous Merapi area, from where they continued guerilla activities for some time.

The brutal murder of the generals and other wanton killings by the Communists in Central and East Java sparked off a bloody holocaust of wholesale slaughter of Communists, fellow travellers, and many innocent bystanders, lasting for several months. Some of these mass executions were carried out by the Army, but most people were killed by members of Muslim youth organizations and P.N.I. equivalents. There are no reliable figures available about the actual number of people murdered; estimates vary wildly from 100,000 to over one million. This frenzied killing spree has been explained by some Indonesian psychologists and sociologists as a gigantic case of running amok; as a sudden explosion of psychic pressure built up during years of privation, economic hardship, instability, fear and disorder. Whatever the reason may be, it is clear that many old scores and vendettas were being settled often without any reference to the Communist issue. In many areas of Java the pattern of killing ran also along the primeval *santri-abangan* division, with large numbers of the latter being exterminated to the last member of the family, including small children.

The full story of the GESTAPU, and the objectives they had in mind, cannot yet be told and perhaps will never be told. The events are still too close to be judged objectively and those Indonesians who could lift the veil of secrecy and uncertainty surrounding the coup are understandably silent and perhaps will never be given the opportunity to state their views freely.

It is clear that the P.K.I. was involved; but the important question is how deeply; and were the Communists the initiators or the followers? It is less clear whether Sukarno had foreknowledge of the coup, as is now alleged by many Indonesians. Others say that he was completely taken by surprise and for once lost his composure and went to Halim airbase in order to escape, if this proved necessary.

The official Indonesian version of the GESTAPU affair puts the blame squarely on the Communists who are charged with plotting to overthrow the state. Others argue that it is inconceivable that the P.K.I. started the affair in such an obvious state of unpreparedness, fully realizing that it would be crushed by the Army immediately. Others argue that the P.K.I. took part in the coup as a preventive action. The Communists feared that if its great protector, Sukarno, died, the Army would immediately pounce upon the party and destroy it. Any regime which would be more strongly committed to the Sukarnoist state philosophy than the existing Army High Command could only be advantageous to the Communist cause. The P.K.I. and also initially Sukarno blamed the coup on a Council of pro-Western generals.

There is also the view presented in the so-called 'Cornell report', an unpublished study by a number of American scholars who carried out detailed fieldwork in the months immediately following the coup. According to this version, a number of relatively junior officers in the Diponegoro and Brawidjaja Divisions, who were dissatisfied with promotion possibilities and were also ideologically opposed to the Army leadership, planned a *putsch* in Djakarta to overthrow Nasution and his followers. In addition to their private ambitions the plotters were moved by their disapproval of the Dutch-speaking, pro-Western, high-living Djakarta generals, who in their view had betrayed the true ideals of the revolution. The coup was therefore designed to bring the whole of the Army more closely into line with Sukarnoist revolutionary thinking. Looking for support in the largely 'hostile' capital, the plotters made contact with the Air Force Commander Omar Dhani and also accepted the help offered by the Communists cadres at Halim. The chances of success became greater when a few months before the coup Colonel Untung, a battalion commander in the Diponegoro Division, was transferred to the Presidential bodyguard in Djakarta. According to the Cornell report the P.K.I. was only involved at the fringes, leaving sufficient leeway to extricate itself if the plot misfired.

Whatever role the P.K.I. might have played and whatever the extent of its involvement, the GESTAPU affair presented the anti-P.K.I. groups within the armed forces and the community as a whole with the opportunity to crush the party.

The 30 September coup also proved to be the beginning of the end of Sukarno, who stubbornly kept refusing to adjust himself to a situation in which he could only retain his position by the grace of the Army.

Indonesians and foreign scholars differ widely in their opinion about Sukarno's involvement in the GESTAPU. Nasution and many top Army officers are convinced that he had previous knowledge of the affair, and in fact Sukarno's presence at Halim airbase on the morning of 30 September make it difficult to absolve the President from any complicity. Moreover, Sukarno's behaviour after the coup could only strengthen the suspicions of his opponents.

During the first few months after the GESTAPU Sukarno refused to give in to the growing pressure of many Army officers and large sections of the general public to ban the P.K.I. and he blandly dismissed the coup as 'a mere ripple in the ocean of the Indonesian revolution'.

Suharto and other Army leaders, although deeply shocked by Sukarno's apparent lack of concern about the murder of the generals and increasingly more suspicious about the President's role in the 30 September affair, were careful not to force an open break too suddenly. Sukarno still commanded a great deal of support from the masses in Central and East Java and from certain sections in the armed forces, such as the K.K.O. And direct action against the President might have caused a civil war.

By October 1965, however, the physical onslaught against the P.K.I. was in full swing and within a few weeks one of the major props supporting Sukarno's power was annihilated. Moreover, many of the university and high school students, who had been so much subjected to Sukarnoist indoctrination, turned against Sukarno to his great chagrin. As with the Communist massacres, the Army stood behind the Students' Action Fronts (KAMI and KAPPI) and actively encouraged them, creating the impression that the Army was following the actions of the people.

Sukarno, however, kept pushing his NASAKOM ideal and exhorted the Indonesian people not to veer away from the ideals of the revolution. On 21 February 1966 Sukarno announced a reshuffle of the cabinet. Nasution was dropped as Minister of Defence, and a number of prominent P.K.I. sympathizers, including Subandrio, the corruptor Jusuf Nuda Dalam, and Air Force Chief Omar Dhani were retained. Installing the new cabinet on 24 February 1966, Sukarno stressed the need to continue the fight against capitalism and imperialism, and in particular against the neo-colonialist stooge Malaysia. And as if to taunt his attackers even further Sukarno on 26 February banned the students' organization KAMI. The students, however, ignored this presidential order—something unthinkable six months earlier—and intensified their campaign against GESTAPU supporters, and now began to attack Sukarno openly.

To stop the growing agitation, Sukarno announced that a great *musjawarah* was to be held in Djakarta Palace on 10, 11, and 12 March with the heads of political parties, the 100 member cabinet, and the territorial commanders of the Army.

On 10 March Sukarno was able to talk the political parties into signing a declaration condemning demonstrations which undermined the authority of the President. The declaration also warned against the subversive activities of NEKOLIM forces. On 11 March the *musjawarah* was suddenly broken up when unidentified troops began to surround the palace and Sukarno, with Subandrio hot on his heels, fled in his helicopter to his Palace in Bogor.

On that same afternoon Sukarno was visited at Bogor by three generals, emissaries of General Suharto, who pointed out to the President that the country was rapidly falling into chaos owing to continuous demonstrations and threats of the destruction of buildings and properties by anti-GESTAPU forces. Sukarno took the hint. After having been assured that he would be allowed to retain his titles, he signed an already typed out document in which he transferred his authority to General Suharto.

On 12 March 1966, Suharto signed a decree banning and dissolving the P.K.I. Encouraged by the turn of events, the students pushed ahead and staged sit-ins in government departments and ministerial residences. In turn Suharto had the major targets of the students' anger arrested such as the Minister of Higher Education, Prijono, the Foreign Minister, Subandrio, and the recently appointed Minister for Basic Education, Sumardjo, all known P.K.I. fellow travellers.

Suharto announced a new cabinet on 4 April in which Sultan Hamengku Buwono was given the post of Vice-Premier and Adam Malik was made second Vice-Premier. The M.P.R.S., the highest sovereign body in the country, met on 20 June, and elected General Nasution as its president and approved the transfer of power to General Suharto.

Sukarno blindly and stubbornly kept pushing his now lost ideals. In a speech on 20 June he again agitated against NEKOLIM, foreign aid, and stressed his concepts of *Berdikari* and RESOPIM.

The M.P.R.S. ended its session on 5 July and resolved to rescind the appointment of Sukarno as President for life, leaving him the titles of 'Great Leader of the Revolution' and 'Plenipotentiary of the M.P.R.S.'. Moreover, Sukarno was forbidden to issue presidential decrees and was to consult with General Suharto on the formation of a new, smaller, and more efficient cabinet before 15 August. The M.P.R.S. also outlawed the dissemination of Marxist teachings, called for a halt to the anti-Malaysia campaign, and directed the government to expend all efforts on improving the living conditions of the people.

Sukarno ridiculed the decisions of the M.P.R.S. and publicly stated that he refused to form a cabinet which was solely concerned with the filling of stomachs. The Presidential speech on the 17 August 1966 again was apparently designed to antagonize his opponents. Sukarno reluctantly agreed to abandon his NASAKOM concept on the condition that it was to be replaced by NASASOS—the SOS standing for Socialism. He also strongly opposed plans to have

Indonesia readmitted to the United Nations, again emphasized *Berdikari*, and maintained that the anti-Malaysia campaign should be intensified.

Sukarno's position, however, quickly eroded during the closing months of 1966. The trial of the former Minister of Central Bank Affairs, Jusuf Muda Dalam, who implicated the President in his shady financial deals and fraudulent practices, did Sukarno irreparable harm. Similarly, the trials of Subandrio and Omar Dhani caused Sukarno's prestige to decline even further. During the course of these trials evidence—which may have been trumped up—was presented charging Sukarno with having attempted to aid Aidit escape after the coup and having approved the training of Communist youth cadres at Halim airbase and the Subandrio arms deal with Peking.

The students in Djakarta and Bandung now denounced Sukarno even more fiercely and demanded that he be tried by a military court. A speech by Sukarno on 19 December 1966 at a big rally arranged by his supporters in Djakarta at which he blandly demanded the reintroduction of guided democracy, caused such a furore in the Army that the President was demanded to explain himself to the M.P.R.S. The much awaited presidential explanation was sent to the M.P.R.S. on 10 January 1967. Djakarta was tense that day. Rumours about the K.K.O. and other pro-Sukarno groups planning an uprising were rife. Sitting with some students that evening in front of a television set, I still remember the expressions on these young men's faces, first of complete amazement, then of disgust which quickly rose into uncontrollable anger, when Sukarno arrogantly declared that the M.P.R.S. had overstepped its powers in requesting the President to explain day-to-day policy decisions. Sukarno then went on to deny any complicity in the GESTAPU and stated that if he was to be put on trial why then should Nasution not also be brought before the court on charges of having planned to overthrow the government. Furthermore, Sukarno refused to take the sole responsibility—and he might have had a point there—for the disastrous state of the economy, and he argued that the whole nation was collectively responsible.

But neither the students nor the Army were in the mood to take Sukarno's recalcitrance any longer. During the next few days the streets of Bandung—a city which had always harboured the most radical elements in the country, including the young Sukarno—were decked out with the slogan '*Ganjang Sukarno, usir Tjina*' ('Hang Sukarno, kick out the Chinese').

Nasution retaliated on 13 February 1967 when in a radio broadcast he squarely laid the blame for the GESTAPU affair on Sukarno, and a few days later the general submitted to the M.P.R.S. a long document containing the evidence for his allegations.

Sukarno's position had now become completely untenable and on 20 February 1967 he transferred all his powers to General Suharto. This decision was legalized by the M.P.R.S. on 12 March 1967, with the further stipulation that Sukarno was to abstain from engaging in politics until after the general elections. Furthermore, the M.P.R.S. made it clear that Sukarno could expect to be put on trial to explain his activities during his term of office.

This was the end of Sukarno's political career and until the end of his life he lived virtually under house arrest.

Why did Sukarno persist in refusing to accept the New Order? And why did it take the Army leaders so long to topple Sukarno from his throne?

One obvious reason for Sukarno's stubborn attempts to whitewash the Communists, was that he needed the party intact in order to maintain his own power. Moreover, with age creeping on—or putting it less charitably, with senility beginning to take its toll— Sukarno's tremendous vanity had been inflated to fantastic proportions not least by his recent great successes after years of suffering, struggling, and unscrupulous political manoeuvring. Success had made Sukarno even more intractable in his belief about his great mission to Indonesia and the world; in the infallibility of his system; and in the historical inevitability of the course of events as he had perceived it.

According to one former close associate of the President the reason for Sukarno's stance after the coup was that he was purposely trying to stir up trouble with the New Order to force the Army to put him—the 'father of the fatherland', the Moses who had led his people out of captivity—on trial. Sukarno speculated—and with good reason—that such a move would cause an outcry among his supporters, who were still strong particularly in Central and East Java, where even a year ago one could be told by scores of people that Sukarno was a just man. Moreover, if he was brought to trial, Sukarno reasoned that his defiant opposition would give heart to his followers whom he firmly believed were preparing themselves to rise *en masse* to put the 'Great Leader of the Revolution' back on his rightful throne.

The danger of civil war was clearly realized by Suharto and many General Staff Officers, who were able to convince Nasution and other more sanguine officers of the Siliwangi Division and the R.P.K.A.D. (Army Para-Commandos) that direct action against Sukarno would be politically dangerous. The Army therefore confined Sukarno to his house in Bogor which was appropriately called *Hing Puri Bima Sakti* (the Dream Palace of the Holy Bima). There the former President was only allowed to dream. The house was strictly guarded to prevent Sukarno from escaping to Central Java where—as many Indonesians agree—his appearance would have caused thousands of people to flock under his banner which would have resulted in widespread disturbances, if not a full-scale rebellion against the new Djakarta government. Perhaps an even greater worry to the Suharto government was the Communist underground movement which was steadily gaining momentum during 1967 and which according to Army intelligence reports was preparing to restore Sukarno to power.[21]

Another important reason for Suharto's policy of slowly demolishing Sukarno's position was that the new regime had to take account of popular sentiment. Even outside the still large circle of Sukarno supporters one could often hear people remark, poor Sukarno, he has fallen from such great heights, why kick a man when he is down. And then there were many Indonesians who had a feeling of *malu*, of being ashamed towards the outside world if Sukarno was to be put on trial, the man whom they had revered and followed blindly for so long.

Another important factor which inhibited many members of the political élite from pressing too strongly for Sukarno's conviction, was that the washing of the total stock of the Presidential linen in public would have undoubtedly implicated a number of people, who were now staunch supporters of the new regime.

Perhaps the most fundamental problem confronting Suharto was to legitimize his government in the eyes of the people and he solved this problem by gradually feeding Sukarno enough rope to strangle himself; by allowing him for a considerable time to publicly oppose the New Order, while at the same time gathering and publicizing evidence about Sukarno's private life and his role in the GESTAPU. This caused the majority of the people to see Sukarno as a bad ruler and Suharto as his legitimate successor.

During the last few years of his life Sukarno was very lonely. He was allowed few visitors and the foreign Press and foreign scholars were barred from meeting him. Bereft of the glitter and excitement for which he had such an insatiable craving, and with very few true friends left, Sukarno finally realized that he had come to the end of the road. He gradually started to decline both physically and mentally. He died on 20 July 1970 in Djakarta from acute kidney poisoning, the disease which had plagued him for most of his life.

CHAPTER VII

Epilogue

WAS Sukarno primarily a nationalist or an egoist? Was he a reformer or a charlatan? Was he a modern Indonesian or was he still basically the product of traditional Javanese civilization?

What is clear is that to understand something of the enigmatic personality of Sukarno and the complexity of the motivation underlying his actions, more than one key is needed. The Javanese *volksgeist* argument, which is presented in such great detail and with such precision by the German scholar Bernard Dahm, highlights only one—although important—element in Sukarno's mental makeup. But to show Sukarno almost solely as a *ksatrijah* figure from the *wajang*, ruled in his actions entirely by idealistic considerations, seems to go too far. A far more blatant simplification is to dismiss Sukarno as a Communist, an anarchist, or one of the other various manifestations of Satan with which some of his enemies are wont to compare him.

Sukarno was neither a saint nor a fallen angel. He was very much a man of flesh and blood. And, as with many men of stature, he was endowed with a strongly developed ego. He was extremely vain and often vindictive. He could be generous and charming, but also ruthless if somebody stood in his way. Sukarno was often a romantic dreamer who conjured up visions of grandeur for his country and himself; but he was also a pragmatist, a Machiavellian of the first order equipped with an acute sense of political timing. His greatest strength lay in his tremendous speaking talent and his charismatic power over the masses. He will no doubt go into the history books as one of the greatest demagogues of the twentieth century.

Sukarno was undoubtedly an important nationalist leader. He struggled passionately against colonialism and he played an important role in the achievement of Indonesian independence. Furthermore, the credit for the creation of a unitary Indonesian state and for preventing the country from disintegrating into various separate units must in a large part go to Sukarno. He became the father of the fatherland, the symbol of Indonesia, the Moses who led his people out of captivity.

Sukarno's nationalism comprised various elements. Apart from a genuine feeling of compassion for his exploited people and the conviction, based on a mixture of Javanistic and Marxist messianic expectations, that capitalism and colonialism were by their very nature bound to fail, Sukarno's struggle for freedom was also motivated by personal considerations. For Sukarno colonial rule was a deep personal insult which had to be revenged. This need to get his own back on the Dutch, and for that matter anybody else who stood in his way, grew into an obsession which sometimes caused him to overreact. Sukarno showed some of the typical characteristics of the *parvenu*: the man who has made it to the top, but who is highly sensitive because he is still discriminated against. It was partly because the colonial upper-classes—and later many Western nations—dismissed him as a *parvenu* that he began to act like one, besmirching and ridiculing everything that was Dutch or Western and rattling his sabre if insufficient notice was taken of his tantrums.

This feeling of rancour together with the inborn and immense pride in Javanese civilization turned Sukarno into a chauvinist. Cutting off the hand that had fed him, he dismissed Western education as too materialistic and too intellectual. He condemned Western civilization as a whole, because it had bred colonialism and capitalism; because it was inhumane, decadent, and on the verge of collapse. The influence of Marxism and of the prophets of doom such as Spengler is also undeniably evident here, although Sukarno selected only from Marxist theory what he thought useful in the construction of his own *Weltanschauung*. Sukarno preached that Indonesia and the world could not achieve true freedom, happiness and prosperity until capitalism and imperialism had been destroyed and a complete change in the value system had occurred. As the West had in his view little to offer in this respect, Sukarno drew heavily on traditional Javanese civilization in constructing his new value system.

From the beginning of his political career Sukarno had struggled to create a national unitary state out of the hundreds of different geographical, ethnic, linguistic, and ideological segments which comprised the Netherlands Indies. He argued—and the history of the period 1949–57 proved him correct—that Western parliamentary democracy with its principle of majority rule was unworkable in the Indonesian situation, because it would exacerbate rather than diminish the existing divisions in the country. To quote Sudjatmoko, an eminent Indonesian scholar and one of the most outspoken opponents of Sukarno:

> Our recent history has shown that quick rises in the power and influence of one party are not seen as the legitimate results of that party's greater political skill, its temporary luck or its increased popular appeal, but as a direct threat to one's own loyalty group, endangering this group's security. Such changes are therefore met with deep hostility, primordial anxieties, triggering potentially violent forces of self-preservation. This means that no single party can move far along the road to political dominance before triggering political reactions strong enough to bring about its fall. All this means that the level of tolerable disagreement and conflict in Indonesian society is low.

In fact the change in the political situation in Indonesia since the abortive coup of 30 September 1965 has been one of degree rather than kind. It is true much of the Sukarnoist doctrine has been discredited; the anti-Western stance has been abandoned, and the economic problem has been taken seriously in hand, but the important structural features of guided democracy, such as strong leadership and functional representation, as well as the *Pantja-Sila* ideology still remain intact.

Sukarno was the great unifier of Indonesia. This is certainly true in the geographical sense. As the great leader, as the symbol of Indonesia, he played an important role in forging the archipelago into a nation. In political terms this statement is debatable, because in fact Sukarno's power depended to a large extent on the continuation of political and ideological division within the country. Guided democracy did not solve the problem of political disunity but only simplified it into a contest between the Army and the Communists. The degree of Sukarno's power was largely dependent on the success with which he was able to stalemate these two contending forces by keeping the Army divided within itself, and to a lesser extent, by keeping the Muslims from putting up a united front.

During the period of parliamentary democracy the political parties were accused—and rightly—of expending all their energies on playing politics in order to obtain the largest possible share of the spoils. These same charges can be levied against Sukarno. In order to maintain his powerful position Sukarno was forced to expend almost all his efforts on keeping the balance of power between the Army and the P.K.I., which were constantly trying to change the situation in their favour. In practice then Sukarno's guided democracy turned out to be a status-seeking device and as such its policies could only be negative and purposely vague. On the surface, Sukarno's diatribes against capitalism, imperialism, and feudalism, sounded revolutionary, but in practice they turned out to be just hollow phrases.

Sukarno's behaviour during the last years of his political career has been compared to that of a traditional Javanese king. Certainly it is astounding to see Sukarno during the early 1960s—urged on by the P.K.I.—mounting an intensified campaign against feudalism, capitalism, and NEKOLIM, while at the same time busily creating a feudal system of his own in which he himself figures as the king-pin. By proving the system of parliamentary democracy morally wrong he attempted to legitimize his own kingship. He attempted to turn Djakarta into the magical-mystical centre of the state and to this end erected large buildings and statues. In his palace he surrounded himself with a clique of sycophants: a new order of *nouveaux riches* '*prijaji*'. His foreign policy, his overseas tours, his sexual exploits were grandiose and befitted a traditional Javanese king.

However, the comparison with traditional Javanese kingship is only a superficial one and cannot be driven too far. First of all, Sukarno's personal behaviour, his style of politics, was purposely *kasar*, partly in order to stay in tune with the revolutionary ethos, but also, so some Javanese argue, to spite the traditional nobility, because they still considered him a *parvenu*.

But in another important way Sukarno's idea of kingship was also fundamentally different from the traditional Javanese one. The Javanese ruler of old was considered to be the mediator between the gods and the people; he himself was of the divine and acted as a transformer of the divine potency. Sukarno started from an entirely different premise: the sovereignty of the people. He was the mouthpiece of the people; the mediator and interpreter of the people's wishes, sufferings and ambitions. The great secret of Sukarno's power and success was that for a considerable time he was able to discern the feelings of the majority of Indonesians. This came easily to him because on the whole these feelings were similar to his own. He speculated on the popular rancour with colonial rule; on hurt pride and the desire to get even; and above all on the messianic expectations of a golden era of prosperity and happiness for all. He made continuous references in his speeches to Indonesian Socialism, but remained silent as to how and when this state of bliss was to be realized. Instead of giving his people more bread Sukarno staged a gigantic circus performance. In Djakarta stadium he made long speeches against capitalism and colonialism of the old and new variety, and against anything else that happened to incur his wrath. He delighted and awed his people with his charismatic speaking talents and linguistic virtuosity; with the brazen way in which he took the great nations of the world to task, his tightrope acts in international politics and with his amatory exploits. Sukarno the great actor, the great poseur, acted out with gusto the roles of great sufferer, clown, hero, and high priest of the Indonesian revolution to the sound of loud applause.

This is not to say that Sukarno did not believe in what he preached. In any case this would have militated against his vanity. Sukarno was absolutely convinced that he had found the key to Indonesia's and the world's problems. And it must be admitted that he put his finger on many of the sore spots in the Western political and economic system.

The blatant injustices of majority rule and electoral jerrymandering; the selling of the national heritage for a plate of lentils; the neo-colonialist attitudes of some politicians and business concerns, have caused Sukarnoist-like reactions in many Western countries including complacent Australia. Moreover, there is a growing conviction in many parts of the Western world that if the immense problems of poverty, exploitation, and pollution, are to be solved, a moral revolution—*eine Umwertung aller Werte*—is needed, in which the obsession with the profit motive will have to be sacrificed.

It was disastrous for Indonesia that Sukarno fell by the wayside and was unable to translate his views into practical solutions to his country's political and economic problems. Sukarno was an innovator but no reformer, unlike some of his greatest political enemies such as Sjahrir, Hatta, and the small band of 'administrators' who in 1949 chose against great odds to continue where the colonial power had left off and lead their country along the difficult road to socio-economic rehabilitation and development.

Sukarno, on the other hand—and many other Indonesians with him—attempted to take the easy way out. There is probably more than an element of truth in Subandrio's observation that Sukarno was a man in a hurry, who because freedom had come fairly late in life wanted to jump over mountains to achieve within his own lifetime what he fervently hoped for and dreamt about for so long: the creation of an Indonesia which was powerful, feared and respected by the nations of the world.

Was Sukarno a traitor to the Indonesian cause? It could be argued that Sukarno betrayed the trust put in him by many of his countrymen to pull Indonesia out of the political and economic quagmire into which it had sunk. To blame Sukarno alone is too severe; he was aided and abetted by those whose only concern was with feathering their own nests during the period of guided democracy.

Was Sukarno planning to hand over the country to the Communists? This seems highly unlikely. He believed—and here his vanity plays an important role again—that the P.K.I. had become a genuine convert to NASAKOM and that the party would put Indonesia first and international Communism second. It is true that Sukarno had always considered the Communists as the storm troops of the revolution: the indispensable stimulus needed to effect socio-economic change. But Sukarno could hardly be expected to agree to a Communist takeover, which he surely must have realized would have done away with the need for his services. The distinct shift towards the P.K.I. during the last years of guided democracy may be partly explained by the fact that for once he was beginning to lose touch with political reality. Senility was beginning to take its toll and during the years he was suffering more severely than ever from a chronic kidney ailment. According to sources close to the President at the time, he began to show definite signs of megalomania; the various assassination attempts had left their mark and stories fed to him by some of the Palace clique and the Communists about supposed rightist plots helped to create in his mind the idea that the world was against him. During the last few years of his Presidency he shut himself off from his old comrades of the nationalist movement and began to live in a dreamworld of NEKOLIM and rightist generals who were ever on the ready to pounce on him.

Whatever Sukarno's mental state might have been, his erratic swashbuckling behaviour during the period of guided democracy gives the distinct impression that success went to his head, and that his vanity and self-importance took on such proportions that he felt he could take on the whole world if necessary.

Sukarno's presence at Halim makes it difficult to absolve him from at least having some foreknowledge of the coup of 30 September 1965, although it is hardly conceivable and entirely out of character that he wanted to take part in a *putsch* designed to help put the Communists in the saddle. If Sukarno was involved, then it seems far more likely that he wanted to redress the balance of power in his favour by annihilating NEKOLIM elements in the Army, be they imaginary or not.

Reviewing Sukarno's life and career, he comes to the fore as one of the greatest leaders of the Indonesian independence movement. Although still influenced in his religious and philosophical views by Javanese tradition, Sukarno was essentially a man of the twentieth century. He was a realist, who devised a system of government which was closely attuned to existing Indonesian conditions. The soundness of the system of guided democracy is proved by the fact that although stripped of much of its original ideological coating its structure is still in use in Indonesia today. It was disastrous for Indonesia that during his long term as President Sukarno turned out to be much more a political opportunist than the great idealist he portrayed himself to be. In particular, during the period of guided democracy Sukarno began to treat Indonesia as his own private domain; and, as Hatta had already perceived, as early as the 1930s Sukarno used the people to wipe his feet on.

Notes

CHAPTER I

1. Hellypradibyo and Herman Pratikno, *Bingkisan Trikora ke-3* (Djakarta, Lembaga Sosial dan Kebudajaan Nasional, 1964), pp. 62–3.
2. Abu Hanifah, *Tales of a Revolution* (Sydney, Angus and Robertson, 1972), pp. 19–20.
3. Prof. G. Reesink, interview in Djakarta in September, 1970.
4. Adams, Cindy, *Sukarno, an autobiography as told to Cindy Adams* (The Bobbs-Merrill Company, Inc., 1965), p. 19.
5. Noble status and rank in Java depended on the degree of blood relationship to the King or vice-regal (bupatih) families. The noble status of descendants would lapse after the fourth generation.
6. After the takeover of Java by the Dutch East India Company (1602–1799) the provincial governors of the King—the bupatihs or Regents—were left with a great deal of independent power in return for allegiance to the Dutch. During the nineteenth century the Regents and their subordinates gradually lost their local independence and many of their feudal privileges. By the end of the century they had been transformed into a corps of civil administrators, the *Inlands Bestuur* (Native Local Government Service), which came under the direct control of Batavia. Appointment to the higher posts was made on the basis of hereditary succession, a principle which was officially legalized as late as 1854.
7. The Regents and their descendants or dignitaries of higher rank such as princes (*pangeran*), are known by the Javanese as *prijaji*. The term is sometimes also used in a wider sense to include all government officials.
8. Abu Hanifah, op. cit., pp. 25–6.
9. Traditional Javanese civilization was feudal in character and

life was centred in and around the divinely ordained king and his court. The example of the *ksatryah*, the blameless, courageous and faithful knight, was the sublime ideal of the basically aristocratic Javanese civilization. And the life of the *ksatryah* formed one of the major themes of classical Javanese literature, dance, and the *wajang* (the shadow play). The *wajang* was also a popular art form which linked the village and the court in the same philosophy of life, the primary purpose of which was to know how to live in harmony with oneself and with society, within the divinely ordained and therefore unchangeable socio-political order and the universe. The result was that in the status-seeking Javanese life all efforts were directed at perfecting and refining life within a given and fixed framework. Art and life became completely intertwined. Life itself became an art.

10. Western education had created a spiritual and psychological impasse for many Javanese. Only a few were able to find complete intellectual satisfaction in Western philosophy or religion, and in order to regain their spiritual equilibrium many joined the Theosophical Society, which was more akin to traditional Javanese philosophy in its teachings. The Theosophical Society, which had been founded in the United States in 1883, aimed at the establishment of an international brotherhood of man, irrespective of race, religion, caste or sex. The society encouraged the study of comparative religion and the occult. In 1910 an independent Netherlands Indies branch was formed which numbered 325 members of which Sukarno's father was one. By 1930 the organization had 2,100 members, 50 per cent of whom were Europeans, 40 per cent Indonesians, and 10 per cent Chinese and other Asians.

11. Adams, Cindy, op. cit., pp. 23–4.
12. Ibid., p. 26.
13. Kroef, J. M. van der, 'Javanese messianic expectations', *Comparative Studies in Society and History*, Vol. 1958–59, pp. 312–13.
14. Kuijk, Otto, and Veen, Bart van der, *Soekarno tabeh* (Amsterdam, Becht, n.d.), p. 56.
15. Adams, Cindy, op. cit., p. 28.
16. Ibid., p. 28.
17. Ibid., pp. 45–6.
18. Abu Hanifah, op. cit., pp. 30–1.
19. Cf. Kuijk, Otto, op. cit., p. 54.
20. Veer, Paul van 't, *Soekarno* (Den Haag, Kruseman, 1964), p. 17.

CHAPTER II

1. McVey, R. T., The Rise of Indonesian Communism (Cornell, 1965), p. 354.
2. Adams, Cindy, op. cit., p. 39.
3. Dahm, Bernard, *Soekarno en de strijd om Indonesie's onafhankelijkheid* (Meppel, Boom, 1966), p. 52.
4. Adams, Cindy, op. cit., p. 48.
5. These three leaders had been exiled to The Netherlands in 1913 after having been convicted of subversive activities.
6. Adams, Cindy, op. cit., p. 64.
7. Tjipto Mangunkusumo, *Koloniaal Onderwijs Congress, 1916, Praeadviezen*, p. 55.
8. Ksatryan Instituut, *Studieplan 1938–1939 van het Nationaal Handelscollegium* (Bandung, 1938).
9. Adams, Cindy, op. cit., p. 74.
10. Suwarsih Djojopoepito, *Buiten het Gareel* (Utrecht, De Haan, 1940), p. 50.
11. Ibid., pp. 54–5.
12. Abu Hanifah, op. cit., pp. 44–6.
13. Mangunsarkoro, S., 'Het nationalisme in de Taman Siswa beweging', *Koloniale Studien*, 1937, p. 295.
14. Mohammad Said, interview in Djakarta, January 1967.
15. Suwardi Suryaningrat, Koloniaal Onderwijs Congress, 1916, *Stenografisch Verslag*, pp. 116 and 278.
16. Palmier, L. H., 'Sukarno, the Nationalist', *Pacific Affairs*, No. 1, 1957, p. 101.
17. Adams, Cindy, op. cit., p. 74.
18. Suwarsih Djojopoespito, op. cit., pp. 57–8.
19. Sunario, 'Perhimpunan Indonesia dan perananja dalam perdjuangan kemerdekaan kita', paper delivered at the Seminar Sedjarah Nasional II, Jogjakarta, August 1970, p. 51.
20. Ibid., p. 54.
21. Abu Hanifah, op. cit., p. 163.
22. Achmad Subardjo Djojoadisurjo, *Inside Story*, manuscript, partly published in the *Djakarta Times*, July 1970.
23. Sutan Sjahrir, *Sjahrazad. Indonesische Overpeinzingen* (Amsterdam, 1945), pp. 60–1 and 127.
24. Sukarno, *Dibawah Bendera Revolusi I* (Djakarta, 1963). pp, 6–7.
25. Dahm, Bernard, op. cit., p. 79.
26. Adams, Cindy, op. cit., pp. 74–5.
27. Sukarno, op. cit., pp. 6–7.

28. Sukarno, op. cit., p. 39.
29. Acronym coined by Sukarno in the late 1950s meaning *Nasional-isme* (Nationalism), *Agama* (Religion), *Kommunisme* (Communism).
30. Dahm, Bernard, op. cit., p. 106.
31. Adams, Cindy, op. cit., p. 87.
32. Dahm, Bernard, op. cit., p. 105.
33. Abu Hanifah, op. cit., p. 76.
34. Ibid., p. 77.
35. Dahm, Bernard, op. cit., pp. 114–15.
36. Adams, Cindy, op. cit., p. 94.
37. Kuijk, Otto, op. cit., p. 79.
38. Ibid., pp. 81–4.
39. Sukarno, *Indonesia Menggugat* (Djakarta, 1953), p. 159.
40. Adams, Cindy, op. cit., p. 114.
41. Sukarno, op. cit., pp. 115–17.
42. Kuijk, Otto, op. cit., p. 85.
43. Mohammad Hatta, *Verspreide Geschriften* (Amsterdam, 1952), pp. 411–18.
44. Dahm, Bernard, op. cit., p. 126.
45. Ibid., p. 126.
46. Kuijk, Otto, op. cit., p. 86.
47. Pluvier, J. M., *Overzicht van de ontwikkeling der nationalistische beweging in Indonesie in de jaren 1930–1942* (s'Gravenhage, 1953), p. 50.
48. Adams, Cindy, op. cit., pp. 61–2.
49. Sukarno, op. cit., pp. 318–22.
50. Ibid.
51. Kuijk, Otto, op. cit., p. 92.
52. Ibid., p. 93.
53. Cindy, Adams, op. cit., pp. 141–4.
54. Abu Hanifah, op. cit., p. 91.
55. Ibid., p. 87.

CHAPTER III

1. Aziz, M. A., *Japans colonialism and Indonesia* (The Hague, 1955), pp. 117–20.
2. Ibid.
3. Benda, H. J., Izikura, James K., and Koichi Kishi, *Japanese*

military administration in Indonesia. Selected Documents (Yale, 1965), pp. 1–3.

4. Ibid., pp. 17–25.
5. Mitsuo Nakamura, 'General Immamura and the early period of the Japanese occupation', *Indonesia*, No. 10, 1970, p. 12.
6. Ibid.
7. Selosoemardjan, *Social Changes in Jogjakarta* (Cornell, 1962), p. 44.
8. Sluimers, L., 'Nieuwe orde op Java', *Bijdragen tot de Taal-Land -en Volkenkunde*, deel 124, 1968, pp. 339 and 347–8.
9. Abu Hanifah, op. cit., pp. 181–2.
10. Sluimers, L., op. cit., pp. 366–7.
11. Ibid., p. 348.
12. Ibid., p. 349.
13. Ibid.
14. Ibid.
15. Cf. note 3, ch. II.
16. Sluimers, L., op. cit., p. 354.
17. Ibid., p. 350.
18. Ibid., p. 351.
19. Ibid., p. 352.
20. Benda, H. J., 'The beginnings of the Japanese occupation', *The Far Eastern Quarterly*, No. 15, 1966.
21. According to Dahm op. cit., p. 198, the colonial government had no intention of transporting Sukarno to Australia.
22. Adams, Cindy, op. cit., p. 154.
23. In 1821 the Dutch interfered in a civil war in Minangkabau, taking the side of the *adat* chiefs against the Paderis, fanatical and Wahabi-influenced reformers who by fire and sword attempted to convert Minangkabau to the true faith. The struggle lasted until 1837 when the last Paderi leader, Tuanku Imam Bondjol, now a revered national hero in Indonesia, was defeated and exiled. The Paderi spirit, however, lived on, and at the beginning of the twentieth century Minangkabau became one of the most important and vigorous centres of Islamic Reformism in Indonesia. In 1908 disturbances broke out and in 1927 an anti-colonial and ostensibly Communist-led rebellion was staged.
24. Adams, Cindy, op. cit., p. 161.
25. Brugmans, I. J., *Nederlands-Indie onder Japanse bezetting, gegevens en documenten over de jaren 1942–1945* (Franeker, 1960), No. 434, p. 584.

26. Adams, Cindy, op. cit., pp. 163–5.
27. Benda, H. J., op. cit., p. 553.
28. Dahm, Bernard, op. cit., p. 206.
29. Adams, Cindy, op. cit., p. 169.
30. Benda, H. J., op. cit., p. 558.
31. Ibid.
32. Sluimers, L., op. cit., pp. 352–3.
33. Sutan Sjahrir, *Out of Exile* (New York, 1949), p. 245.
34. Adams, Cindy, *My friend the dictator* (Indianopolis, Bobbs-Merrill, 1967), pp. 203–5.
35. During the revolution of 1945–1949 this situation was different and war crimes were committed by both Dutch and Republican forces.
36. Cf. p. 17, ch. II.
37. Sluimers, L., op. cit., p. 354.
38. Ibid., p. 357.
39. Adams, Cindy, *Sukarno, an autobiography*, p. 174.
40. Sluimers, L., op. cit., p. 354.
41. Ibid.
42. Ibid., pp. 360–1.
43. Dahm, Bernard, op. cit., p. 217.
44. Sluimers, L., op. cit., p. 358.
45. Brugmans, I. J., op. cit., No. 406, p. 556.
46. Ibid., No. 407, pp. 557–8.
47. Sluimers, L., op. cit., p. 361.
48. Brugmans, I. J., op. cit., No. 410, p. 561.
49. Ibid., No. 409, pp. 560–1.
50. Dahm, Bernard, op. cit., p. 210.
51. Raden Gatot Mangupradja, 'The Peta . . .', *Indonesia*, pp. 105–6 and 121.
52. Abu Hanifah, op. cit., pp. 132–4.
53. Brugmans, I. J., op. cit., No. 410, p. 561.
54. A kain or sarong is a long piece of cloth which is wrapped around the waist.
55. A pitji is a cap of black velvet, which has become the national headgear of Indonesian men and boys.
56. Brugmans, I. J., op. cit., No. 351, pp. 506–7.
57. Adams, Cindy, op. cit., p. 193.
58. Abu Hanifah, op. cit., pp. 123–4.
59. Brugmans, I. J., op. cit., No. 433, pp. 582–3.
60. Benda, H. J., *The Crescent and the Rising Sun* (The Hague, Van Hoeve, 1958), p. 178.

61. Ibid., p. 181.
62. Dahm, Bernard, op. cit., p. 255.
63. Raden Gatot Mangupradja, 'The Peta and my relations with the Japanese', *Indonesia*, No. 5, 1968, p. 124.
64. Brugmans, I. J., op. cit., No. 437, p. 590.
65. Adams, Cindy, op. cit., pp. 196-7.
66. Sukarno, *The Birth of Pantjasila* (Djakarta, 1957), p. 18.
67. Ibid., p. 35.
68. Adams, Cindy, op. cit., p. 199.
69. Dahm, Bernard, op. cit., p. 276.

CHAPTER IV

1. Brugmans, I. J., op. cit., No. 443, p. 596.
2. Mohammad Hatta, *Verspreide Geschriften*, p. 333.
3. Sutan Sjahrir, *Out of exile*, p. 254.
4. Mohammad Hatta, op. cit., p. 333.
5. Adams, Cindy, op. cit., p. 209.
6. Abu Hanifah, op. cit., p. 145.
7. Achmad Subardjo Djojoadisurjo, op. cit., p. 114.
8. Mohammad Hatta, op. cit., p. 334.
9. Ibid., pp. 338-9.
10. Achmad Subardjo Djojoadisurjo, op. cit., p. 116.
11. Adams, Cindy, op. cit., pp. 212-14.
12. Achmad Subardjo Djojoadisurjo, op. cit., p. 144.
13. Ibid., p. 156.
14. Muskens, M. P. M., *Indonesie. Een strijd om nationale identiteit* (Bussum, Paul Brand, 1970), pp. 76-7.
15. Ibid., p. 161.
16. Smail, John R. W., *Bandung in the early Revolution, 1945-1946* (Cornell, 1964), p. 27.
17. Ibid., p. 28.
18. Ibid., pp. 29-31.
19. Dahm, Bernard, op. cit., p. 286.
20. Smail, John R. W., op. cit., p. 39.
21. Wehl, David, *The birth of Indonesia* (London, Allen and Unwin, 1948), p. 15.
22. Ibid., p. 32.
23. Ibid., p. 34.
24. Sutan Sjahrir, *Our struggle* (Djakarta, 1945), pp. 15 and 22.

25. Sukarno, *Sarinah, de taak van de vrouw in de strijd van de republiek Indonesie* (Amsterdam, Van Ditmar, 1963), pp. 215–16.
26. Ibid., p. 238.
27. Ibid.
28. Kahin, George McT., *Nationalism and Revolution in Indonesia* (Cornell, 1952), pp. 196–7.
29. Ibid., pp. 292–3.
30. Ibid., p. 293.
31. Sukarno, *To My People* (MS., translated by Mrs Molly Bondan of Djakarta).
32. Abu Hanifah, op. cit., p. 310.
33. Veer, Paul van 't, op. cit., p. 70.
34. Abu Hanifah, op. cit., p. 318.
35. Adams, Cindy, op. cit., pp. 262–3.

CHAPTER V

1. Pringgodigdo, A. K., *The office of the president in Indonesia as defined in the three constitutions in theory and practice* (Cornell, 1957), p. 22.
2. Feith, H., *The decline of constitutional democracy in Indonesia* (Cornell, 1968), pp. 111–12.
3. Soedjatmoko, 'Indonesia: Problems and opportunities', *Australian Outlook*, Vol. 21, No. 3, Dec. 1967, pp. 266–7.
4. Muskens, M. P. M., op. cit., p. 182.
5. Feith, H., op. cit., pp. 247–8.
6. Ibid., p. 258.
7. Ibid., pp. 258–9.
8. Ibid., p. 269.
9. Muskens, M. P. M., op. cit., p. 188.
10. Ibid., p. 188.
11. Ibid., p. 189.
12. Ibid., p. 191.
13. Feith, H., op. cit., p. 443.
14. Muskens, M. P. M., op. cit., p. 199.
15. Feith, H., *The Indonesian elections of 1955* (Cornell, 1957), p. 76.
16. Muskens, M. P. M., op. cit., p. 199.
17. Ibid., p. 202.
18. Kuijk, Otto, op. cit., p. 119.
19. Muskens, M. P. M., op. cit., pp. 203–6.
20. Ibid., pp. 209–10.

CHAPTER VI

1. Muskens, M. P. M., op. cit., p. 223.
2. Interview with Ali Sastroamidjojo in September 1970.
3. Abu Hanifah, op. cit.
4. Feith, H., 'Politics of economic decline', T. K. Tan, *Sukarno's Guided Indonesia* (Brisbane, Jacaranda, 1967), pp. 47–8.
5. Weatherby, Donald E., *Ideology in Indonesia: Sukarno's Indonesian revolution* (Yale, 1966), p. 41.
6. Sukarno, *RE-SO-PIM* (Djakarta, 1961), p. 18.
7. Ibid., p. 35.
8. Weatherby, Donald E., op. cit., p. 43.
9. Modelski, George, *The New Emerging Forces. Documents on the Ideology of Indonesian foreign policy* (Canberra, A.N.U., 1963), pp. 56–7 and 59.
10. Weatherby, Donald E., op. cit., p. 60.
11. Ibid., p. 61.
12. Jones, Howard Palfrey, *Indonesia. The possible dream* (New York, Harcourt, 1971), p. 186.
13. Sukarno, *A Year of Triumph* (Djakarta, Department of Information), pp. 8, 11, 13, and 14.
14. Kuijk, Otto, op. cit., p. 133.
15. Tan, T. K., 'Sukarnian Economics', *Sukarno's Guided Indonesia*, p. 33.
16. Ibid., p. 37.
17. Arndt, H. W., 'Economic disorder and the task ahead', T. K. Tan, op. cit., pp. 129–30.
18. Tarzi, Vittachi, *The fall of Sukarno*, 1968, p. 18.
19. Interview with Ali Sastroamidjojo, September 1970.
20. Kuijk, Otto, op. cit., p. 138.
21. Kroef, J. M. van der, *Indonesia since Sukarno* (Singapore, Asian Pacific Press, 1971), pp. 74–5.

Selected Bibliography

Unpublished sources

Abu Hanifah, *Tales of a revolution* (MS., 1968).

Akira Nagazumi, *The origins and the earlier years of the Budi Utomo 1908–1918* (Ph.D. thesis, Cornell, 1967).

Deliar Noer, *The rise and development of the modernist Muslim movement in Indonesia during the Dutch period 1900–1942* (Ph.D. thesis, Cornell, 1963).

Mohammad Said, *Taman Siswa (Garden of Pupils)*, stencilled paper, n.d., n.p.

Subardjo Djojoadisurjo, A., *Inside Story*, (MS., partly published in the *Djakarta Times* July, 1970).

Sukarno, *To my people*, (MS., translated by Mrs Molly Bondan, n.d.)

Veur, P. W. van der, *Introduction to a socio-political study of the Eurasians of Indonesia* (Ph.D. thesis, Cornell, 1955).

Collections and collective publications

Benda, H. J., Izikura, James K., and Koichi Kishi, *Japanese military administration in Indonesia. Selected documents* (Yale, 1965).

Brugmans, I. J. *et al.*, *Nederlands-Indie onder Japanse bezetting, gegevens en documenten over de jaren 1942–1945* (Franeker, 1960).

Encyclopaedie van Nederlands-Indie (The Hague, 1917–39).

Hatta, M., *Verspreide Geschriften* (Amsterdam, 1952).

Kahin, G. Mc. T. (ed.), *Governments and politics in South-East Asia* (Cornell, 1963).

Ki Hadjar Dewantoro, *Karja . . .*, bagian pertama: *Pendidikan* (Jogjakarta, Taman Siswa, 1962).

McVey, R. T. (ed.), *Indonesia* (New Haven, 1963).

Modelski, G., *The new emerging forces: Documents on the ideology of Indonesian foreign policy* (Canberra, A.N.U., 1963).

Sukarno, *Dari Proklamsai sampai Resopim* (Djakarta, 1963).

——, *Dibawah Bendera Revolusi*, 2 vols (Djakarta, 1963–4).

Tan, T. K., *Sukarno's Guided Indonesia* (Brisbane, Jacaranda, 1967).

Wal, S. L. van der, *De opkomst van de Nationalistische Beweging in Nederlands-Indie. Een bronnenpublikatie* (Groningen, Wolters, 1967).

——, *Het onderwijsbeleid in Nederlands-Indie, 1900–1940, een bronnenpublikatie* (Groningen, Wolters, 1963).

Monographs

Adams, Cindy, *My friend the dictator* (Indianapolis, The Bobbs-Merrill Company Inc., 1967).

——, *Sukarno, an autobiography, as told to Cindy Adams* (Indianapolis, The Bobbs-Merrill Company Inc., 1965).

Alisjahbana, Takdir, *Indonesia, social and cultural revolution* (Kuala Lumpur, 1966).

Anderson, Benedict R. O. G., *Mythology and the tolerance of the Javanese* (Cornell, 1965).

Aziz, M. A., *Japan's colonialism and Indonesia* (The Hague, 1955).

Benda, H. J., *The Crescent and the Rising Sun* (The Hague, Van Hoeve, 1958).

Bone, R. C., *The dynamics of the Western New Guinea (Irian Barat) problem* (Cornell, 1958).

Brackman, Arnold C., *The Communist collapse in Indonesia* (New York, Norton, 1969).

——, *Indonesian Communism, a history* (New York, 1963).

Brouwer, B. J., *De houding van Idenburg en Colijn tegenover de Indonesische beweging* (Kampen, 1958).

Dahm, Bernard, *Soekarno en de strijd om Indonesie's onafhankelijkheid* (Meppel, Boom, 1966).

Djajadiningrat, A., *Herinneringen van . . .* (1936).

Feith, H., *The decline of constitutional democracy in Indonesia* (Cornell, 1968).

——, *The Indonesian elections of 1955* (Cornell, 1957).

Geertz, C., *The religion of Java* (M.I.T., 1960).

Hanna, Willard A., *Bung Karno's Indonesia* (New York, 1961).

Hellypradibyo and Herman Pratikno, *Bingkisan Trikora ke-3* (Djakarta, Lembaga Sosial dan Kebudajaan Nasional, 1964).

Higgins, B., *Indonesia: the crisis of the millstones* (Princeton, 1963).

Hindley, Donald, *The Communist Party of Indonesia* (Los Angeles, 1964).

Jones, Howard Palfrey, *Indonesia. The possible dream* (New York, Harcourt, 1971).

Kahin, George Mc. T., *Nationalism and Revolution in Indonesia* (Cornell, 1952).

Koch, D., *Om de vrijheid. De nationalistische beweging in Indonesie* (Djakarta, 1950).

Koloniaal Onderwijs Congress, 1916 and 1919, *Praeadviezen and Stenografische verslagen.*

Kroef, J. M. van der, *Indonesia since Sukarno* (Singapore, Asian Pacific Press, 1971).

——, *The Communist Party of Indonesia: its history, program, and tactics* (Vancouver, 1965).

——, *Indonesia in the modern world* (Bandung, 1956).

Ksatryan Instituut, *Studieplan 1938–1939 van het Nationaal Handelscollegium* (Bandung, 1938).

Kuijk, Otto, and Veen, Bart van der, *Soekarno tabeh* (Amsterdam, Becht, n.d.).

Legge, J. D., *Indonesia* (Englewood Cliffs, Prentice Hall, 1964).

McVey, R. T., *The Rise of Indonesian Communism* (Cornell, 1965).

Mintz, J. S., *Mohammad, Marx and Marhaen: the roots of Indonesian Socialism* (London, 1965).

Mook, H. van, *Indonesie, Nederland en de wereld* (Amsterdam, 1949).

Muskens, M. P. M., *Indonesie. Een strijd om nationale identiteit* (Bussum, Paul Brand, 1970).

Nasution, A. H., *Towards a People's Army* (Djakarta, 1964).

——, *Menegakkan Keadilan dan Kebenaran*, 2 vols (1967).

Niel, R. van, *The Emergence of the Modern Elite* (The Hague, 1960).

Nieuwenhuyze, C., *Aspects of Islam in post colonial Indonesia* (The Hague, Van Hoeve, 1958).

Palmier, L. H., *Indonesia and the Dutch* (London, 1965).

Pauker, Guy J., *The rise and fall of the Communist Party of Indonesia* (Santa Monica, Rand Corporation, 1969).

Pluvier, J., *Confrontations: a study in Indonesian politics* (Oxford, 1965).

Pluvier, J. M., *Overzicht van de ontwikkeling der nationalistische beweging in Indonesie in de jaren 1930–1942* (s'Gravenhage, 1953).

Pringgodigdo, A. K., *The office of the president in Indonesia as defined in the three constitutions in theory and practice* (Cornell, 1957).

Rutgers, F., *Idenburg en de Sarekat Islam in 1913* (Amsterdam, 1939).

Selosoemardjan, *Social changes in Jogjakarta* (Cornell, 1963).

Sartono Kartodirdjo, *Religious movements of Java in the 19th and 20th centuries*, paper No. 52 at the International Conference on Asian History at Kuala Lumpur (Jogjakarta, 1970).

Sjahrir, S., *Onze strijd* (Amsterdam, 1946).

——, *Out of exile* (New York, 1949).

——, *Sjahrazad: Indonesische overpeinzingen* (Amsterdam, 1945).

Smail, John R. W., *Bandung in the early revolution, 1914–1946* (Cornell, 1964).

Sukarno, *A Year of Triumph* (Djakarta, Department of Information, 1963).

——, *Indonesia Menggugat* (Djakarta, 1953).

——, *RE-SO-PIM* (Djakarta, 1961).

——, *Sarinah, de taak van de vrouw in de strijd van de republiek Indonesie* (Amsterdam, van Ditmar, 1963).

——, *The birth of Pantjasila* (Djakarta, 1957).

Sunario, *Perhimpunan Indonesia dan peranannja dalam perdjuangan kemerdekaan kita*, paper delivered at the Seminar Sedjarah Nasional II, August 1970, at Jogjakarta.

Suwarsih Djojopoespito Buiten het gareel (Utrecht, De Haan, 1940).

Veer, Paul van 't, *Sukarno* (Den Haag, Kruseman, 1964).

Vittachi, T., *The fall of Sukarno* (1968).

Weatherby, Donald E., *Ideology in Indonesia: Sukarno's Indonesian Revolution* (Yale, 1966).

Wehl, David, *The Birth of Indonesia* (London, Allen and Unwin, 1948).

Wertheim, W. F., *Indonesian society in transition* (The Hague, Van Hoeve, 1959).

Wolf, Ch., *The Indonesian story: the birth, growth and structure of the Indonesian republic* (New York, 1948).

Articles

Benda, H. J., 'The beginnings of the Japanese occupation', *The Far Eastern Quarterly*, No. 15, 1966.

Castles, L., 'Coup and counter-coup in Indonesia', *Australian Neighbours*, 1965.

Dommen, A., 'The attempted coup in Indonesia', *China Quarterly*, 1966.

Feith, H., and Lev, D. S., 'The end of the Indonesian rebellion, *Pacific Affairs*, 1963.

Gatot Mangupradja, 'The Peta and my relations with the Japanese', *Indonesia*, No. 5, 1968.

Glassburner, B., 'Economic policy-making in Indonesia 1950–1957', *Economic Development and Cultural Change*, 1962.

Graaf, H. de, 'The Indonesian declaration of independence', *Bijdragen tot de Taal-Land- en Volkenkunde*, deel 115, 1959.

Hindley, Donald, 'Indonesia's confrontation with Malaysia', *Asian Survey*, 1964.

——, 'President Sukarno and the Communists: the politics of domestication', *The American Political Science Review*, 1962.

Kroef, J. M. van der, 'Gestapu in Indonesia', *Orbis*, 1966.

——, 'Javanese messianic expectations', *Comparative Studies in Society and History*, Vol. 1958–59.

——, 'Sukarno and Hatta: the great debate in Indonesia', *Pacific Quarterly*, 1958.

——, 'Sukarno and the selfmade myth', *World Review*, July, 1965.

Lev, D. S., 'Indonesia 1965: the year of the coup', *Asian Survey*, 1966.

——, 'The political role of the army in Indonesia', *Pacific Affairs*, 1963–1964.

Mackie, J. A. C., 'Indonesian politics under Guided Democracy', *Australian Outlook*, 1961.

Mangunsarkoro, S., 'Het nationalisme in de Taman Siswa beweging', *Koloniale Studien*, 1937.

Palmier, L. H., 'Sukarno, the nationalist', *Pacific Affairs*, 1957.

Mitsuo Nakamura, 'General Immamura and the early period of the Japanese occupation, *Indonesia*, No. 10, 1970.

Pauker, Guy, J., 'Indonesia in 1964: toward a People's Democracy?', *Asian Survey*, 1965.

Penders, C. L. M., 'Sukarno, the social and ideological background', *World Review*, October, 1966.

——, 'Indonesia's Army—the emergence of military power in Indonesian politics', *World Review*, March, 1968.

Sasrasoegondo, 'Op welke wijze kan bij de opvoeding van de landskinderen de Inheemse cultuur meer tot haar recht komen?', *Djawa*, 1924.

Sluimers, L., 'Nieuwe orde op Java', *Bijdragen tot de Taal-Land- en Volkenkunde*, deel 124, 1968.

Soedjatmoko, 'Indonesia: problems and opportunities', *Australian Outlook*, 1967.

Sutter, J. O., 'Two faces of Konfrontasi: "Crush Malaysia" and the Gestapu', *Asian Survey*, 1966.

Wertheim, W. F., 'Indonesia before and after the Untung Coup', *Pacific Affairs*, 1966.

Index